Bible
Speaks
today

T0334965

the message of

1 CORINTHIANS

Series editors:
Alec Motyer (OT)
John Stott (NT)
Derek Tidball (Bible Themes)

the message of

1 CORINTHIANS

Life in the local church
Revised edition

David Prior

INTER-VARSITY PRESS
36 Causton Street, London SW1P 4ST, England
Email: ivp@ivpbooks.com
Website: www.ivpbooks.com

First published 1985
Reprinted 1987, 1988, 1990, 1991, 1992
Second edition (with study guide) 1993
Reprinted 1995, 1997, 1999, 2000, 2002, 2004, 2006, 2008
This edition published 2020

British Library Cataloguing-in-Publication Data
A catalogue record for this book is available from the British Library.

ISBN: 978–1–78974–151–3
eBook ISBN: 978–1–78359–054–4

Set in 9.5/13pt Karmina
Typeset in Great Britain by CRB Associates, Potterhanworth, Lincolnshire
Printed and bound in Great Britain by Ashford Colour Press Ltd, Gosport, Hampshire

Produced on paper from sustainable forests.

Inter-Varsity Press publishes Christian books that are true to the Bible and that communicate the gospel, develop discipleship and strengthen the church for its mission in the world.

IVP originated within the Inter-Varsity Fellowship, now the Universities and Colleges Christian Fellowship, a student movement connecting Christian Unions in universities and colleges throughout Great Britain, and a member movement of the International Fellowship of Evangelical Students. Website: www.uccf.org.uk. That historic association is maintained, and all senior IVP staff and committee members subscribe to the UCCF Basis of Faith.

*For Rosemary, who shares life in the local church with me,
who knows its full cost more deeply, and without whom
I could not adequately sustain its sorrows
or appreciate its joys.*

Contents

Bible Speaks Today

GENERAL PREFACE

The Bible Speaks Today describes three series of expositions, based on the books of the Old and New Testaments, and on Bible themes that run through the whole of Scripture. Each series is characterized by a threefold ideal:

- to expound the biblical text with accuracy
- to relate it to contemporary life, and
- to be readable.

These books are, therefore, not 'commentaries', for the commentary seeks rather to elucidate the text than to apply it, and tends to be a work rather of reference than of literature. Nor, on the other hand, do they contain the kinds of 'sermons' that attempt to be contemporary and readable without taking Scripture seriously enough. The contributors to The Bible Speaks Today series are all united in their convictions that God still speaks through what he has spoken, and that nothing is more necessary for the life, health and growth of Christians than that they should hear what the Spirit is saying to them through his ancient – yet ever modern – Word.

ALEC MOTYER
JOHN STOTT
DEREK TIDBALL
Series editors

Author's preface

Paul's letter to the Christian church at Corinth first came alive to me in the city of Cape Town – a city, like Corinth, dominated by a mountain; like Corinth, a cosmopolitan and heterogeneous seaport; like Corinth, the meeting point of many different cultures, creeds and cults; like Corinth in the fifties of the first century, the focus in the 1970s for a remarkable outpouring of the Spirit of God on his church.

In the early months of 1974 the people of God in the parish of Wynberg, a suburb of Cape Town, wrestled with the text of 1 Corinthians in a weekly Bible school. As the renewing power of God's Spirit percolated through the parish, we all struggled with the tensions and the joys inherent in any such situation. Opportunities emerged for sharing the studies and the life in other contexts – with fellow clergy on a diocesan retreat; with a mixed group (in all senses) of Christians in the university city of Grahamstown; with another parish in Durban. Then, in 1976, there came an opportunity to be exposed to the church in renewal in a totally different culture from either England or Southern Africa: a month spent experiencing new life in the church in Chile and among the people of God in Buenos Aires.

There have been other contexts – in England, the USA, Canada, Brazil, Jamaica, Zimbabwe, Uganda and South Africa – where the issues raised in 1 Corinthians have been debated, often during conferences or missions – not least between October 1979 and March 1980 at St Aldate's Church, Oxford.

In other words, this book is the result of living and ministering on the *inside* of what is (conveniently but misleadingly) called Renewal with a capital 'R' – and that in a rich diversity of cultures.

From this diverse experience over the last seventeen or eighteen years has come the ever-increasing conviction, not simply that 'the Bible speaks today', but that 1 Corinthians is uniquely a tract for the times. Perhaps we ought to say 1 *and* 2 Corinthians, because the Corinthian correspondence as a whole so clearly holds in balance the double vocation of God's people – to glory and to suffering.

C. K. Barrett, whose two superb commentaries in the A&C Black series consistently illumine the text of Corinthians, has put it memorably:

> I believe that the church in our generation needs to rediscover the apostolic Gospel; and for this it needs the Epistle to the Romans. It needs also to rediscover the relation between this Gospel and its order, discipline, worship and ethics; and for this it needs the 1st Epistle to the Corinthians. If it makes these discoveries, it may well find itself broken; and this may turn out to be the meaning of the 2nd Epistle to the Corinthians. (1967)

> . . . Yet an earthenware vessel that contains such treasure need not fear breaking; it is the apostolic vocation to carry about the killing of Jesus and those who accept it are apt to find the funeral transformed into a triumph, as they learn to trust not in themselves but in Him who raises the dead. (1972)

I owe an immense debt to Anne Johnson and Betty Ho Sang, who helped tirelessly with typing and retyping the manuscript. I am very grateful to John Stott for his encouragement and incisive comments, and also to Frank Entwistle and members of the IVP Editorial Committee for their shrewd appraisal of style and content.

It is inevitable that any treatment of 1 Corinthians will not please, let alone satisfy, some readers. My prayer is that this book will enable many churches, directly and indirectly, to recognize and to tackle the problems inherent in being God's people in the world today. It is good to remember that 'God is faithful', especially in and through all our trials and tribulations. 'The grace of the Lord Jesus be with you.'

DAVID PRIOR

Chief abbreviations

Of the many commentaries on the Corinthian correspondence, the following were most frequently consulted:

Allo	Le P. E.-B. Allo, *Saint Paul, Première Épître aux Corinthiens* (J. Gabalda, Paris, 1956)
Barclay	W. Barclay, *The Letters to the Corinthians* (The Daily Study Bible, The Saint Andrew Press, 1954)
Barrett	C. K. Barrett, *A Commentary on the First Epistle to the Corinthians* (Black's New Testament Commentaries, A&C Black, 1968)
Bruce	F. F. Bruce, *1 and 2 Corinthians* (The New Century Bible Commentaries, Eerdmans and Marshall, Morgan & Scott, 1971)
Conzelmann	Hans Conzelmann, *1 Corinthians* (Hermeneia, Fortress Press, 1975)
Dods	Marcus Dods, *The First Epistle to the Corinthians* (The Expositor's Bible, Hodder & Stoughton, 1889)
Godet	F. Godet, *Commentary on St Paul's First Epistle to the Corinthians* (T&T Clark, 1889), 2 volumes
Goudge	H. L. Goudge, *The First Epistle to the Corinthians* (Westminster Commentaries, Methuen, 1903)
Hodge	Charles Hodge, *A Commentary on the First Epistle to the Corinthians* (Geneva Series, Banner of Truth, 1958)
Morgan	G. Campbell Morgan, *The Corinthian Letters of Paul* (Oliphants, 1947)
Morris	L. Morris, *1 Corinthians* (Tyndale New Testament Commentaries, Inter-Varsity Press, 1958)

Ruef   John S. Ruef, *Paul's First Letter to Corinth* (Pelican New Testament Commentaries, Penguin, 1971)

In addition, considerable use was made of Arnold Bittlenger, *Gifts and Graces* (Eng. tr., Hodder & Stoughton, 1967) – an exegetical commentary on chapters 12 to 14.

Introduction

Corinth stood on a narrow isthmus, only 4 miles across, linking the southern part of Greece with the rest of the country and countries to the north. In this important position it inevitably became a prosperous centre of trade and commerce: by land everyone came through Corinth; by sea sailors usually chose to use Lechaeum and Cenchreae, the two seaports flanking Corinth at either end of the isthmus, rather than circumnavigating the dangerous waters of Cape Malea at the southern tip of Greece (a distance of over 200 miles). For large ships it was a matter of unloading at one port and having the cargo carried by porters to the other, to be re-embarked on another ship. Small ships could be placed on rollers and dragged across the isthmus, to be relaunched the other side. Nero, Emperor of Rome from AD 40 to 66, actually made an abortive attempt to build a canal across the isthmus. The Corinth Canal was completed only in 1893.

Like most seaports, Corinth became both prosperous and licentious – so much so that the Greeks had a word for leading a life of debauchery: *Korinthiazein*, that is, to live like a Corinthian. Homer[1] talks of 'wealthy Corinth' and Thucydides[2] refers to its military importance, which it owed to its control of the seaports of Lechaeum and Cenchreae. The Isthmian Games, second in importance only to the Olympic Games, were held at Corinth.

Dominating the city was the 'Acrocorinth', a hill of over 1,850 feet, on which stood a large temple to Aphrodite, the Greek goddess of love. The thousand priestesses of the temple, who were sacred prostitutes, came down into the city when evening fell and plied their trade in the streets.

---

[1] *Iliad* 2.570.
[2] Thucydides 8.7.

'The cult was dedicated to the glorification of sex.'[3] The worship of Aphrodite is parallel to that of the Ashtoreth (taken from Syrian worship of Astarte) in the days of Solomon, Jeroboam and Josiah.[4]

At the foot of the Acrocorinth was the worship of Melicertes, patron deity of navigation – the same as Melkart, the chief god or 'baal' of the city of Tyre (whose cult was introduced into Israel in the ninth century BC when Ahab married Jezebel, daughter of the ruler of Tyre and Sidon – cf. 1 Kgs 17ff.). Thus, Astarte and Melkart, goddess and god at Corinth, were the direct result of oriental influence.

In addition, there was the temple of Apollo in the city itself – Apollo, the god of music, song and poetry; also, the ideal of male beauty. Nude statues and friezes of Apollo in various poses of virility fired his male worshippers to physical displays of devotion with the god's beautiful boys. Corinth was therefore a centre of homosexual practices (cf. Rom. 1:26ff.).

Historical factors also played a significant part in forming the culture of the Corinth which Paul reached in AD 50. In 146 BC the Achaean League of Greek city-states, which had been defying Roman expansion for some time, collapsed and Corinth (which had led the opposition to Rome) was levelled; its citizens were killed or sold into slavery. Thus the strategic site remained for a century, until Julius Caesar (who knew a good thing when he saw it) refounded Corinth as a Roman colony.

> A Roman colony was a little Rome planted in other lands amid a non-Roman population to be a centre of Roman life and to maintain the Roman peace. Along the great Roman roads – those military highways which ran from Rome to the various frontiers of the Empire – these colonies of Roman citizens were planted at strategic points and they played an important part in the imperial organization.[5]

From that date, 46 BC, Corinth emerged into new prosperity and with an increasingly cosmopolitan character. As a Roman colony, Corinth received its share of veterans from the Roman army, who were given land in Corinth to enable them to set up home as settlers. This powerful minority ensured a Roman flavour to the new city, but it soon became

---

[3] J. C. Pollock, *The Apostle* (Hodder & Stoughton, 1969), p. 120.
[4] Cf. 1 Kgs 11:1–9, 33; 2 Kgs 23:13.
[5] F. F. Bruce, *The Spreading Flame* (Paternoster, 1958), p. 13.

a hotchpotch of races, creeds, languages and cultures. Those with commercial interests, entrepreneurs and the like, began to take up residence, including many Jews. Farrar describes Corinth as 'This mongrel and heterogeneous population of Greek adventurers and Roman bourgeois, with a tainting infusion of Phoenicians; this mass of Jews, ex-soldiers, philosophers, merchants, sailors, freedmen, slaves, trades-people, hucksters and agents of every form of vice.'[6] Barclay characterizes her as a colony 'without aristocracy, without tradition and without well-established citizens'.[7]

Corinth was a rough, tough place in the middle of the first century. It is not difficult to imagine something of its reputation and its reality. Nor is it a reflection on modern cities such as San Francisco, Rio de Janeiro or Cape Town to see them as counterparts of that urban challenge to the apostolic gospel.

Pollock puts the situation Paul faced like this:

Corinth was the biggest city Paul had yet encountered, a brash new commercial metropolis . . . It squeezed nearly a quarter of a million people into a comparatively small area, a large proportion being slaves engaged in the unending movement of goods. Slaves or free, Corinthians were rootless, cut off from their country background, drawn from races and districts all over the empire . . . a curiously close parallel to the population of a 20th Century 'inner-city' . . .

Paul had seen a Christian church grow and flourish in the moderately-sized cities he had found in Macedonia. If the love of Christ Jesus could take root in Corinth, the most populated, wealthy, commercial-minded and sex-obsessed city of eastern Europe, it must prove powerful anywhere.[8]

1. Paul at Corinth

In view of these factors, it is not all that surprising to discover that Paul talks of his arrival in Corinth as full of 'fear and in much trembling' – he was very scared indeed (1 Cor. 2:3). However confident he was in the power of the gospel, whatever the proper interpretation of the nature and

---

[6] Quoted in Barclay, p. 4.
[7] Ibid.
[8] Pollock, *The Apostle*, p. 121.

impact of his preaching to the Athenians immediately before coming to Corinth, however shell-shocked he had been by savage treatment up north in Macedonia a few weeks earlier – Paul would have been less than normal if he had not been considerably affected by the reputation of Corinth in the Mediterranean world. The fact that he makes a strong point of his 'fear and . . . trembling' would indicate that he found Corinth distinctively, if not uniquely, awesome.

A narrative of Paul's eighteen months' stay in Corinth (longer than anywhere he visited except for Ephesus) is provided in Acts 18:1–18. From this we can gather a few outline facts about his ministry. As in Ephesus, he practised his trade as a tentmaker, at least in the opening weeks of his ministry until he had worked himself into the situation and had become known as a preacher and a teacher. A love-gift from the churches in Macedonia and Philippi, brought later by Silas and Timothy, also gave him freedom to concentrate on his preaching and teaching ministry. If his daily timetable in Ephesus is anything to go by, Paul might well have given as many as eight hours a day to his manual work, leaving perhaps 11 am to 4 pm for his ministry of the Word.[9] In the hot months of the year in a Mediterranean climate, this represents a rigorous daily schedule for a man obviously not blessed with the best of health.

A closer study of Luke's account of Paul's time in Corinth will further bring to life the apostle's relationship with the Christians in that city.

Compared with his rough treatment at the hands of the Macedonians, especially at Philippi, Paul had a relatively straightforward time in Athens – the usual combination of mockery and interest, but not many believers. However, the church was founded in Athens. He came to Corinth feeling weak in every way – physically battered, spiritually unexcited by the Athenian experience, emotionally deprived of the partnership of Silas and Timothy, and naturally rather in trepidation at the prospect of coming face to face with the city of love.

It is reasonable to infer that Paul reached Corinth in about March 50 and stayed there until about September 51 (the dates may be a year or so out). The most probable date for 1 Corinthians is in the early months of 54, or possibly towards the end of 53 (i.e. about the middle of his two and a half years in Ephesus).

---

[9] Cf. NRSV margin of Acts 19:9, together with the description of his daily lifestyle contained in his farewell address to the elders of the church at Ephesus in Acts 20:18–35, especially verse 34. See also 1 Thess. 2:9.

Walking through the streets, his attention was drawn inevitably to traders in his own occupation of tentmaking (or, more widely, leatherwork). Apparently Paul, as a rabbi, would have found it necessary to have some other source of income, because rabbis were expected to perform their religious and legal functions without demanding a fee. One of the local crafts in his own province of Cilicia was tentmaking, with the cloth made from goats' hair (known as 'cilicium'). He would most naturally have been attracted to such an indigenous craft, finding as much pride and pleasure in doing his work creatively as no doubt Jesus himself did in his carpentry. He recognized a fellow Jew when he saw one in Aquila, and it does not require much imagination to visualize their initial conversation. Aquila and Priscilla were already accustomed to a fairly mobile life and would readily have offered the hospitality of their home to this lonely preacher, who had also found completeness and 'shalom' in Jesus.

It is difficult to overestimate the encouragement this encounter would have brought to Paul in his 'weakness'. Indeed, God seems to have given him very significant encouragement all the way through his eighteen months in Corinth. Aquila and Priscilla were the first example; then comes the arrival of Silas and Timothy, not only bringing good news of the Macedonian churches, but making a powerful team of five to penetrate this crucial provincial capital with the gospel. Such shared ministry is fundamental: it needs to be based on strong friendship and partnership, not merely doing 'Christian' activities together but sharing the whole of life. Aquila and Priscilla became close partners with Paul and were prepared to move home and job at the summons of the Spirit in furtherance of the gospel.

As always, Paul initially concentrated on the synagogue and, in spite of direct and (later) concerted opposition from the Jewish community, found great encouragement in the conversion of Crispus, who was responsible for running the synagogue (Acts 18:8). Indeed, it looks very likely that Crispus's replacement, Sosthenes (Acts 18:17), was also converted to Jesus. His is an uncommon name and it appears, alongside Paul's, as co-author of 1 Corinthians (1 Cor. 1:1). No wonder the Jews were so incensed by the impact of Paul's preaching.

When he was no longer allowed access to the synagogue, Paul decided to hold his meeting next door. The owner of the house, one Titius Justus (obviously a Gentile), is likely to have had the third name of Gaius and to be the man of that name mentioned in 1 Corinthians 1:14 and Romans 16:23.

So Paul was provided with an ideal location, from which he could contact both Jewish and Gentile Corinthians. Indeed, 'many . . . became believers and were baptized' (Acts 18:8).

The church was growing apace. There were many reasons for confidence and buoyancy. Yet it appears that Paul was still low in spirits, uncertain and prone to depression. As John Pollock imagines the situation,

> He would never win another Corinthian to Christ, see the sparkle of new life in a man's eyes. And he dreaded the physical agony of another stoning or beating with rods; the desolation of being flung out again with winter now on them, the seas turbulent, and nowhere to take his stiff, aging joints but the mountain trails of the Peloponnese. He wanted to give up, stop preaching, take himself away to live quietly at peace, back to the Taurus, to Arabia, to anywhere.[10]

Then the Lord, who understood the pressures, the depression, the desire to opt out, spoke directly to Paul in a vision, rallying his spirits, guaranteeing much more fruit in Corinth, and lifting the fear of more physical battering at a time when he knew Paul had had enough. Paul would have cherished very precious memories of those Christians in Corinth; they became to him living proof of the faithfulness of a God who cares for and encourages his wearied servants.

The rest of the time in Corinth seems to have been relatively straightforward, as Paul spent the time 'teaching the word of God among them' (Acts 18:11), steadily building up the church, binding it together, extending its frontiers. There was a slight hiccough, when a new Roman proconsul took over the province – Gallio, brother-in-law of Seneca, Nero's tutor and philosopher. The Jews glimpsed a chance to have Paul locked up and to put an end to this Christian menace. But Gallio knew how to keep his distance from Jewish troublemakers, and Paul did not even have a charge to answer. If Sosthenes was by this time a Christian, he was the one to receive the beating for the name of Jesus. That must have been hard for Paul to watch, but certainly it would have bound them even closer together in the fellowship of Christ's sufferings.

---

[10] Pollock, *The Apostle*, p. 124.

So Paul left Corinth after eighteen months' effective ministry, together with Aquila and Priscilla. He always looked back on his time in Corinth with great affection. He had arrived feeling nothing but weakness; but he left having experienced the secret of all Christian ministry – that God's power is made perfect in weakness (2 Cor. 12:7–10). It is always difficult to leave a community of God's people among whom we have been taught similarly deep lessons. It is very much like a bereavement, as though losing part of oneself. That is how Paul felt about the church at Corinth. The Christians there were part of him and, when he wrote to them, he wrote to brothers and sisters in Christ who had been a refreshment and an encouragement to him in times of real depression. God had said: 'there are many in this city who are my people' (Acts 18:10), and those many people were to Paul 'the seal of my apostleship in the Lord' (1 Cor. 9:2).

It was at Corinth that he learnt thoroughly the lesson which he uses to conclude the major teaching of this letter: 'Therefore, my beloved, be steadfast, immovable, always excelling in the work of the Lord, because you know that in the Lord your labour is not in vain' (1 Cor. 15:58).

2. The Corinthian correspondence

Because of his deep attachment to the Christians in Corinth, Paul was bound to put pen to paper when strange teachings began to divide the church. As C. K. Barrett says,

> Many winds of doctrine blew into the harbours and along the streets of Corinth, and it must have been very difficult for young Christians to keep on a straight course . . . Corinth would undoubtedly have received Christian visitors in addition to Paul and some of them preached the same gospel, others did not . . . Some of those whom Paul had in mind indulged in speculative theology based on the themes of knowledge (*gnosis*) and wisdom (*sophia*) . . . It may well be right to see in Corinth an early form of that confluence of Hellenistic, Oriental, Jewish and Christian streams which makes up full-blown Gnosticism . . .
>
> Paul was dealing with men who wished to be at the centre of, and to control, their own religion, and had not yet learned what it meant to walk by faith, not by sight.[11]

---

[11] Barrett, pp. 36ff.

There is full discussion in C. K. Barrett of the complex details within the correspondence between Paul and the Corinthian church. The most helpful guide through these intricacies is William Barclay.[12] The basic fact to remember is that 1 and 2 Corinthians as we have them do not (by their own testimony) comprise the entire correspondence. Mention is made of a letter previous to 1 Corinthians (1 Cor. 5:9). At the end of 2 Corinthians[13] Paul talks of paying the Corinthians a *third* visit: the first is that described by Luke in Acts 18, but the second is unknown. In 2 Corinthians 7:8 Paul talks of another letter of such sternness that Paul almost wished he had never sent it. This cannot be 1 Corinthians, and the first nine chapters of 2 Corinthians are certainly not stern: indeed they are probably the most tender, warm and irenic of all his human correspondence. This leaves 2 Corinthians 10 – 13 which, by his own admission, contains very traumatic material which could well be the material Paul wishes he had never despatched. This leaves us with the following possible sequence of events, as laid out by Barclay:

   i. The 'Previous Letter', which *may* be contained in 2 Corinthians 6:14 – 7:1 (NB 6:13 runs very smoothly into 7:2).

   ii. 'Chloe's people' (1 Cor. 1:11) bring to Paul at Ephesus news of division at Corinth.

   iii. 1 Corinthians chapters 1–4 are written in reply and Timothy is about to take it to Corinth (1 Cor. 4:17).

   iv. Three men (Stephanas, Fortunatus and Achaicus: 1 Cor. 16:17) arrive with more news and a letter from Corinth: Paul immediately writes chapters 5 and 6 and pens chapters 7–16 in reply to this letter. Timothy then takes the whole of 1 Corinthians to Corinth.

   v. The situation gets worse and Paul makes a disastrous visit to Corinth after which things get even more painful for Paul (cf. 2 Cor. 2:1).

   vi. He then sends the 'Severe Letter' (2 Cor. 10 – 13) by the hands of Titus (2 Cor. 2:13; 7:13).

   vii. Paul is so worried that he cannot wait for Titus to return; he sets out to meet him in Macedonia (2 Cor. 7:5–13), and then writes 2 Corinthians 1 – 9, the 'Letter of Reconciliation'.

---

[12] Barclay, pp. 6–9.
[13] 2 Cor. 12:14 and 13:1–2.

1 Corinthians 1:1–9

1. The perfect church

Before we look at Paul's description of the church at Corinth from God's perspective, it is worth taking a bird's-eye view of its main characteristics as they are shown in these two letters.

It was a large church – many Corinthians were converted to Christ. It was full of cliques, each following a different personality. Many Christians were very snobbish: at fellowship meals the rich kept to themselves, and the poor were left alone. There was very little church discipline: a lot of laxity was allowed, both in morals and in doctrine – an all-too-common combination. They were unwilling to submit to authority of any kind and the integrity of Paul's own apostleship was frequently questioned. There was a distinct lack of humility and of consideration for others, some being prepared to take fellow Christians to court and others celebrating their new-found freedom in Christ without the slightest regard for the less robust consciences of fellow believers. In general, they were very keen on the more dramatic gifts of the Spirit and were short on love rooted in the truth. This is the church Paul greets.

1. Paul's greeting to the church at Corinth (1:1–3)

Paul describes himself in almost the same way as at the beginning of Romans, 2 Corinthians, Galatians, Ephesians and Colossians: that is, as an apostle commissioned by God. Thus from the outset he makes plain his apostolic calling to those at Corinth who questioned it.

The greeting fills out the conventional Greek and Hebrew words of welcome with specifically Christian content: instead of *chaire* (= greetings),

Paul uses *charis* (= *Grace*); and he takes the Hebrew *šālôm* and invests it with emphasis on Jesus Christ the Lord.

In verse 2, Paul uses a number of pungent phrases to describe the church at Corinth. On closer investigation, there seems to be a deliberate play on the root word *kalein* (= call) – a theme which is central to Paul's thinking, particularly in these opening paragraphs of the letter: 1:9, 'God is faithful; by him you were *called* into the fellowship of his Son, Jesus Christ our Lord'; 1:23–24, 'we proclaim Christ crucified . . . to those who are the *called* . . . Christ the power of God and the wisdom of God'; 1:26, 'Consider your own *call*, brothers and sisters; not many of you were wise by human standards, not many were powerful, not many were of noble birth.'

Clearly this sense of *calling* is uppermost in Paul's mind as he ponders the relationship between the Corinthian church and himself, and as he recollects the circumstances in which the Christian community came into being at Corinth. Fundamentally, he is conscious of God's initiative in his own call and in the call of the Christians at Corinth, both individually and corporately. He seems to be saying this: 'God called me to be an apostle, God called each one of you to be a saint, to enjoy the fellowship of his Son, Jesus.' If God had not thus called, he would not have become an apostle and they would not have found Jesus Christ to be the wisdom and the power of God, let alone come to share in him and be his special people, his saints. This almost self-conscious harping on God's call would indicate that Paul's use of the word *ekklēsia* (literally 'a company of those called out') to describe the church at Corinth is also not accidental.

Thus God calls each individual by name, and a person responds by calling on *the name of our Lord* (cf. verse 2). The fact that these Corinthians, and countless others *in every place, call on the name of our Lord Jesus Christ* is proof positive that God has already made his call sound clearly enough for them to hear and respond.

All those who thus hear God's call and respond are members of the *ekklēsia* of God. They have been set apart by God in that call, and are reserved for Jesus Christ (*sanctified in Christ Jesus*). There is as close a unity between such people *in every place* as there is between Paul and the Christians of Corinth in that single place.

Paul does not talk of 'my church', but of *the church of God*. He was as responsible for the birth and life of that church in Corinth as it is possible for any human to be: but it was *God's* church, not Paul's. We often speak too loosely of 'my church' or 'our church'. It is a healthy corrective to note Paul's example. Many problems in a church in fact revolve around a selfish possessiveness, by pastor and congregation, towards its life and activities. It also needs to be said that no individual Christian, or group of Christians, has any special claim to Jesus: he is *both their Lord and ours*.

For Paul himself there was probably no distinction in time between his call to be a saint, along with every other believer, and his call to be an apostle: the one included the other, the former being a calling he shared with others and the latter being something which set him apart from others.

A concise summary of what was involved in the unique apostleship entrusted to Paul, as to the original disciples of Jesus, can be found in 'Gospel and Spirit', a statement first published in 1977.[1] This says:

> Through divine revelation and inspiration these men were authoritative spokesmen for, witnesses to and interpreters of God and his Son. Their personal authority as teachers and guides – authority bestowed and guaranteed by the risen Christ – was final, and no appeal away from what they said was allowable.

When God called Paul from his bitter persecution of the Christian church, he called him into his apostolic ministry. That vocation was not a second call after the initial call. Each Christian is similarly called: our appointed ministry is part of what it means to be saved. It may take some time to discover it, certainly to slot into it; but nevertheless each Christian is called to serve.[2]

Of course, Paul's call to be an apostle, though admittedly in many ways very different from that of the other apostles,[3] was crucial in establishing his credentials in front of the Corinthian church when it was being harassed by others who styled themselves not merely apostles, but far more authoritative and effective apostles than Paul.[4] Paul found it necessary to ask himself searching and painful questions about his call to be an apostle. We may not have that particular struggle to face, but we

---

[1] Joint Statement of the Church of England Evangelical Council and the Fountain Trust, published as *Theological Renewal*, Occasional Paper No. 1, April/May 1977.

[2] Cf. Acts 26:15ff. and Gal. 1:15ff.

[3] Cf. 1 Cor. 15:8–9.

[4] Cf. 1 Cor. 4:18–19 and the material in 2 Cor. 10 – 13.

need to remind ourselves that a call to salvation is necessarily a call to service.

Paul does not refer to the community of God's people at Corinth as *part* of the church, but as *the church of God* as it is at Corinth. Equally, in a letter almost certainly written later at Corinth, he talks of the church as it is in the house of Aquila and Priscilla (Rom. 16:5). In other words, whether we are thinking of the Christians gathered in a geographical area or in someone's home, there is nothing lacking except numbers. The church as a whole is present, in microcosm. Indeed, there is good scriptural justification for seeing the church in someone's home as primary and working out from that basic unit.[5]

The presence of a person by the name of *Sosthenes* as co-writer with Paul of 1 Corinthians is intriguing. Although by no means an unknown name at the time, it is sufficiently uncommon for us to assume that this is the same Sosthenes who replaced Crispus as ruler of the synagogue in Corinth when the latter turned to Christ.[6] The fact that Paul included Sosthenes without comment indicates that he was well known to the Christians at Corinth. The conversion to Christ of two leading officials in the Jewish community one after the other must have thrown them all into some disarray. A parallel situation emerged at Oxford University in the early 1960s in the heyday of the Humanist Society. Its president was converted to Christ, which led to an extraordinary general meeting of the Society. The person then elected was himself converted within a few weeks, thus necessitating another extraordinary general meeting. The Sosthenes affair should spur our faith in presenting the claim of Jesus Christ to those who seem most entrenched in the official opposition.

2. Paul's confidence in the church at Corinth (1:4–9)

The one fact most people have at their fingertips concerning the Corinthian church is that it was a mess – full of problems, sins, division, heresy. It was, in this sense, no different from any modern church. The church is a fellowship of sinners before it is a fellowship of saints. Even those churches which have glowing reputations are known all too well by their members and pastors to be full of weaknesses and sins. The sad thing

---

5 For further implications of this perspective, see the author's *The Church in the Home* (Marshalls, 1983).
6 See Acts 18:8, 17.

is that dissatisfied church members will often naively think that another church in the area will somehow be better than the one they now attend. From this restlessness comes the common habit of church-swapping. Perhaps one of the best antidotes for this kind of malaise is to look again at what Paul says in 1:4–9 about the notoriously messy church at Corinth.

We need to register this primary truth – Paul looks at the Corinthian church as it is *in Christ* before he looks at anything else that is true of the church. That disciplined statement of faith is rarely made in local churches. The warts are examined and lamented, but often there is no vision of what God has already done in Christ. If the first nine verses of this letter were excised from the text, it would be impossible for any reader to come to anything but a fairly pessimistic view of the church at Corinth. The statements of faith, hope and love that occur at frequent intervals in the text would have no context; they would degenerate into pious dreams. For lack of the kind of vision spelt out in verses 4–9, the people of God today are, in many places, perishing: either going through the motions of being the church with no real expectation of significant growth into maturity, or desperately urging one another to more effort, more prayer, more faith and more activity – because those seem to be the right things.

If it is true that the church in the home or in a given area lacks nothing except numbers, then what Paul says of the church at Corinth *in Christ* is an accurate description of *every* church of God. His confidence in the church at Corinth is based on God's generosity and faithfulness.

a. The church is fully endowed with all the gifts of God's grace (1:4–7)

The grace of God that has been given you . . . in every way you have been enriched in him . . . you are not lacking in any spiritual gift – three statements which speak of the lavish generosity of God towards these redeemed sinners at Corinth. It is important immediately to point out that these statements are about the church of God at Corinth, not about individual believers. If we are to know the fullness of God's blessing, if we are to experience all the gifts of his grace which are ours in Christ, it has to be together in fellowship. No individual Christian can claim to be 'not lacking in any spiritual gift' – as chapters 12 and 14 of 1 Corinthians make abundantly plain.

But the local church potentially *does* have every spiritual gift within its corporate life, and should prayerfully expect God to bring them into mature expression. In giving us his Son Jesus, God has given us all he has; he can give us no more; we have everything in him. If we are gradually to make these gifts a reality in our life together, we shall need to enter more fully into the richness of his grace; we shall also need to keep our eyes skinned for his *revealing* (7), his unveiling. Such a hope has its own inner incentive to move forward as those destined to be the bride of Christ, because it is then (and only then) that we shall enter into the full reality of all that is ours in Christ.

In talking of the gifts of God's grace,[7] Paul specifically stresses that the church has been enriched *in speech and knowledge*. The two words here are *logos* and *gnōsis*, both bundles of dynamite in the early church. It is quite likely that Paul concentrates on these two clusters of gifts because the Corinthians majored on them.[8] There is also, without doubt, an early reference here to the pervasive teachings of Gnosticism: the second-century heretical hotchpotch (already discernible in the middle of the first century) about which it is still difficult to be precise, but which created a spiritual elite who claimed alone to possess true knowledge, alone to be able to put it into words and alone to have proper authority to guide and control the life of the church.[9]

Paul is adamant that God has fully endowed the whole congregation with these gifts of knowledge and speech, and no doubt Paul is thinking of particular friends at Corinth with different gifts. On the speaking side he would have included such gifts as prophecy, teaching, preaching, evangelism, speaking in tongues and interpretation of tongues, and any use of the gift of speech which contributes to the building-up of the church. As far as knowledge is concerned, the church as a body has access to all the wisdom, insight, discernment and truth which it needs (Col. 2:3). It needs no special gurus to bring it to them.[10]

Two important points are made (somewhat cryptically) about preaching in the rather difficult phrase in verse 6: *just as the testimony of Christ has been strengthened among you*. The meaning probably is this: as Paul

---

[7] NB *charis* (= grace) and *charisma* (= gift) come from the same root.

[8] Cf. chapters 12–14.

[9] For a helpful summary of the Corinthian brand of Gnosticism, as far as we can trace it in these letters, it is worth consulting C. K. Barrett, *2 Corinthians* (Black's New Testament Commentaries [A&C Black], 1973), pp. 36–42. In *The Message of Colossians and Philemon: Fullness and Freedom* (IVP, 1980), Dick Lucas identifies seven aspects of what has been called the 'Colossian heresy', many of which were probably present in embryo in Corinth (pp. 22–24).

[10] Cf. 1 John 2:20, 27.

himself proclaimed 'the boundless riches of Christ' (Eph. 3:8) to the church of God at Corinth during those busy eighteen months, so they began to appreciate and gradually to experience the richness of their inheritance as children of God. In other words, they were enriched in proportion to the quality and the clarity of Paul's preaching. The two points here about preaching, therefore, are these. First, the privilege and the responsibility of the preacher is to uncover and explain all that is ours in Christ; second, bare preaching is not adequate – it must be confirmed (more literally 'secured') in the lives of the hearers, and that requires the work of God's Spirit (1 Thess. 1:5), bringing conviction, illumination and faith.

The church is thus fully endowed with all the gifts of God's grace. These need to be discovered, explained and appropriated. For this to happen, preaching must testify to the boundless riches of Christ. Such preaching requires the power of the Spirit to secure those riches in the life of the Christian community.

b. The church will be completely sustained by the faithfulness of God (1:8–9)

Not only is Paul very positive about the present resources of the church of God at Corinth; he is also full of confidence in the Lord for its future. Whatever ups and downs it might face, Paul is sure of the faithfulness of God: he has called them into the fellowship of his Son; he will 'sustain' (*strengthen*; this is the same word as in verse 6 = 'make secure') them to the end. The phrase in verse 9 '*koinōnia* of Jesus Christ' could mean either that the church is *the fellowship* of Jesus Christ, that is, the company of people who call Jesus Lord and belong to him; or that God calls us to share in his Son, Jesus. The latter interpretation is more likely, especially as that truth is picked up later to pinpoint the sinfulness of division on the grounds of allegiance to those who are simply 'Servants through whom you came to believe, as the Lord assigned to each' (1 Cor. 3:5).

If we have been called, on the initiative of God himself, to share in his Son, Jesus Christ, then God will not abandon us or go back on his promises. That is the force of the word *pistos* (= *faithful*). We can totally depend on God: he is not a human being, he cannot deny himself, he will keep his word. The church is his responsibility: he is committed to 'the perfecting of the saints' (Eph. 4:12, AV; cf. Rom. 8:28–30).

God's terminus is not merely the end of each individual's lifespan, which he certainly guards with personal care, but *the day of our Lord Jesus*

Christ (8). If we take the teaching on this subject in this letter, we discover that this day marks the full disclosure (literally 'unveiling') both of Jesus Christ as he really is, and of the true quality of our service for Christ (3:10–15), as well as of the inner purposes and motives of our hearts (4:5). It is a day, anticipated with joy in each celebration of the Lord's Supper (11:26), when the dead in Christ shall be raised (15:23, 52) to an incorruptible life in what Paul calls 'a spiritual body' (15:44). It is a day, therefore, for which Paul longs in the prayer at the end of his letter (16:22): *Maranatha* – 'Our Lord, come!'

God's faithfulness extends to that day, and beyond it into the fullness of eternity. He will keep his people *blameless* in that day: that is, when the secrets of people's hearts are disclosed and we might have had legitimate fear of being finally found guilty before him. God will ensure that absolutely no charge or accusation is laid against his people, whether by human beings or by Satan, the great 'accuser of our brothers' (Rev. 12:10, margin). On that day it will be plain to all that it is God who justifies, and that those whom he has justified he has also, in the selfsame act, glorified (cf. Rom. 8:33). It is Jesus who matters on that day; it is his day; he calls the tune; he determines the issues. Because we have been called to share in Jesus, we share in his supremacy on that day. We are not under judgment for sin on that day. If anything, the New Testament teaches that we shall exercise judgment along with Jesus Christ (cf. 1 Cor. 6:2–3).

If we have been called to share in Jesus, let us abide in him (1 John 2:28f.) – the only way of gradually becoming like him. When we have become like him through the grace of God continuously at work in us, it will be impossible for any guilt, or even cause for guilt, to exist. To such a radical purpose God has committed himself in calling us into fellowship with his Son.

The practical implications of this 'glorious hope' in terms of our vision for the local church are relatively straightforward. It must surely mean that we are unreservedly committed to the church of God where he has placed us; that we are unhesitatingly confident about God's desire and ability to make his church in that place like Jesus Christ; that we are uncompromisingly certain about the call for us to be holy, as he is holy. It is these implications which Paul works out in the rest of this letter.

1 Corinthians 1:10–17

2. Cliques at Corinth

Paul's high view of the church – at Corinth and in general – pinpoints the sadness he must have felt at hearing news of division among the Corinthian Christians: *it has been reported to me by Chloe's people that there are quarrels among you, my brothers and sisters* (11). All the indications are that Paul found this news extremely painful. He knew enough about the realities of local church life not to be surprised. But still he was deeply hurt. This is shown by the double reference to *brothers and sisters* in verses 10 and 11. The fact of Christian brotherhood is the ground of his appeal for unity: if Jesus Christ has by his grace made them one and if they share in him, then they must 'become what they are': *I appeal to you . . . by the name of our Lord Jesus Christ . . .*

What exactly caused this division at Corinth? We can see both explicit and implicit causes in verses 12–17. Obviously personality cults were emerging, taking three major figures in the early church as their focus, almost certainly with absolutely no encouragement from either Paul, Apollos or Cephas (Peter). But there may well be other clues to the trouble in the way Paul argues in verses 13–17: for example, it looks as if baptism was becoming an issue. There may well have been also some incipient heresy separating 'the Jesus of history' from 'the Christ of faith'.[1]

Whatever the causes of these developing cliques, the situation had become one of 'strife'; *quarrels* (11) is too weak a translation. The different

---

[1] C. K. Barrett writes along these lines in his introduction to 2 Corinthians (see especially pp. 41–42) and his commentary on 2 Corinthians 5:16 and 11:23 in *2 Corinthians* (Black's New Testament Commentaries [A&C Black], 1973).

stages on the road to division are worth spelling out. In 1 Corinthians 11:18–19 Paul refers again to these 'divisions'. There he deprecates the fact that inevitable 'factions' have been allowed to sunder the body of Christ and to produce 'strife'. In other words, there are bound to be different emphases and ideas within the local church: the word translated 'factions' in 11:19 is *haireseis* (from which we get the word 'heresy'), and it has the root meaning of 'choose'. All Christians select different aspects of the truth at different times for particular emphasis. Such selection inevitably brings the focus away from other strands of truth on to one or two specific matters. That is allowable, if not necessary, so long as what is being done is recognized for what it is, namely, selectivity. When a Christian, or a group of Christians, becomes totally absorbed with one aspect of the truth to the neglect, exclusion or even denial of the whole truth as it is in Jesus, then the danger point has been reached. That is when selectivity becomes heresy and it can be readily seen who is 'genuine' (11:19) and who is false.

Paul is concerned that the church at Corinth should learn the right way of dealing with what we have called 'selectivity'. When a few Christians begin to stress one aspect of the truth, they need to be aware of what they are doing, and the rest must refuse to react negatively. The Corinthians had allowed such emphases to develop into cliques, who were refusing to share together in fellowship. Selectivity had produced splinter groups (the word translated *divisions* is *schismata*, from which we get 'schism', and which literally means to 'cut apart'). Now there was open strife between the different groups.

1. The four groups

The major problem was that these cliques had all managed to take their eyes off the Lord Jesus Christ. Each rallied support around one personality or another.[2] Each had its own slogans. It is important to understand the nature of each clique, because they all recur regularly in the church. In fact, it is interesting (though sad) to discover that Clement of Rome (writing about AD 95) talks about the same cliques and divisions at Corinth in his day – though he does not mention the 'Christ-party'. So, forty years on, the trouble had not been eradicated. This indicates that we should

---

[2] NB The word for 'strife' (*quarrels*, verse 11) has the overtones of a clash of personality.

expect and be on our guard against these divisive tendencies at all times. Let us look at each group.

a. The Paul-party

'I became your father in Christ Jesus through the gospel' (4:15). Obviously there were many at Corinth who were for this fundamental reason very strongly attached to Paul. He had brought them to faith and they were for ever in his debt. The total transformation God had effected in their lives, from the darkness of utter paganism to the marvellous light of the gospel, made them doubly grateful for Paul's labours on their behalf. So whatever Paul said, or was imagined to have said, these folk accepted verbatim. They probably regarded everyone else as second-rate anyway. True, Paul had been gone for several years now, but his memory lived on. There is probably no pastor of a church with any history behind it who has not discovered a Paul-party of this kind within his congregation. They have taken their eyes off the Lord in the passage of time and are consequently always harking back to 'the good old days'.

Barclay suggests that the Paul-party emphasized Christian freedom and the end of the law. The fact that Paul specifically mentions personalities, rather than matters of theology, suggests that this interpretation is unlikely. Very often what happens in a local church today is that differences grow around personalities (either from within the church fellowship or from the wider church) and then become articulated around matters of doctrinal dispute. There may well be genuine theological disagreement, but the 'strife' emerges because personal relationships are not good. When the love of God is truly controlling such relationships within a church, areas of disagreement find their proper perspective and do not necessitate 'strife', let alone 'schism'.[3]

So-called 'clashes of personality' often, on analysis, are nothing much more than a failure, or even a refusal, to let God's love change us in our attitudes to one another. We allow theological differences (instead of the love of God) to determine the quality, openness and depth of our relationships. For example, our Western tendency to be detached and objective in discussing a situation enables us to analyse differences in the church in what we believe to be a careful, biblical way. We can pursue

---

[3] Francis Schaeffer writes helpfully about the matter of Christian truth and its need for a proper context of Christian love in *The Mark of the Christian* (IVP, 1971).

such a course sitting in the same room as those with whom we disagree – and never meet one another as people, let alone as brothers and
sisters in Christ. We part company convinced that the *real* problem is
theological, when in fact we have managed, by our very detachment, to
prevent the love of God from bringing harmony and mutual acceptance.
We then declare that theological differences are the cause of the schism
between us.

This seemed to be classically the case over the division which emerged
in the church in the 1960s and 1970s over charismatic renewal in Britain.
Fifteen years of doctrinal disagreement preceded any committed attempt
on a national level to build loving relationships. Out of the doctrinal
debate came division; out of the bridge-building between people came a
marked degree of mutual trust and acceptance.[4] If (as Paul says in 1 Cor.
13) love is of fundamental and pre-eminent importance, then it is
imperative to build and foster good relationships in which we can discuss
theological differences in the love of God.

The Paul-party almost certainly emerged in reaction to others in
Corinth forming groups around the other figures mentioned here. Until
the others emerged, everyone would have presumably supported Paul. In
other words, those supporting Paul reacted in kind, forming their own
group. It is so easy to respond to fleshly (as Paul calls it in 3:1–4) behaviour
in the church with equally fleshly methods, instead of taking up God's
armour in the power of the Spirit.

b. The Apollos-party

Although there is relatively little information to hand about Apollos, what
we do know gives us a clear portrait and provides a satisfactory, though
speculative, explanation for his becoming the focus for a developing
clique at Corinth. According to Acts 18:24 – 19:7, Apollos came from Alexandria in Egypt, probably the most respected and creative university city
of the Mediterranean. Tarsus was 'no mean city', but it was no Alexandria:
when Apollos came to Corinth with his intellectual ability, his fine
speaking, his expository skill in the Old Testament Scriptures, his accurate
teaching about Jesus, his fervent enthusiasm, his powerful confrontation

---

[4] The statement 'Gospel and Spirit', published in 1977, was the fruit of this coming together for four day-
conferences over a period of eighteen months. The statement begins: 'We are glad that we did so [i.e. met in
this way], and acknowledge that our failure to do so earlier may have helped to prolong unnecessary misunderstandings and polarisations.' (See above, p. 11, n. 1.)

of the Jews in public and his bold preaching – it is no wonder that he began to attract a personal following.

Aquila and Priscilla took him under their wing in Ephesus and carefully redirected his ministry (Acts 18:26). Apollos then had an invaluable ministry with young believers in Christ. Luke particularly remarks that 'he greatly helped those who through grace had become believers' (Acts 18:27), both in his proclamation of Jesus as Messiah and by giving them more thorough teaching to strengthen Christians in their encounters with hostile Jews.[5]

Some feel that Apollos, with such a background, might have been unwittingly responsible for introducing something of an intellectual elite into the Corinthian church. Young Christians certainly can be sucked into a personality cult around the gifts and graces of impressive speakers, particularly those with a genuinely helpful teaching ministry. Apollos probably did not stay that long in Corinth, but it was long enough for some to start comparing him favourably with Paul, who did not lag behind in fervour or mastery of the Old Testament Scriptures or intellectual ability, but who by his own admission did not display great eloquence.[6] It is certainly not necessary to blame Apollos for intellectualizing Christianity, as suggested by Barclay. At the same time, when a group of Christians begins to take its teaching only from its chosen guru, schism is not far off.[7]

c. The Peter-party

It seems to be generally agreed that 'the Cephas-group represented Jewish Christianity in some form'.[8] Peter may have visited Corinth himself, which would explain the emergence of such a clique. Some of his followers may also have visited Corinth and pushed the party line. There is ample evidence of legalistic tendencies in the church at Corinth, particularly in the debate about the rights and wrongs of eating food offered to idols in chapters 8–10. We only have to read the account (in Gal. 2) of Paul's clash

---

[5] Alexandria was the centre of Old Testament exegesis and exposition, and had seen the foundation of the Septuagint, the Greek version of the Old Testament.

[6] Cf. 2 Cor. 10:10 and 1 Cor. 2:3–4.

[7] The first Christianity of which we do hear at Alexandria was characterized by Gnostic tendencies. Howard Marshall has written: 'It would not be surprising if Apollos had picked up some garbled understanding of Christianity there . . . We can presume that he was instructed (by Aquila and Priscilla) in the distinctive Pauline doctrines' (*Acts*, Tyndale New Testament Commentaries [IVP, 1982], pp. 303f.).

[8] Barrett, p. 44.

with Peter about food laws to realize that the 'kosher' issue may well have continued to be a smouldering fire between the apostle to the Gentiles and the one 'entrusted with the gospel for the circumcised' (Gal. 2:7). From the very beginning there had been among Corinthian Jews significant conversions to Jesus as the Christ and the temptation to return to legalism must have been very strong, especially in the notorious profligacy of Corinthian society.

The first flush of new life in the Spirit can often give way to a very negative and restrictive legalism, particularly in the family life of those converted from rank paganism to the liberty of the gospel. When the fire of enthusiasm dies down, a 'safe' way emerges, which is often the letter without the Spirit. This tendency reflects our natural desire to have clear guidelines for faith and behaviour, rather than to walk the tightrope of obedience to the Spirit between the two extremes of licence and legalism.

There are today many examples of a genuine renewal in the Spirit sliding into this kind of legalism, in which certain teachers emphasize the importance of particular outward patterns of behaviour, of strict duties towards the church and of specific structures for pastoral oversight. Many Christians feel secure in such straitjackets. It even reaches the stage where real spirituality is assessed by such outward evidence.[9] It is arguable that uncritical calls for the church to return to primitive apostolic practice as recorded in the Acts of the Apostles represent a similar 'back to Jerusalem' tendency. What is clear is that we need constantly to be vigilant against any reduction of what it is to be Christian to a series of rules or prohibitions: 'You must do this. You must not do that.'

d. The Christ-party

At first sight the existence of a group with the watchword 'I belong to Christ' seems strange and unlikely.[10] Experience today, however, would strongly underline the timeless accuracy of Paul's words here. Wherever the Spirit of God is at work, there always emerges a group of folk who sit very lightly indeed to any human leadership. The very presence of three cliques at Corinth, each paying excessive attention to an individual leader, would have been likely to produce a fourth group to whom all this 'hero

---

[9] For example, the East African revival (called the 'Balokole' movement) now has a movement within a movement for the 're-revived', but its distinctives are to be found in special behaviour.

[10] It has been suggested that the phrase 'I belong to Christ' could have been Paul's exasperated response to the other three positions.

worship' would have been anathema. With a strong dose of anti-authoritarianism built into them, they would have taken the very plausible line: 'Who needs leaders anyway? Christ is our leader. He is the head of the body. We depend on him alone and we go straight to him. He tells us what to do and, when we wait on him, he lets us know his will.'

If all the other three groups had (and have) plausibility, this group is the most difficult to evaluate. Their emphasis and their language are usually above reproach and their 'hotline' to God can be very intimidating. The net result of their presence in the church is that most others feel spiritually inadequate: 'We do not get clear messages from the Lord; we have no comparable sense of immediacy in prayer; we cannot match such unswerving certainty about the will of the Lord.' There is always a faint, but discernible, air of spiritual superiority when members of this group are present. It is not easy to cope with comments such as 'The Lord has told me that . . .'

Often the psychological basis for this kind of emphasis lies in a mixture of strong individualism and latent insecurity. This leads to an inner resistance to being told what to do and manifests itself in the need to bolster uncertainty with statements expressing the validity of strong subjective experiences. Such people hold that their experiences cannot be evaluated, let alone shown to be wrong, because they are above analysis. They maintain that it is neither relevant nor right to evaluate such experiences, because they are not up for discussion.

There can be little doubt that this Christ-party would have given considerable impetus to Gnostic tendencies at Corinth. Whereas the Apollos-group could have been responsible for introducing an intellectual elite into the Corinthian church, this group would have readily spawned a super-spiritual elite. Both tendencies have stayed with the Christian church down the centuries. It is conceivable that this Christ-party was a spillover from the mystery-religions of Corinth, with their emphasis on spiritual experiences which bypass the mind completely.

The interesting point about such a Christ-party is that they tend (sooner rather than later) to hive off and form their own 'church', mainly because they come eventually to feel that the average local church is not spiritual enough. This in itself may account for the fact that Clement of Rome does not mention the Christ-party at Corinth, when he does refer to the other three parties, in his epistle about the Corinthian church written in AD 95.

However inevitable such distinctive groupings may have been at Corinth, Paul is not prepared to ignore their potential divisiveness. He makes a very strong appeal for unity in verse 10 and then proceeds to give three powerful arguments against disunity in verses 13–17. The appeal contains three words with a political flavour – *agreement, divisions* and *be united*. The first word means, literally, 'say the same thing' and is found on the first-century gravestone of a married couple, indicating, not the 'yes-man' mentality, but working together in a harmonious relationship. Paul believes and urges that these four groups should work together. Each has an important emphasis, and that emphasis must be brought fully and unreservedly into the life of the Christian community. All must be on the lookout for imminent schism, refusing to allow differences of emphasis to produce division.

Paul was keen, in other words, on harmony – not unison. He believed that it was not merely possible for Christians of many different kinds to live together in harmony, but that this was their calling from God. Such mutual recognition, giving each person the freedom to express his or her convictions and insights, would lead to a restoration of true unity *in the same mind and the same purpose* (*nous* and *gnōmē*).[11]

2. Focus on Jesus Christ

Paul's arguments against disunity all focus on Jesus Christ and it needs to be said uncompromisingly that both then in Corinth and generally today division and disunity arise because the eyes of Christians are elsewhere than on Jesus Christ. These arguments revolve around the wholeness of Christ, the cross of Christ and the Lordship of Christ.

a. The wholeness of Christ

Has Christ been divided? or, literally, 'Has Christ been parcelled out?' (13). Paul is asking the Corinthians, with all their division, 'Do you suppose that

---

[11] Both these words denote wrestling with and arriving at the truth (no unity without content). The word used here at the end of verse 10 (*united*) is that used for resetting a dislocated bone or for mending nets (cf. Mark 1:19), i.e. bringing back to their former condition. The same word is used by Paul in Eph. 4:12 for the impact of the four/fivefold ministry (apostles, prophets, evangelists, pastors and teachers) on the church as a whole in 'equipping' it for 'the work of ministry'. This would suggest two things: one, that the unity of mind and opinion is part of the 'givenness' of unity in Christ which we are to maintain (cf. Eph. 4:3): two, that we need the ministry mentioned in Eph. 4:11 to bring us back to this unity. This latter point underlines the truth of Barrett's comment: 'neither at this point nor later does Paul suggest that the church can be mended by ecclesiastical politics' (p. 42).

there are fragments of Christ that can be distributed among different groups? If you have Christ, you have all of him. Jesus cannot be divided.' We cannot have half a person, as though we said: 'Please come in, but leave your legs outside.' This, incidentally, throws light on such common phrases as 'wanting more of Christ'. It cannot be; we should rather be allowing Christ to have more of us. We are the disintegrated ones whom Christ is gradually making whole, so that we become more like him – integrated and entire. The same argument applies to wanting more of the Holy Spirit. If he is personal, a Person, than we either have him living within us or we do not; again, our desire and prayer should be for the Holy Spirit to have more of us.

b. The cross of Christ

Paul's second argument against disunity is, if anything, even more vivid: *Was Paul crucified for you?* (13). He is challenging the Corinthians to drop their personality cults and to fix their attention once again on 'Jesus Christ, and him crucified'. That was the focus of his message when he first preached in Corinth (2:2). That was the message which had attracted them from the outset. They owed their brand-new life to Jesus Christ. He it was who had died for their sins and brought them forgiveness and cleansing – not Apollos, or Peter or Paul. They knew the reality of being ransomed and changed. They were indebted to Jesus Christ, whichever group they espoused now.

Whenever Christians give their allegiance to any human personality, such as a gifted preacher or pastor, they have taken their eyes off Jesus Christ and there will inevitably be disunity. Jesus is the only one who can unite men and women and he does so through his cross, because we can come to God only via the cross of Christ and the ground there is level: all are equal at the cross. We never move on from the cross. When we do, we move from the place of reconciliation – with God and with others (cf. Col. 1:19–22).

This explains the importance of the Lord's Supper as a sacrament of this reconciliation. To be continually reminded of the cross in this way is one of the healthy results of regularly sharing in the service of Holy Communion. When faced with the fact of disunity in the Christian church today, it seems odd to many Christians that this particular service should be seen by some as the *last* focus for unity, rather than the first. Some Christians argue that *not* being able to share together at the Lord's Table is the penalty we pay for our disunity and that we can do so only when we are more fully united. We would argue strongly that reconciliation and unity between Christians is the *fruit* of the atoning sacrifice of Christ at Calvary, and that the service of Holy Communion is therefore where we *begin* to demonstrate that unity which is God's gift to us through the reconciling work of his Son. To suggest that we have to work towards visible unity *before* we can share together in the Lord's Supper looks dangerously like adding our good works to the grace of God enacted at Calvary. We all come together to the Lord's Table as sinners redeemed by his blood; we there acknowledge the disunity caused through our sin and guilt, then gratefully and joyfully celebrate our unity in forgiveness and cleansing. There is no single truth more eloquent or productive of true unity between Christians than the cross of Christ.

c. The Lordship of Christ

This argument against disunity is subsumed in the third rhetorical question in verse 13: *Or were you baptized in the name of Paul?* To be baptized in (*eis*, literally 'into') the name of someone was to have one's life signed over to that person, to come under his authority and to be at his beck and call. Paul makes the self-evident point that the Corinthians had, in baptism, become the possession of Jesus Christ – and of nobody else. He was clearly very sensitive to the possibility of people regarding themselves as his own disciples. That was what happened to the people baptized by John the Baptist. Paul was determined (like John – John 3:30) that he should decrease and that Jesus should increase in the affections and loyalties of the believers.

It seems likely that Paul was actually addressing a situation in Corinth where baptism per se was assuming exaggerated importance. He is certainly very keen to play down the importance of the one who performs the ceremony: *I thank God that I baptized none of you except Crispus and Gaius* (14). The last thing Paul wants is for anyone to talk as if he or she was baptized in the name of Paul (15). From the outset of his ministry, therefore, it would appear that Paul left to others the actual taking of baptisms. He was well aware of the personality cults that so easily arise around baptism. Still today we have people who talk, with a large amount of ignorance, as though the identity of the baptizer is important.

If Paul *had* baptized all those converted through his ministry, there would have been room for very great misunderstanding. He seems actually to have forgotten precisely whom he did baptize at Corinth; his memory has to be jogged in order to recall *the household of Stephanas*.[12]

Although, therefore, it is correct to say that Paul plays down baptism in terms of his own ministry (verse 17: *Christ did not send me to baptize but to proclaim the gospel*), it is important to underline the significance of baptism as the third lynchpin for Paul's plea for unity among the Christians of Corinth. He recognizes the foundational significance for every believer of his or her baptism. He takes each Christian back to that sacrament and he rams home the point that this was no empty ceremony, but that it indicated a total dedication to the Lordship of Jesus Christ. They now all belong to Christ, not to Apollos or to Peter or to Paul. For Paul it is the deep meaning of baptism that counts, not the manner in which the sacrament is administered or the person who performs it. He stresses the distinctive nature of the baptized life, and this would seem pastorally to be the necessary emphasis today in continuing debates about baptism.

On these three grounds – the wholeness of Christ, the cross of Christ and the Lordship of Christ – Paul appeals to the Christians at Corinth to express their God-given unity in Jesus Christ. We, like Paul, are under orders *to proclaim the gospel* (17), and so to preach it that in no way do we detract from the cross of Christ. It is very easy to do the latter, notably when we pander to the wisdom of the world. And this leads into Paul's first main theme: true and false wisdom.

---

[12] Examples of such household baptisms are found in Acts 16:15, 32–33.

1 Corinthians 1:18 – 2:16

3. Wisdom – true and false

Throughout this section Paul contrasts the wisdom of the world with the wisdom of God. Although many characteristics of both will become plain as we look at the text, it will be valuable to take an overview of the theme as a whole. The root word (*sophos* or *sophia*) occurs over twenty times and 'it is possible, though not certain, that Paul is taking up a slogan from Corinth'.[1]

Barrett has shown helpfully that Paul uses the word 'wisdom' in four senses, two bad and two good.[2] A bad example of wisdom is referred to in 1:17 ('eloquent wisdom'), where it describes a particular way of speaking – that is, in the skilled marshalling of human arguments. In 1:19 Paul is describing not so much a way of speaking as a way of thinking – that is, an attitude to life which is based on what I *wish* to believe and to do.

In contrast to these examples of human wisdom, Paul writes of God's wisdom, also in two senses (according to Barrett). He describes (1:21 and 2:7) God's *plan of salvation* as determined by his wisdom; but he also sees Jesus Christ as the very wisdom of God and thus the actual *substance of salvation* (1:24 and 30). For Paul, therefore, any attempt to establish salvation except on the foundation of Jesus Christ and him crucified is complete foolishness.

Paul saw two fundamental ways in which the unbelieving world attempted to construct such a way to God: the Jews wanted God to meet

---

[1] Conzelmann, p. 37.
[2] Barrett, pp. 67–68.

all their criteria by providing irrefutable and tangible proof on which they could base their convictions.

> Their demand was for evidence, and their interest was in the practical . . .
> In the light of this they demanded a sign from the Lord (e.g. John 6:30).
> They thought of the Messiah as One attested by striking manifestations
> of power and majesty. A crucified Messiah was a contradiction in
> terms.[3]

The Greeks preferred to speculate their way towards God through reasoning and argument. Having used their intellect to create a god in their own image, they found it impossible to conceive of God in personal terms:

> to the Greek idea the first characteristic of God was *apatheia* . . . the total
> inability to feel. The Greeks argued that God cannot feel . . . A God who
> suffers was a contradiction in terms . . . God of necessity was utterly
> detached and remote.[4]

Inevitably the Greek mind found the preaching of the cross, that is, that God was in Christ reconciling the world to himself, both incomprehensible and ridiculous.

To Paul, therefore, the wisdom of the world (both Jewish and Greek) seemed to arise clearly out of human beings' rebellion against God, their refusal to bow the knee and their determination to make God fit their own ideas and desires. Because God is determined to root out all such human pride, any wisdom is to be rejected which is not based on 'Christ crucified' (and on the derivative truths which spring from that gospel, e.g. the essential sinfulness of human beings and the gracious provision of salvation by a holy and loving Creator God).

It seems clear that such worldly wisdom stalked the streets and the lecture halls of Corinth. Conzelmann in fact quotes some catchphrases in the popular philosophy of the day: 'The wise man is king' and 'To the wise man all things belong.'[5] Paul rejected this worldly wisdom. He also rejected the form in which much of it was purveyed, namely, with

---

[3] Morris, p. 45.
[4] Barclay, pp. 20–21.
[5] Conzelmann, p. 15.

persuasive eloquence. 'The Greeks were intoxicated with fine words.'[6] They were concerned not so much with the truth or otherwise of what was said, as with the articulacy and cleverness with which it was said.

But we would be naive to assume that Paul was writing this letter simply to contrast Christian preaching and Christian truth with contemporary Greek and Jewish wisdom. The intellectual (academic or popular) climate of the day always infects the Christian church in many subtle ways. As Barrett writes,

> it is not the world's false boasting in its wisdom and ability that caused Paul to write 1 Corinthians, but the same false boasting in the church . . . where Christians were glorying in men and wrongly evaluating their gifts. They can only do this because they have forgotten that their Christian existence depends, not on their merit, but on God's call and the fact that the Gospel is the message of the Cross.[7]

It takes much time, consistent study of the Scriptures and constant illumination by the Holy Spirit to reproduce 'the mind of Christ' in a Christian community. That process involves un-learning the wisdom of the world, as much as absorbing the wisdom of God. It is important, therefore, for Christians today to appreciate the ways in which our thinking has been influenced by the secularism of our own age, in the same way as Paul found it necessary to uncover for the church at Corinth the emptiness and the folly of contemporary thinking.

In uncovering the empty foolishness of worldly wisdom, Paul in no sense underestimates its significance or its impact. The essential characteristic of worldly wisdom is that it can empty the word of the cross of its power (1:17). That is the measure of its serious threat to the gospel and to the church. We are dealing, therefore, not with anything peripheral or superficial, but with a subtle enemy that strikes at the very heart of our message. If we cannot identify it and isolate it, our gospel will be puny and empty.

Paul clearly admits the effectiveness of this wisdom. In verses 17–21 he uses four phrases which encapsulate his view: such wisdom is 'eloquent'

---

[6] Barclay, p. 22.
[7] Barrett, p. 59.

(17), indeed 'clever' (19, RSV); but, because it is nothing but words (20), it is completely unsatisfactory in terms of our basic needs and desires (21).

The word 'wise' (19) actually comes in a quotation from Isaiah 29:14. The context of that passage describes a situation in the life of the kingdom of Judah in the eighth century BC. People were thinking, planning and acting in a way which effectively ignored the reality, let alone the relevance, of a transcendent God who can significantly affect the actual situation here and now. In their cleverness they were relying on purely human ingenuity and resourcefulness. Of such clever wisdom Christians, as much as unbelievers, have often had a surfeit.

One of the marks of purely human wisdom is its reliance on eloquent, persuasive presentation, complete with a plethora of words. The Swedish film director Ingmar Bergman once remarked: 'When God is dead, the Christians chatter.' Jesus himself warned plainly about a religion which is expressed in orthodox language but does not result in a changed lifestyle.[8] Paul knew the right place of persuasive argument in proclaiming Christ: at Corinth he had 'dialogued' in the synagogue week by week, trying 'to convince Jews and Greeks' (Acts 18:4). But he personally discounted the effectiveness of persuasive speech by itself in bringing about faith in Jesus and life-transforming knowledge of God.

To up-and-coming Christian leaders like Timothy and Titus Paul hammered home the futility and the menace of endless verbal debates. The precise details of the practices condemned in the Pastoral Epistles remain unclear, but the main thrust is obvious: Paul was looking for changed lives, manifesting faith, love and holiness. He was against any kind of wordiness, which sounds full of religious content but is confined to 'myths', 'speculations', 'meaningless talk', 'profane chatter', 'wrangling over words', 'quarrels', 'stupid controversies'. His advice can be summed up in two words: 'Avoid them.'[9]

In both content and method of presentation, therefore, the wisdom of the world endangers 'the word of the cross'. Paul would presumably not have rejected *all* the knowledge, wisdom and philosophy of the non-Christian world (although he does not express such sentiments in 1 Corinthians). He probably recognized its merits within its inevitable and considerable limitations. Such wisdom may indeed achieve many things,

---

[8] Cf. Matt. 7:21; Luke 6:46.
[9] Cf. 1 Tim. 1:3–7; 4:6–7; 2 Tim. 2:14ff.; Titus 3:8–11.

may also impress many people, produce great impact and bring considerable kudos – but it never satisfies the hungry soul with forgiveness and peace with God.

In this passage (1:18 – 2:16) Paul unfolds the wisdom of God from three perspectives: the word of the cross (1:18–25), the ways of God (1:26–31) and the ministry of the Spirit (2:1–16). It may not be coincidental that these have a trinitarian appearance: in chapter 2 Paul's teaching seems to have an explicitly trinitarian content.

1. The word of the cross (1:18–25)

It is important to note the emphasis Paul places on the *message* (18) and on preaching (21 and 23). However much he denounces and renounces the wordiness of human wisdom, he passionately believes in the rational nature of God's revealed wisdom. Not only is Jesus himself both the wisdom and the word of God, but Paul writes explicitly (2:13) of imparting the wisdom of God 'in words . . . taught by the Spirit'. Neither the preaching nor the receiving of this message can be done with merely human resources, but we must never allow that fact to take away our responsibility to preach the gospel in words both relevant and 'taught by the Spirit'.

The wisdom – and the foolishness – of God is seen in *the message about the cross* (18).[10] The parallel phrase in 1:23, *we proclaim Christ crucified*, stresses the content of this word. The phrase *the cross* is often used in too vague a way, without spelling out the fact of a particular Person being strung up on that Roman gibbet. God's wisdom is seen in the Messiah hanging on a tree. To the Jews that presents *a stumbling-block*, a complete scandal (Greek *skandalon*), because 'Cursed is everyone who hangs on a tree.'[11] How could the all-conquering Messiah, he who is to come, end his days hanging on a tree? That simply proves he cannot be the Messiah. There is no wisdom in that message; it is all non-sense. But Paul insists, 'We preach Christ, the anointed one, the Messiah, having been crucified.' It may look complete non-sense, foolishness, stupidity to unbelieving Jews and Greeks, but that serves to underline that they are among *those who are perishing* (18).

---

[10] This phrase (*logos tou staurou*) seems a deliberate play on the word *logos* which also occurs in verse 17 ('eloquent wisdom'), where the literal translation is 'the wisdom of word(s)' (*sophia logou*).

[11] Deut. 21:23; cf. Gal. 3:13–14.

Whereas Jews want *signs*, the Greeks constantly *desire wisdom* (22); but, until they give up their reliance on their own insight and understanding, they will never be able to receive the wisdom of God in Jesus Christ. For the Son of God to be born in human form, then to grow up into manhood virtually unrecognized, to go about doing good and healing all kinds of sickness, to surrender his life into the hands of unscrupulous men, to die the death of crucifixion as a common criminal – all this defies human wisdom and understanding.

As long as the Greeks cling tenaciously to their search for wisdom along the tramlines of their own understanding, they will continue to go round in circles, on the spiral that descends ultimately to destruction. The word *perishing* (18) stands for

definitive destruction, not merely in the sense of the extinction of physical existence, but rather of an eternal plunge into Hades, and a hopeless destiny of death, in the depiction of which such terms are used as 'wrath and fury, tribulation and distress'.[12]

The key question becomes: does Jew or Greek want to be *saved*, rather than to perish? Will the one hang on to the demand for convincing signs, rather than ask to be saved? Will the other perish in seeking for wisdom, instead of admitting the need of a saviour from such destruction? It is precisely to this certain sense of 'eternity in a person's soul' that God addresses the word of the cross.

C. S. Lewis wrote:

It is hardly complimentary to God that we should choose him as an alternative to hell. Yet even this he accepts. The creature's illusion of self-sufficiency must, for the creature's sake, be shattered. And by trouble, or fear of trouble on earth, by crude fear of the eternal flames, God shatters it, unmindful of his glory's diminution. I call this 'divine humility', because it's a poor thing to strike our colours to God when the ship is going down under us, a poor thing to come to him as a last resort, to offer up our own when it is no longer worth keeping. If God were proud, he would hardly have us on such terms. But he is not proud. He stoops to conquer. He would have us even though we have shown that

---

[12] A. Oepke in Kittel, *Theologisches Wörterbuch zum Neuen Testament*, Vol. 1, p. 396.

we prefer everything else to him, and come to him because there is nothing better now to be had.[13]

The wisdom of human beings, the wisdom that the Greeks constantly seek, will not allow such matters of conscience, of the need of salvation, of the prospect of eternal destruction, of a complete inability to find God and to know God, to bring them to their knees and to say, 'Lord, save me.' God has made himself unknown to and unknowable by human wisdom. He has made himself known in this crucified Messiah. He has decided to save from eternal destruction, not those who have particular wisdom or who do good deeds to the best of their ability, but *those who believe* (21) in this crucified Christ. In this way God has indeed destroyed the wisdom of the wise (19).

When people, Jews or Greeks, do bow the knee to Jesus Christ as Lord, they begin to taste God's power to save (18). Just as they have hitherto been sinking helplessly in the downward spiral of sin and death, so now they experience increasingly the upward call of God in Christ Jesus (24). Here it is important to stress that God does not argue with those who argue with him. God's answer to all the wisdom of the world is to *act* in *power* (Greek *dynamis*, from which we have 'dynamite'): thus the gospel's best defence is men and women *who are being saved* (18) as they respond to *the message about the cross*. This wisdom may seem both foolish and weak, but it is far, far wiser and stronger than anything worldly wisdom can offer (25).

Thus, however rational and meaningful is 'the word of the cross', we should never fall into the trap of responding to the arguments of worldly wisdom merely with words, even 'words taught by the Spirit'. It is the power of God to save and to change men and women that is the most effective response of all: *Christ the power of God and the wisdom of God* (24), for God has made him our 'wisdom . . . and righteousness and sanctification and redemption' (1:30).

2. The ways of God (1:26–31)

'It pleased God . . . to save those who believe' (21, RSV). So God chose to rescue from destruction those humble enough to rest their lives (past,

---

[13] C. S. Lewis, *The Problem of Pain* (Fontana, 1957), p. 85.

present and future) on 'Jesus Christ, and him crucified': these believers he has called to share his own life (2 Pet. 1:3–4).

We see more precisely God's wisdom in the way that he operates: he saves those who believe, not the wise or the clever, and thus expresses his own determination to knock all human pride. 'God opposes the proud' (1 Pet. 5:5) and his set purpose is *that no one might boast in the presence of God* (29 – cf. Isa. 2:11–17). Those who prefer to rely on their own wisdom and insights may continue to do so, but not in the presence of God: they thereby excommunicate themselves. In fact, God is so intent on breaking down all human pride that he deliberately acts in such a way as to reveal its emptiness.

He did so at Corinth: *God chose what is foolish in the world to shame the wise, God chose what is weak in the world to shame the strong, God chose what is low and despised in the world, things that are not, to reduce to nothing things that are* (27–28). New life and love, new purity and peace, new hope and happiness were manifestly evident in the Christian community at Corinth – and nowhere else in that degraded city. Yet *not many of you were wise by human standards, not many were powerful, not many were of noble birth* (26). All the noblemen, all the philosophers, all the business executives and landed gentry, all the people walking the corridors of power – all these were notable by their virtual absence from the church at Corinth. There were one or two exceptions, but *not many.*

Corinth was by no means unusual, because Christianity spread most rapidly among the lower classes of Mediterranean society, and this single fact (in class-conscious Greek and Roman society) was partly the cause of its being so offensive. The riff-raff were being converted, saved, changed. God picked out the scum of the earth and made them kings and priests in his kingdom (Rev. 5:9–10). This was precisely what Jesus had himself indicated when announcing his own ministry: 'he has anointed me to bring good news to the poor' (Luke 4:16ff.). This is the way of God, his wisdom, the power of the gospel.

By using such methods God is overthrowing one of the false standards of the world, namely, the notion that those who matter to him are the wise, the well-bred, the articulate, the gifted, the wealthy, the wielders of power and influence. Such standards die very hard even in the Christian church. They were a powerful force at Corinth; they stifle the glory of God today. James had a stinging rebuke for Christians adopting such standards in his day (Jas 2:1–9) by giving special treatment to influential people in church gatherings.

God's way is to give special position and honour only to his Son, Jesus. God has made him to be everything to us: *for us wisdom . . . and righteousness and sanctification and redemption.*[14] If a man or woman is looking for those things, they will be found only in Jesus: depth, status, purity, freedom – they are in Jesus alone through his death on the cross. If God's way is to exalt and glorify Jesus, wise people will follow God's way, humble themselves before the crucified Saviour, renounce any reliance on worldly assets and *boast in the Lord* alone: that is true wisdom. The grammar of the Greek in verse 30 indicates that Paul is saying 'wisdom equals righteousness, sanctification and redemption': to know those three is to be truly wise.

In seeing God's wisdom in the way in which he operates, it is worth noting also that it is in his love that he resists the proud. He saves only those who are humble enough to turn to Jesus Christ to save them, and he longs for all to be saved and to come to the knowledge of the truth (1 Tim. 2:4). God is constantly and deliberately bringing proud people to their knees, so that they can enter his presence in repentance and faith. People who glory in their intelligence and insight will be put to shame by those who, by worldly standards, are ignoramuses but who know God in Jesus Christ. Immensely powerful people are shown up in all their vulnerability by the impressive inner strength of very weak individuals who love God. Insignificant and very ordinary people often get under the skins of the wealthy and the influential, who would normally ignore and despise them. In these and other ways human pride is punctured by the wise love of God.

We are urged as Christians to humble ourselves under the mighty hand of God (1 Pet. 5:6); but, if we are not wise enough to do that, God will see to it that we are humbled – often through the most unlikely people. These are the loving ways of our wise God. It is shown, then, how true it is that

> my thoughts are not your thoughts,
>> nor are your ways my ways, says the LORD.
> For as the heavens are higher than the earth,
>> so are my ways higher than your ways
>> and my thoughts than your thoughts.
> (Isa. 55:8–9)

---

[14] For a superb exposition of verse 30, see Barrett, pp. 60–61.

The context of these words from Isaiah is even more apposite to this part of 1 Corinthians, because the previous two verses describe God's free and abundant pardon extended to all who seek the Lord 'while he may be found', who 'call upon him while he is near'. This complete and eternal acceptance of the repentant sinner who calls on God to be saved is completely alien to worldly wisdom and to the ways and thoughts of human beings. Without exception human ways call for human effort, good deeds, wise words as the path of salvation. The ways of God spell out the message: 'Seek the LORD . . . call upon him . . . return to the LORD . . . and to our God, for he will abundantly pardon.'

Let the one who boasts, boast in the Lord (31). This is a quotation from a particularly relevant passage in Jeremiah:

> Thus says the LORD: Do not let the wise boast in their wisdom, do not let the mighty boast in their might, do not let the wealthy boast in their wealth; but let those who boast boast in this, that they understand and know me, that I am the LORD; I act with steadfast love, justice, and righteousness in the earth, for in these things I delight, says the LORD. (Jer. 9:23–24).

3. The ministry of the Spirit (2:1–16)

The work of the Holy Spirit is stressed repeatedly in chapter 2. Yet it is a chapter explicit with the doctrine of the Trinity: for example, 2:2, *Jesus Christ, and him crucified*; 2:8, *the Lord of glory*; 2:16, *the mind of Christ*; while God as such is mentioned in 2:1, 5, 7, 9, 10, 11, 12 and 14. The other primary truth embedded in the chapter is the close relationship between the cross and the Spirit. P. T. Forsyth called these two 'inseparable bedfellows', and the whole discussion of wisdom in chapters 1 and 2 makes that very plain. God's wisdom is revealed in Jesus Christ and him crucified, and this wisdom is revealed by its original witnesses through the ministry of the Spirit (2:10 and 13).

In verses 1–5, Paul recalls his arrival at Corinth *in fear and in much trembling* (3), such was the reputation of the city and his own sense of vulnerability at all levels. He made a conscious, deliberate and determined decision to abandon any natural or worldly wisdom, and to concentrate on *Jesus Christ, and him crucified* (1–2). The plausible persuasiveness of the contemporary philosopher was rejected: instead Paul relied on and was in his own person a demonstration of the power of the Spirit (4). That decision ensured that the consequent results in the lives of transformed Corinthians rested securely *not on human wisdom but on the power of God* (5).

This paragraph provides the perfect touchstone for all preaching, as much as in what Paul rejected as in what he determined to pursue. There are searching questions here for the preacher. Is our preaching genuine proclamation? Do we proclaim the mighty acts whereby God has borne witness to himself in Jesus? Do we obscure our proclamation with *lofty words* (1) or anything else? Have we made a firm decision to make Jesus Christ and him crucified both the theme of our preaching and the centre of our living? Do we experience proper tentativeness and do we taste our own vulnerability as preachers of the gospel in a pagan, hostile world? Does our preaching demonstrate the power of the Spirit? Do the *results* of our preaching demonstrate the power of the Spirit? Are people's lives being changed? Do they know the power of the Spirit in their own lives?

At verse 6 Paul's language and direction alter. From 1:18 he has been painting in vivid colours the contrast between the wisdom of the world and God's wisdom. He has exposed the emptiness of all schemes of salvation created by and centred on human beings. He has effectively emptied such human wisdom of all ultimate value and of any consequent attractiveness. The net impact might well have been the conclusion that Paul was not interested in wisdom of any kind – none except the 'foolishness' of the gospel. The single word *Yet* (6) therefore introduces Paul's riposte to any such conclusion: *Yet among the mature we do speak wisdom.*

It is important to note the switch in 2:6 from the first person singular (2:1–5, 'I') to the first person plural (2:6–16, 'we'). This is even more notable because Paul reverts to 'I' from 3:1 onwards. One explanation of this change is that Paul is referring in this paragraph to the normal practice of the apostles, including himself, in teaching the church: that is, that the apostles normally taught spiritual truth to spiritual people in the power of the Spirit (cf. verse 13); but the immaturity, indeed the infantile condition, of the Corinthians precluded such teaching in their case. If this is the proper interpretation, the difficult and challenging phrase in verse 16, *we have the mind of Christ*, becomes a claim made by the apostles in their unique role in building the church.

It has been argued that there is no particular significance in the switch from 'I' to 'we' and back to 'I'. It is then suggested that Paul is describing the norm in most churches, stressing the wealth of divine wisdom available to those who are not immature like the Christians at Corinth. Those who are 'spiritual' and press forward in experiencing through the Spirit all that God has given to us in Jesus (cf. verse 12) can then say, with Paul, *we have the mind of Christ*.

In verse 6 Paul reasserts that God's wisdom is not *a wisdom of this age*. It does not originate in this passing world, nor does it reveal the characteristics of the world, nor can it be obtained through worldly acumen. The phrase *of this age* comes again in 1:20 and 3:18. Because this age is *doomed to perish*, any worldly wisdom will show all the inbuilt characteristics of this age. This wisdom, which comes from or is seen mainly in *the rulers of this age*, will pass away as they will, because they are mortal, temporary and fleeting.

What does Paul mean by *the rulers of this age* (6 and 8)? It could be earthly rulers, such as Pilate and Caiaphas, representing Roman and Jewish wisdom; or it could refer to demonic powers. Without ever *identifying* demonic powers with the power structures and human rulers of the world, the Bible nevertheless strongly suggests a worldview in which the powers of evil manifest their grip particularly in situations where human power is most effectively wielded.[15] Paul seems, therefore, to be indicating that the most influential human wisdom is that which controls the decisions and actions of those in authority.[16] Yet even that immensely powerful wisdom passes away, as the rulers who imbibe and express it pass away.

Even such influential wisdom pales into insignificance in the face of God's *secret and hidden* wisdom (7). This wisdom has been revealed, embodied and made available in Jesus Christ. If the rulers of this age had perceived the true identity of Jesus, they would never have *crucified the Lord of glory* (8). That ignorance, that blindness, that destructiveness, reveals the full folly of human wisdom.

In the remarkable phrase in verse 7, where Paul describes God's wisdom as that *which God decreed before the ages for our glory*, we have a perspective from eternity to eternity. In brief, Paul is saying that in his wisdom God decided on *Jesus Christ, and him crucified* as the way of salvation long before time and space began, long before he created us in his own image

---

[15] Cf. John 16:11; Eph. 6:12.

[16] This contrast between a wisdom influenced by evil forces and the wisdom from God is drawn clearly in Jas 3:13ff.

(*before the ages*). More than that, from eternity he planned to bring all his 'saints' to share his glory.

It is most important to note that

> the mystery of which Paul speaks here is not something additional to the saving message of Christ crucified: it is in Christ crucified that the wisdom of God is embodied. It consists rather in the more detailed unfolding of the divine purpose summed up in Christ crucified.[17]

We never, therefore, move on from the cross of Christ – only into a more profound understanding of the cross. 'Paul does not have a simple gospel of the cross for babes, and a different wisdom-gospel for the mature. All Christians are potentially mature in Christ, though only some are actually what all ought to be.'[18]

This *secret and hidden* wisdom of God is, therefore, nothing more nor less than *Jesus Christ and him crucified*. Though hidden and secret for generations, he has now been revealed as the Son of God and as the Saviour of the world. The word *secret* (Greek *mystērion*) has a double stress: human beings cannot penetrate the secret, but God has in his love unlocked it to those who humble themselves before him. It remains *secret and hidden* to those who still rely on human wisdom. 'The three great sources of human knowledge – seeing, hearing and thought – alike fail here. Hitherto this wisdom has been a mystery, a thing hidden. Now God has himself revealed it.'[19] He has revealed it *through the Spirit* (9–10).

In a few deft strokes Paul has given the immature Corinthians a glimpse of God's glorious wisdom.[20] He longs for them to show that maturity which would liberate him to expound his wisdom to them. The word *mature* (6) is one of Paul's favourite and important words. It was used in the Greek mystery-religions of the 'initiated', but Paul has in mind that growth into full maturity by the whole church which is the goal of his entire ministry.[21] A key passage is Philippians 3:8–15, which we can effectively summarize as follows: 'I want to know Christ; I have not yet fully reached that point; but I am straining forwards to reach that goal; I forget where I have been

---

[17] Bruce, p. 38.
[18] Barrett, p. 69.
[19] Dods, p. 66.
[20] Several commentators (e.g. Dods and Bruce) think that Paul expands this wisdom more fully in Ephesians, especially 3:1–13.
[21] Cf. Eph. 4:13; Col. 1:28.

before, I am striving forwards . . . and anyone who is mature will have precisely the same attitude.' In a word, for Paul, to be mature is to know I have not yet arrived and to press forwards. In this sense, the newest Christian can be 'mature', and old stagers can often get into a rut and stop moving on in the Lord. Maturity is, therefore, a process, not a plateau.

Perhaps the key to this process of maturing comes in the last phrase of verse 9, where Paul affirms that the Holy Spirit reveals the wisdom of God to *those who love him*. For the Corinthians, knowledge mattered more than love; for Paul, the key to knowing all that God has prepared for us is in loving him. Apparently the quotation contained in verse 9 (which is mainly from Isaiah 64 and 65) came to be a watchword of the Gnostics in later years, as they laid claim to superior knowledge and standing before God. Paul is making it clear that such wisdom is open to all, and the way in is to love God.[22] 'Anyone who loves God is known by him' (1 Cor. 8:3).

In verses 10–16, Paul explains in some detail the ministry of the Holy Spirit in revealing to us Jesus as the wisdom of God. This ministry is essential because, without it, we could never understand *what is truly God's* (11). The Spirit *searches . . . even the depths of God*, and he enables all believers (i.e. all who have received the Spirit, 12) to come to know, to impart and to interpret all that God has given us in Jesus (12–13).

It is in this section (12–13) of the paragraph (2:6–16) that the 'we' vocabulary most naturally refers to the specific ministry of Paul and his fellow apostles. Although every Christian is potentially enabled by the Spirit to understand, impart and interpret all that God in his grace has bestowed on us, the apostolic teaching about the salvation of God in Jesus has unique authority of the kind described in verse 13: *we speak of these things in words not taught by human wisdom but taught by the Spirit*. As well as rejecting once again the eloquence of worldly wisdom, Paul here maintains that his teaching, in its language as well as in its substance, is supplied by the Holy Spirit. The words he uses verbalize the thoughts of God, and thereby are enshrined by the authority of God.

The inspiration of the Holy Spirit is necessary for the instruction, illumination and enabling not only of apostolic messengers, but also of those who hear them. Those who have not received the Spirit (14, *Those who are unspiritual*) do not have the resources to recognize, appreciate or welcome what the Spirit wants to impart through his messengers. In

---

[22] It could well be that the Gnostic interpretation of 1 Cor. 2:9 is explicitly rebutted in 1 John 1:1.

verses 12–14 Paul thus uses six important verbs to describe the ministry of the Spirit in those who teach and those who hear the gospel: the former he enables to know, to declare and to explain; the latter he enables to receive, to understand and to appreciate. Without such ministry from the Spirit there can be no communication and no growth into maturity: the truth is incomprehensible and the things of the Spirit are even regarded as foolishness (14).

We can begin to see why Paul must have felt so frustrated by the sheer fleshliness, or carnality, of the Christians at Corinth. They, like all Christians, had access to the very *mind of Christ* (16); but they were precluding themselves from the privilege of being able, by the work of the Spirit, to *discern all things* (15) through God's self-revelation in Jesus Christ, the very wisdom of God. Vast tracts of human experience, endeavour and adventure lay beyond the grasp of these Christians at Corinth, so long as they remained *unspiritual* (14). The Greek word here is *psychikos*, which refers to 'everything that belongs to our heritage from the first Adam'[23] who was made a living *psychē* (cf. 15:45). Paul is saying that Christian believers can revert to behaving like unbelievers. When people have been born again by the Spirit of God, they become potentially 'spiritual people', but they are not automatically going to continue walking in the Spirit.

We must beware any tendency to sit back on our haunches and to feel that we have 'arrived'. We must determine to love God with every fibre of our being. We must link closely with our fellow believers in the body of Christ, because to have the mind of Christ is essentially a corporate experience: '*we* have the mind of Christ' (16). As we pursue these priorities, the Spirit will unfold to us more and more of the wisdom of God in Jesus Christ, our crucified and risen Lord.

---

[23] Bruce, p. 40.

1 Corinthians 3:1 – 4:21

4. Fools for Christ's sake

One of the major failures in the Corinthian church was their wrong view of Christian leadership. This has already become apparent in 1:11–16. They were far too ready to put the spotlight on individuals, to play one off against another, to compare this person with that person. They needed straight teaching on the nature and the function of Christian leadership. Actually, to use the word 'leadership' is to beg the question. As Paul proceeds to show in chapters 3 and 4, such a concept, if seen through secular spectacles, is virtually absent from and fundamentally alien to the New Testament. Because today there is such a focus in secular circles on the need for leadership, and often for one particular model of leadership (according to one's political leanings), it is important that the church rediscovers what the Scriptures really teach about genuinely Christian leadership. These two chapters give us many clues.

In correcting the false and boastful wisdom of the Corinthians, Paul's fertile and imaginative mind calls into play several vivid metaphors, of which we will examine six, together with the final paragraph of chapter 3 concerning worldly wisdom.

1. Babies and adults (3:1–4)

We have already noted Paul's lament (1) that the church at Corinth was not in any sense *spiritual*. 'For in the one Spirit we were all baptized into one body' – yes; 'and we were all made to drink of one Spirit' – yes (12:13). But following the Spirit's direction, walking in the Spirit's power, demonstrating the unity of the Spirit? Certainly not. The Corinthians themselves reckoned that they were very spiritual, that they were wise and mature Christians, not least because of a multiplicity of spiritual gifts on view in their life together. But Paul is firm: *And so, brothers and sisters, I could not speak to you as spiritual people.* He does not hesitate to call them *brothers and sisters*, but he has to call them also *people of the flesh* (1, 3), *merely human* (4). In fact, he calls them *infants*; babes *in Christ*, certainly, but still in their nappies (or 'diapers', as Americans say), hardly able to speak any words at all in terms of real wisdom from above.

Apparently, this had been the case with the Corinthians from the beginning: *I fed you with milk, not solid food, for you were not ready for solid food. Even now you are still not ready* (2). Interestingly, Paul reckoned it was in order for new believers to be given 'meat' as well as 'milk', but not at Corinth. They were not ready for it, even some years on from their conversion to Christ. 'Mere lapse of time does not bring Christian maturity' (Barrett).

On what grounds does Paul put these Christians on a par with ordinary men and women without Christ? *For as long as there is jealousy and quarrelling among you, are you not of the flesh, and behaving according to human inclinations?* (3). Jealousy was rife in the church at Corinth. They were constantly looking over their shoulders at one another, envying the gifts of others. There was little love at Corinth, only competitiveness. There was no appreciation of the different contributions brought under God by people like Paul himself and Apollos – only breaking off into cliques and refusing to mix with certain people of different views.

Such behaviour is puerile, says Paul. We can almost hear him mentally screaming, 'Grow up! Stop behaving like babies!' This is, in fact, how young children behave when they shout, 'I want that toy, that present!', or when they stamp their feet and say, 'I'm not going to play with you – you're not my special friend.' This is also what ordinary men and women, men and women without Christ and without his Holy Spirit, are like. As James says: 'if you have bitter envy and selfish ambition in your hearts, do not be boastful and false to the truth' (Jas 3:14).

2. Planting and watering (3:5–8)

Paul now goes right to the heart of the matter. *What then is Apollos? What is Paul?* Asking the questions in this disdainful way, and not even saying '*Who* is Apollos? *Who* is Paul?', immediately defuses the personality cult controversy. Some looked up to one, some to the other: but Paul is quite clear – we are both *servants, diakonoi* (= deacons). We wait at table to serve you; we wait on God for his instructions. As we obey his wishes, so you are blessed. We move at his bidding. He has assigned to us our responsibilities.

I planted, Apollos watered (6). Both activities are vital. Each depends on the other. It is no good one planting seeds where the other cannot water them, and the one who waters does not achieve much if he waters everywhere except where the seeds have been sown. Both functions are important, but useless unless *God* gives *the growth*. Both the one who plants and the one who waters are completely dependent on God – and on each other: 'God's servants' (9), equal in his sight and equal in value (8). Both need to work hard and both can expect to be rewarded at the end (cf. 14): *each will receive wages according to the labour of each* (8).

This emphasis on serving is crucial for recovering a biblical perspective on leadership. Jesus taught precisely the same:

> the greatest among you must become like the youngest, and the leader like one who serves. For who is greater, the one who is at the table or the one who serves? Is it not the one at the table? But I am among you as one who serves.
> (Luke 22:26–27)

Division, rivalry, jealousy arise in the church because certain leaders lord it over the flock and God's people often love to have it so; it is less demanding, less disturbing. Authority in the church, truly Christian authority, comes from those who lay down their lives for their brothers and sisters in service and availability. Any other authority is worldly authority and is to be rejected.

Although the major thrust of these verses is to diminish the importance of individual leaders, it is worth pointing out that Paul does not fall into the trap of dismissing the parts played by Apollos and himself as irrelevant. Indeed, he stresses that through the ministry both of himself and of Apollos the Corinthians had come to faith in God (5, *Servants through whom you came to believe, as the Lord assigned to each*). They are insignificant compared with God himself, *who gives the growth* (7), but they are vital to the divine scheme of things. Each has his distinctive work to do, and that work requires strenuous toil (cf. 15:10) for him, as indeed it does

45

for every Christian (15:58). So each individual's contribution to the work of God is essential: 'Paul forbids the man either to assert himself against the community or to merge himself into it' (Barrett).

If this is the proper way to understand the ministry of those entrusted with leadership in God's church, then let the Corinthians stop saying 'I belong to Paul' and 'I belong to Apollos' – the emphasis falls on the personal pronoun in these phrases. Both Paul and Apollos are gifts from God to the church at Corinth and are to be received as such.

3. Foundations and buildings (3:9–17)

In verse 9 Paul switches from an agricultural to an architectural metaphor: *you are God's field, God's building.* A building needs both a foundation and a superstructure. Just as God gave him the task of planting the seed of the gospel in the hearts of the Corinthians, so God in his grace enabled him to lay the foundation for a strong church at Corinth.

Paul likens himself to *a skilled master builder,* one who brings all his experience and knowledge to the work and assigns tasks to individual workmen. The Greek word gives us the English 'architect' and it is obvious, most of all to architects themselves, that they cannot do everything and that they depend on the skill, the craftsmanship and the sheer hard labour of many other fellow workers. Paul has done his particular job: he has laid the foundation, by clearly proclaiming Jesus Christ and him crucified (2:2). His reason for doing that was to ensure that the faith of the Christians at Corinth rested securely in the power of God on Jesus himself, the only sure foundation (cf. 2:5 and 3:11).

Some in Corinth were talking as though Paul himself was the foundation stone of their church life: but no human being can sustain the life of any church or any Christian. Pastors and preachers move on and die: only a church built on Jesus Christ survives. There may even be an oblique reference here to the Peter-party who could have been relying on Peter, the rock, as the foundation of the church.[1]

Once the foundation has been securely laid, the building must go up. Paul laid the foundation, *and someone else is building on it* (10). Indeed, several people are involved in building the church at Corinth, and Paul is

---

[1] There is a hint of the same possibility in Paul's description of his confrontation with Peter, James and John in Gal. 2, where he mentions these three apostles as 'acknowledged pillars' (2:9).

concerned all the way through this letter that the church should be built up in faith and love. That is the explicit thrust of chapters 8, 10 and 14; but it is the heartbeat of the whole letter.

It is common to interpret verses 12–15 in terms of an individual Christian's quality of life as revealed on *the Day* of the Lord. In its context Paul is, in fact, describing the quality of workmanship done by those contributing to building up the church at Corinth. *Each builder must choose with care how to build on it* (10) – both Apollos and Peter, the local leadership, and indeed anyone involved in the life of the church at Corinth.

Paul sees the day coming (cf. 1:8) when the true nature of every Christian's work will *become visible* (13) and be plain for all to see, *because it will be revealed with fire.* That fire *will test what sort of work each has done*, that is, its quality. It will not be a matter of how successful, or effective, or popular, or commended by men and women. The materials used will be exposed: will they turn out to be *gold, silver* and *precious stones*? Or will they actually be nothing but *wood, hay* and *straw*? Will the work of Christians in Corinth prove to be what God has done by his Spirit, or what men and women have erected in their own resources, for their own benefit and glory? It is easy to cover up the materials of which a building is made, so that it looks sturdy as well as impressive. *The Day will disclose it.*[2]

If we are involved, therefore, in building up the life of God's church, we need to pray both that our good resolutions and our acts of faith may be impregnated with the power and grace of God, and that our motivation may be solely that the name of Jesus Christ may be glorified. If that is the character of our Christian service, we shall *receive a reward* (14). No doubt every Christian's work is mixed in quality; no doubt we all shall have the awesome sadness of seeing much of our work *burned*. This should inspire all Christians to take more thorough care how we are building. Yet, whatever the extent of the loss we shall suffer, nothing in the eternal justice of that fire can tear us away from the love of God or from his salvation. Because of what Jesus Christ has done on the cross, it has 'pleased God . . . to save those who believe' in him (1:21, RSV). No amount of wood, hay, straw and other such rubbish can put us back on the downward spiral to eternal destruction: *if the work is burned, the builder will suffer loss; the builder will be saved, but only as through fire* (15).

---

2 Cf. Mal. 3:1ff.; 2 Thess. 1:6–12.

Those who have believed in Christ crucified for forgiveness, cleansing and eternal life need fear no condemnation, even from the holy God who knows our innermost secrets. Jesus himself has said: 'Very truly, I tell you, anyone who hears my word and believes him who sent me has eternal life, and does not come under judgement, but has passed from death to life' (John 5:24). These verses in 1 Corinthians 3 urge us to take with full seriousness *both* the certainty of eternal life *and* the scrutiny which the Lord will bring to our daily service as Christians. He is passionately concerned for the church, his building (9): it is his temple; his Spirit dwells in the church, in each local church (16). It is not surprising, therefore, that he is prepared to *destroy* anyone who uses his or her God-given talents to suck the life out of his church, to destroy God's temple (Jas 4:5).

This is both a warning and an encouragement: *God's temple is holy, and you are that temple* (17). God will not let anyone maltreat, let alone destroy, his own living temple. Therefore we must not let anyone abuse us, nor must we abuse ourselves. *God's Spirit dwells in you* (16), that is, all members of the church together as the body of Christ (at Corinth or anywhere). Later, Paul will be stressing that God's Spirit dwells in each Christian's actual body, that this is also 'a temple of the Holy Spirit' (6:19). As we shall see, the practical implications of that truth for personal purity are equally penetrating.

4. Worldly wisdom (3:18–23)

The final paragraph of chapter 3 reverts to the theme of worldly wisdom and the futility of any kind of boasting about powerful personalities as leaders. That is certainly how the world thinks, but *the wisdom of this world is foolishness with God* (19). Those who are truly wise in God's sight are those who deliberately reject such worldly wisdom and adopt an attitude to people and to things which everyone else will call foolish (18). This attitude sees nothing as grounds for boasting, because everything and everybody is a gift from God to undeserving sinners – including apostles and teachers like Paul, Apollos and Cephas, not to mention the whole wide world, life and death, the present and the future. So it is totally out of place to boast about people and things which, quite undeservedly, have been placed in our laps by a lavishly generous God. Indeed, concludes Paul, the fact that they belong to us as gifts of his grace must be held firmly in the context that we belong to Another – to Christ himself: *you belong* to *Christ* (23). He brings the argument full circle by stressing also that *Christ belongs to God* (23), presumably indicating the dependence of the Son upon the Father and the submission of the Son to the Father (cf. 15:28).

5. Servants and stewards (4:1–7)

If the Corinthians have a completely wrong view of Paul, Apollos and Peter, what is the correct one? *Think of us in this way, as servants of Christ and stewards of God's mysteries* (1). Being people-centred, the Corinthians were giving their allegiance to people, people of God, but only people. That was the way the world behaved and taught – and still does, not least because of the powerful impact of the media. Whenever the church follows big names and becomes people-centred, it is aping the world. No, says Paul, do not boast of men and women; you are not servants of such people: they are your servants. The word for *servants* is unusual, literally meaning an under-rower, that is, someone who was simply responding to higher authority and doing his job. This authority is that of Jesus Christ.

The second word, *stewards*, is fairly common in the New Testament. The Greek *oikonomos* was a housekeeper or overseer (often a slave) charged with providing the establishment of a large estate with food and all things needful. He was responsible, not to his fellows, but to his lord. He was not expected to exercise his own initiative, still less his own personal authority. He simply did his master's bidding and looked after his affairs. So Paul sees himself as responsible, not to the Corinthians or to *any human court* (3), but to *the Lord* (4) alone. He is very much aware that he must render account of his stewardship, and this sensitivity keeps him more than alert to the needs of the Corinthians. He will not lord it over them. He is not going to curry favour with them. He is not going to play fast and loose with them. He is not going to deprive them of what God has provided for them. Like a good steward, he will ensure that the right nourishment is provided at the right time. He has nothing to give them except what he has himself received from his master. Paul's supreme motivation as a minister of God to the Corinthians is this: 'One day I will have to render account to God.'[3]

---

[3] Cf. Heb. 13:17; Jas 3:1.

Because Paul sees himself and the others as *stewards*, he exhorts the Corinthians not to slip into any judging attitude: do not condemn us, and also do not eulogize us. Leave that to the Lord: he will do all the judging. If a person deserves to be commended for his or her stewardship, then that person will indeed be commended by the Lord (5). *Do not pronounce judgment before the time*, that is, before all the evidence is out in the open, which will be only when *the Lord comes*. He *will bring to light the things now hidden in darkness and will disclose the purposes of the heart* (5), a disclosure a good servant or steward will not fear. Paul is free of any sense of guilt about the way he has so far discharged his stewardship (4), but a clear conscience in itself is not the same as full acquittal: only God, the righteous judge, can pronounce that. Paul is more than content to leave his case with God.

Verse 4 is of special interest. The first part of the verse can be interpreted like this: 'My conscience says nothing against me, but I have not been justified on that basis.' Paul's understanding of the role of conscience is seen in Romans 2:14–16:

> When Gentiles, who do not possess the law, do instinctively what the
> law requires . . . [t]hey show that what the law requires is written on their
> hearts, to which their own conscience also bears witness; and their
> conflicting thoughts will accuse or perhaps excuse them on the day
> when, according to my gospel, God, through Jesus Christ, will judge the
> secret thoughts of all.

Paul himself told the Roman governor of Judaea, Felix, 'I do my best always to have a clear conscience towards God and all people' (Acts 24:16). Even if this conscience did accuse him, there were two cleansing and strengthening secrets, summed up in these two passages: '. . . how much more will the blood of Christ . . . purify our conscience from dead works to worship the living God!'; and 'God is greater than our hearts, and he knows everything.'[4]

Greek and Roman philosophers (e.g. Plato and Seneca) regarded conscience as passing final judgment on a person. For Paul, only God can do this. The essential ground for Paul's clear conscience is the fact that God 'justifies the *ungodly*' (Rom. 4:5) by virtue of the cross of Christ. So,

---

[4] Heb. 9:14; 1 John 3:20.

when Paul says in verse 4 that, because there is nothing on his conscience, he is not thereby justified, he is actually pointing to the only grounds of justification and the only source of a clear conscience – Jesus Christ and him crucified. No wonder he made that the kernel of his preaching.

The final phrase of verse 5 is interesting because the emphasis in the original falls on the first and the last words: *Then . . . from God*, that is, then, and not before, certainly not now, when all judgment cannot be anything but '*pre*-judice'; commendation *from God*, and not from anybody else, in Corinth or anywhere else.

In the teaching of this paragraph there is a door open into true freedom for Christian workers. Paul had a grim past as a vicious opponent of Jesus Christ, as he himself readily admits later (15:8–9); but, such is his experience of the grace of God in forgiving him, he can boldly say, *I am not aware of anything against myself* (4). The remainder of his life (after the Damascus road experience) is consecrated to being a servant of Christ and a steward of the mysteries of God.[5] He knows that the Lord's criterion, in ultimately scrutinizing his ministry, will be neither success nor popularity, but faithfulness: *Moreover, it is required of stewards that they should be found trustworthy* (2).[6]

The short paragraph of 4:6–7 summarizes the teaching not just of this section (4:1–5), but of chapters 3 and 4. *All this* (6) probably refers to the material in these two chapters thus far. Paul is affirming that his analysis of the nature of Christian leadership is valid for all time, but is here being applied to himself and Apollos for the benefit of the Corinthians. These Christians saw even the gifts of God as grounds for boasting. But, says Paul, they are no different from any other church. *What do you have that you did not receive? And if you received it, why do you boast as if it were not a gift?* (7). All true ministry in the church, whoever brings it and of whatever kind it is, is provided by God: it is ridiculous to *be puffed up in favour of one against another* (6).

---

[5] The phrase 'the mysteries of God' refers, by analogy with the Greek mystery-religions, to all that God has to share with his people, i.e. all the riches of heaven. The phrase can never be applied narrowly to what happens at the heart of the Eucharist, however true it is that the death of Christ is the event which has made these riches available to us.

[6] We learn the same liberating lesson from Jesus himself: 'Who then is the faithful and wise slave, whom his master has put in charge over his household, to give the other slaves their allowance of food at the proper time? Blessed is that slave whom his master will find at work when he arrives' (Matt. 24:45–51). The parallel passage in Luke (12:41–48) ends with the classic challenge to all involved in Christian ministry: 'From everyone to whom much has been given, much will be required.'

The yawning void in the life of the Corinthian church was caused by the absence of love: 'love is not puffed up' (13:4, AV). On the contrary, 'love builds up' (8:1), whereas 'Knowledge puffs up.' This 'knowledge', this false wisdom, of the Corinthians was clearly taking them *beyond what is written* (6). This is a difficult phrase, which Barrett interprets as enjoining 'life in accordance with Scriptural precept and example'.[7] The phrase 'going beyond Scripture' has been seen as the characteristic and the watchword of the Christ-party, in the sense that they saw the Old Testament Scriptures as a thing of the past, which 'mature' Christians had left behind. It could well be, alternatively, that 'Nothing beyond what is written' was a Jewish formula brought to Corinth by the Peter-party. We shall never know the full significance of what is clearly a topical allusion of some importance. The major point of these two verses is the foolishness of boasting among people who owe everything to the grace of God.

6. Kings and paupers (4:8–13)

At the heart of the boasting at Corinth was the conviction that they were really a very successful, lively, mature and effective church. The Christians were satisfied with their spirituality, their leadership and the general quality of their life together. They had settled down into the illusion that they had become the best they could be. They thought they had 'arrived'. Hence the irony in Paul's double *Already* in verse 8: *you have all you want . . . you have become rich . . . you have become kings* – already! This word indicates Paul's own conviction that this is a valid part of the Christian message, but it is not one to be fully experienced in this life on earth: we have been filled, enriched, lifted to reign with Christ (cf. 1:4–9); but we shall not enter fully into that inheritance here and now. It is a theology of glory, but it has to be placed in the context of a theology of the cross, which Paul proceeds to do in verses 9–13.

He readily acknowledges that he would love to be set fully free in Christ, together with the Corinthians: *Indeed, I wish that you had become kings, so that we might be kings with you!* (8). He would love to be beyond all the persecution, the batterings, the depression and the sheer slog of being *fools for the sake of Christ* (10). They may have arrived, but he has not. They reckon they are strong, but he is all too aware of his weakness. They

---

[7] Barrett, p. 106.

glory in their reputation and respectability in worldly society, but he is mocked and scorned by the world. In a passage reminiscent of his powerful statements in 2 Corinthians about his weakness and his vulnerability,[8] Paul paints the authentic marks of Christ's own ministry. 'A servant is not greater than his master',[9] and for Christ's sake he has become the scum of the earth (13). Paul sees the apostles as supremely called to this suffering. He imagines a Roman general's triumphal procession on his return to Rome. The captives and the booty are paraded as a spectacle for the public to relish, culminating with the captured general or king, who was already *sentenced to death*. The apostles are in such a position.

For people who, like the Corinthians, are concerned for their own status, reputation and popularity, authentic Christian ministry is immensely difficult to accept, let alone to embrace. The truth that God's strength is made perfect in our weakness gets through to us very slowly. To be *a spectacle to the world, to angels and to mortals* (9) goes against the grain, because it means being constrained to live our lives under the critical, often scornful, scrutiny of all and sundry. We tend, in our natural inclinations, to erect a screen around our privacy and our real selves, allowing only those whom we choose to penetrate and see us as we really are.

It is no sociological or circumstantial phenomenon that the Christian church is growing most noticeably among the poor in countries of the Global South: this growth reflects accurately the way these Christians approximate more closely to the pattern of Christian life and ministry described in the New Testament. 'God *chose* what is foolish . . . what is weak . . . what is low and despised' (1:27–28, emphasis added). It is this divine wisdom which so intrigues, not just us, but angels (when they are given the chance to see it in operation). Angels have always been fascinated by the message of the gospel (cf. 1 Pet. 1:12), and the church has been commissioned to make 'the principalities and powers' (rsv) aware of God's wisdom in the cross of Christ (cf. Eph. 3:8–11).

Three principles for Christian ministry need to be stressed from this metaphor of kings and paupers. First, if we are among those being blessed in our Christian life and work, it is axiomatic that others are being buffeted. Second, if we are experiencing the buffeting and the authentic

---

[8] 2 Cor. 4:7–11; 6:3–10; 11:23–33.
[9] Cf. John 13:16; 15:20.

cost of Christian ministry, then we can be assured that it is genuinely releasing blessing in others whose lives we are touching – consciously or unconsciously, directly or indirectly (cf. 2 Cor. 4:12). Third, all Christians are, at one and the same time, *both* kings *and* paupers – that is, it is the authentic Christian experience to be wealthy in Christ and yet despised by the world. We never reach our perfect bliss here: we shall not have perfect health, we shall not have instant guidance, we shall not be in constant, beautiful contact with the Lord. We are still human; we are still in the world; we are still mortal; we are still exposed to sin, the world, the flesh and the devil; we must still wrestle and watch and pray; we shall still fall and fail. There *is* victory; there *is* power; there *is* healing; there *is* guidance; there *is* salvation – but we have not yet arrived. We live in two worlds and there must therefore be tension. Paul describes the true situation in these terms: 'For he has graciously granted you the privilege not only of believing in Christ, but of suffering for him as well' (Phil. 1:29).

7. Fathers and children (4:14–21)

In verse 14 Paul seems to recognize that he has been verging on sarcasm in the previous paragraph, and he pulls himself up by assuring the Corinthians that he is not trying *to make you ashamed*, not in any wrong way. He is not averse to arousing in them a proper sense of shame,[10] but here he emphasizes that he is speaking as a father to his *beloved children* (14).

Before we trace the way in which Paul sees himself as a father to the Christians at Corinth, it is necessary to stress that he does *not* see it as an authority position, let alone as one invested with status. He would have known the words of Jesus himself: 'call no one your father on earth, for you have one Father – the one in heaven . . . The greatest among you will be your servant' (Matt. 23:9–11). The way the title 'Father' is given to, and accepted by, the ordained ministers of certain denominations flies in the face of this teaching. Indeed, many other sections of the church often manifest a paternalistic, over-dominant style of leadership, even if they do not use the title 'Father'. The folk-religion which lies behind this is not nearly so serious as the unbiblical theology which gave rise to and still endorses such an understanding of status and authority in the church.

---

[10] Cf. 1 Cor. 5:2; 6:5; 11:22; 15:34.

This false teaching is arguably the strongest barrier to the growth and health of the church in our day. It affects church unity, evangelism, worship, lay ministry, the ministry of women and theological training. Indeed, virtually every aspect of the mission of God's church is hampered, so long as this anti-Christian view of leadership in the church is perpetuated.

Positively, Paul sees himself as father to the Christians at Corinth (and particularly to Timothy, *my beloved and faithful child in the Lord*, verse 17) in the sense that he proclaimed the gospel to them and was, therefore, responsible on a human level for their faith in Christ. Like any father, and because children always copy their father, he has striven to set them an example in daily life of the behaviour expected of Christians; *I appeal to you, then, be imitators of me* (16). Timothy's task was *to remind* them of Paul's *ways in Christ* (17). This consistent example was the number one priority for Paul wherever he went (*as I teach them everywhere in every church*, 17). It underlines the vital importance of exemplary behaviour in the daily lives of all called to leadership in the church. The Corinthians had not seen Jesus in the flesh: they had no Bible; but they had seen Paul (cf. 11:1). Many others had pointed the way to Christ,[11] but he was the first to come all the way to them with the gospel: *in Christ Jesus I became your father through the gospel* (15).

It is, then, as their father that Paul now promises to come to them. When the father has been absent from his family for some time, he wants to come home *with love in a spirit of gentleness* (21), not *with a stick*. Many of those in Corinth whom he had brought to faith in Christ were now behaving in an arrogant and boastful way, writing off him and his ministry and causing great trouble and division in the church. Paul's fatherly heart was deeply hurt by this behaviour and something of that pain can be gauged by his comments elsewhere: 'My little children, for whom I am again in the pain of childbirth until Christ is formed in you' (Gal. 4:19).

Children often make loud claims in a boastful way: it is a reflection of their immaturity. There is a lot of talk, and not very much power to put the big words into action. So Paul ends these two chapters in the same mood as he began – with a strong (and strongly felt) plea to the Corinthians to stop boasting and to grow up: *the kingdom of God depends not on talk but*

---

[11] The word *guardians* in verse 15 is 'pedagogue', the word Paul uses in Gal. 3:24 of the function of the law in making people ready for the coming of Jesus Christ as Saviour.

on power (20). He does not often use this phrase *the kingdom of God*, so common in the Synoptic Gospels; but, when he does, it always refers to fundamentals. He does not ever explain its meaning; he accepted it as the heart of the gospel – and proclaimed it day by day.[12]

---

[12] Cf. comments on 6:9–10, below.

1 Corinthians 5:1–13; 6:9–20

5. Flee fornication

Another major problem at Corinth was that of sexual immorality, which again underlines the serious immaturity of their discipleship. There seems to have been a particularly unpleasant case of sexual deviation, to which Paul now addresses himself.

1. The problem stated (5:1–2a)

We recall that Corinth was a sex-obsessed seaport. Hardly a Corinthian convert would have been left uncontaminated, directly or indirectly, by sexual immorality of one kind or another. Its tentacles would have clung tight and its poison run deep. In such a context it would have been very tempting to compromise the Christian position, either by judgmental expressions of horror at sexual deviation or by easy-going tolerance.

The particular problem presented to Paul is recorded like this: *It is actually reported that there is sexual immorality among you, and of a kind that is not found even among pagans; for a man is living with his father's wife.* The Greek phrase literally says, 'A man has his father's wife', probably indicating his having his stepmother either as wife or as a concubine while his father was still alive. This was forbidden by the Torah,[1] and 'the prohibition was taken over into the church'.[2] Morris[3] is not sure whether

---

[1] Lev. 18:8; Deut. 22:30; 27:20.
[2] Bruce, p. 53.
[3] Morris, p. 86.

it means that the offender has seduced his stepmother, or that she was divorced from his father, or that the father had died, leaving her a widow . . . What is quite clear is that an illicit union of a particularly unsavoury kind had been contracted.

It was a case of incest,[4] and even pagan thinkers were appalled by it.[5]

Although Paul has such a distinctively unpleasant problem presented to him, the nub of the matter is contained in the more general word translated *immorality* in 5:1. The Greek word is *porneia*, which has the literal meaning of 'resorting to prostitutes'. In Corinth the priestesses of the temple to Aphrodite were sacred prostitutes and the practice of *porneia* was particularly prevalent in such an atmosphere. The word came to mean, by consistent New Testament usage, any sexual behaviour which transgresses the Christian norm, that is, all premarital, extramarital and unnatural sexual intercourse. 'The word is used in a comprehensive sense, including all violations of the seventh commandment.'[6]

The history of the church shows that strong temptation in sexual matters is one of Satan's most frequent tactics in attempting to quench spiritual vitality. Here in chapter 5 Paul is writing very specifically about a particularly brazen form of immorality. We must beware of applying his teaching uncritically to every way in which Christians might 'go over the top' in the area of sexual morality. In 6:9–20 he draws out very clearly the general principles for the Christian community as a whole. What chiefly concerns him at present is the total lack of concern among the Christians at Corinth about the implications of what is happening. Indeed he seems, if anything, less bothered about the immorality itself than about the blasé, arrogant attitude being displayed towards it: *And you are arrogant! Should you not rather have mourned . . . ?* (5:2).

This arrogance was one of the besetting sins of the church at Corinth. Before stressing (in 13:4) that it is something which true Christian love never manifests, Paul has at least three other occasions to puncture the pride of the Corinthians. These balloons are personal rivalry (4:6), dismissive attitudes towards Paul himself (4:18–19) and the accumulation of special knowledge (8:1). This inflated quartet is not uncommon today.

---

[4] According to Morris, but not Barrett (p. 121).
[5] Cf. Cicero, *Pro Cluentio* 5.14: 'An unbelievable crime – one, moreover, completely unheard of except in this one particular case.'
[6] Hodge, p. 81.

Paul feels very deeply the total absence of proper sensitivity in the Corinthians about one particular sin, which actually gives the opponents of Christianity even stronger cause for damning and dismissing its claims. 'A living church, which had in it the power of its Head, would have risen as one man, and gone into a common act of humiliation and mourning, like a family for the death of one of its members.'[7]

Such a situation highlights three needs: for discipline (5:2b–13), for clear convictions (6:9–11) and for purity (6:12–20), all of which must be centred on Jesus Christ.

2. The need for discipline (5:2b–13)

The discipline can be summarized in a simple sentence: *he who has done this would [be] removed from among you* (2b). It is worth noting that Paul has nothing to say about the woman in question, presumably because she was not a Christian and was therefore beyond the scope of Christian discipline, or because Paul regards the man in such a situation as the more blameworthy. We need to be clear about the radical nature of this discipline: the man is to be taken *ek mesou*, that is, out of the midst of the believing and worshipping community. This is excommunication, being unable to take part in the Lord's Supper and therefore out of fellowship completely. Why is such thoroughgoing discipline necessary? For the good both of the individual and of the Christian community.

a. Discipline is necessary for the good of the individual (5:3–5)

The need for individual discipline is best summarized in the phrase *that his spirit may be saved on the day of the Lord* (5). That is the proper perspective for our attitude to all people everywhere – their salvation. If, in the eyes of God, it is right and good for a particular person to suffer in this life in order that he or she might ultimately be saved, then let it be so.

The language used to describe the details of the offender's punishment is extremely powerful. The finality and the absolute authority of the pronounced sentence are presumably due to the full weight of apostolic authority being brought to bear, even from a distance. Paul has *already pronounced judgement in the name of the Lord Jesus on the man who has*

---

[7] Godet, 1, p. 242.

done such a thing (3–4). However disinclined to accept Paul's authority as an apostle, the Corinthians would have felt the force of that assertion.

Without entering into all the possible renderings of the original, it seems most likely that Paul is placing the whole disciplinary procedure in three contexts: the total authority of Jesus Christ as Lord (*in the name of the Lord Jesus*), the corporate presence of the whole Christian community at Corinth (backed up by his own presence *in spirit*, 3), and the sovereign control of the Lord over whatever Satan is permitted to do, even to a rebellious Christian. In other words, there is no talk here either of arbitrary ecclesiastical discipline exercised by a few leaders, or of unilateral decision-making without reference to Paul himself (i.e. as the Lord's authoritative apostle). Still less is there any question of a Christian, even one guilty of the kind of gross sin here described, forfeiting his or her hope of eternal salvation and moving beyond a state of grace. On the contrary, the very worst that Satan can do (*the destruction of the flesh*, 5) is totally under the authority of Jesus Christ. Indeed, the church community has no right to consign anyone to the tentacles of Satan except *with the power of our Lord Jesus* (4).

The failure in today's church to exercise proper church discipline often stems from a misplaced – and perhaps cowardly – conviction that such matters are the province of the leadership, rather than of the gathered congregation. Paul here addresses his words of stinging rebuke ('Should you not rather have mourned . . . ?', verse 2) to the whole church, not to its leadership. Once again, we notice the Corinthian fallacy about the proper role of leadership in the church (cf. chapters 1–4). Hodge comments:

> It is a right inherent in every society, and necessary for its existence, to judge of the qualification of its own members. This right is here clearly recognized as belonging to the church . . . The power was vested in the church at Corinth, and not in some officer presiding over that church. The bishop or pastor was not reproved for neglect or discipline; but the church itself, in its organized capacity.[8]

Where, then, the behaviour of an individual Christian has affected the corporate life of a local church (either through the prominence of that individual or widespread knowledge of such behaviour in the congregation as

---

[8] Hodge, p. 83.

a whole), there discipline needs to be exercised and explained when the church as a whole is gathered together. There will, of course, be far more occasions when such public action is not necessary or appropriate, and any relevant discipline can be carried through privately.

Any number of reasons can prevent a congregation taking up its proper responsibilities in this respect. Sheer lack of genuine fellowship between brothers and sisters in Christ is the most common and the most destructive. Because Christians are not used to sharing their lives in any real way, it seems out of place (if not presumptuous) to talk in terms of preserving a proper standard of Christlike behaviour. Another barrier is presented by the sheer largeness and lack of 'integratedness' within many congregations; because few people truly know one another, there cannot be any due sense of mutual accountability.

A third common problem is the gap between leaders and led, as a result of which the former are put on a pedestal and the latter prefer to have it so. Thus, when a Christian transgresses God's law, whether leader or led, there is an almost hypocritical sense of shock.

Among other Christians there is a rather different obstacle: they think that, rather than showing any condemnation and judgment on immoral behaviour, the church ought to express understanding of the pressures inherent in living in today's world, by not holding firm to any moral absolutes of the kind spelt out in the New Testament. In one local church, a married man (latterly divorced) had been living with a woman for over four years, while serving in leadership in their local church in very public ways and with the full acceptance of their pastor. They decided to get married, requested permission for the union to be blessed in the context of the regular weekly Communion service of the church, and invited their friends and family to join them in thus celebrating their marriage. What does such an action say to the unbelieving community about what it means to be Christian?

The implications of this passage are very encouraging as well as admonitory. The very worst that Satan, the 'adversary' of God and human beings, can do lies entirely within the authority of Christ through his church. Jesus said plainly to the disciples that 'whatever you bind on earth will be bound in heaven, and whatever you loose on earth will be loosed in heaven' (Matt. 18:18). If it is drastically necessary for Christians – such as this Corinthian or, presumably, Ananias and Sapphira (Acts 5:1–11) or Hymenaeus and Alexander (1 Tim. 1:20) – to be handed over to Satan for some kind of physical punishment, terminal or temporary, then the very worst that can happen does not take the person beyond the control of God.

The same lesson is obvious in the saga of Job, as indeed in the whole sequence of Jesus' own ministry. The sovereign purposes of God *include* the destructive potency of Satan. Precisely what form Satan's *destruction of the flesh* (5) might take is uncertain. In Job's case, he was delivered to Satan for the affliction of 'his bone and his flesh' (Job 2:5). Paul himself talks of his 'thorn . . . in the flesh' as being 'a messenger of Satan' (2 Cor. 12:7). But neither Job nor Paul was being punished for notorious sin. They were being purified for greater usefulness as servants of God.[9]

It is hard to appreciate the extreme spiritual vulnerability created in a person, hitherto protected by and privileged within the community of God's people, once he or she has been excommunicated from such security. It is equivalent to being dropped, defenceless and disowned, in enemy-occupied territory. The sheer shock of such an experience could produce something like a heart attack, and such impact from strong church discipline need not stretch our credulity too far. After all, it seems to have been operative in the case of Ananias and Sapphira.[10]

It is important to stress that this man would have lost all the potential usefulness of his life on this earth, and therefore all hope of being rewarded for his faithful stewardship of God's gifts when he reaches the fullness of eternal life (cf. 1 Cor. 3:11–15). He would be saved, but even more by the skin of his teeth than the person who wastes all his or her God-given opportunities as a Christian.

On the other hand, unless he is thus excommunicated and handed over to Satan for the destruction of his earthly body, he is likely to degenerate into a complete apostate, who actually tramples on the Son of God, crucifies him afresh and becomes one of those whom it is totally impossible to restore (cf. Heb. 6:4–6). In this respect I remember a most experienced Christian minister saying (after over thirty years of ministry) that he knew of only two people to whom he would apply the term 'apostate' – and one of those two has, it seems, returned to Christ since that minister's death. In other words, it was definitely for his own good

---

[9] Bruce thinks that 'more than mere affliction or sickness may be indicated by the strong word "destruction"' (p. 55). Morris believes that Paul has in mind a process of being so totally abandoned to 'the flesh' (used in its Pauline sense of our lower nature) that complete revulsion towards and consequent rejection of such fleshly lusts would result.

[10] Both Morris and Bruce find it difficult to conceive of such results actually following an excommunication.

that this Corinthian Christian needed to be disciplined in this radical way. He had chosen to trample on his conscience, like Hymenaeus and Alexander (1 Tim. 1:20), and he needed to have his conscience re-sensitized to the eternal consequences of such 'blasphemy'.

b. Discipline is necessary for the good of the Christian community (5:6–8)

Paul returns to the arrogance of the Corinthians: *Your boasting is not a good thing* (6) is a masterly understatement. He has been concerned for the salvation or wholeness of the individual Christian at Corinth; he is concerned now for the wholeness, the salvation, of the church. It seems very likely that he is writing these words in the build-up to the annual celebration of the feast of the Passover, because its details are vivid in his mind as he unfolds the crucial importance of proper discipline in the Christian community.

At Passover each year, the Jews recalled the way God had delivered them from bondage in Egypt (cf. Exod. 12).

> One feature of current passover observance was the solemn search for and destruction of all leaven[11] before the festival began (for seven days unleavened bread only might be eaten). This purging out of all leaven was done before the Passover victim was offered in the temple.[12]

The Passover celebrations were pre-eminently a celebration of the believing community; thus Paul is drawing attention to the devastating contradiction in the Corinthians' tolerance of leaven in the lump; the Passover lamb (i.e. Jesus) has already been sacrificed; the festival celebrations (which normally lasted a week for the Jews) have already begun and should be a permanent feature of the redeemed community. But still there is leaven in the community, and a very large piece of leaven too. The very nature of the Christian community was based on the new Passover lamb's sacrifice and thus demands absolute purity.[13]

---

[11] Leaven is normally used in the Bible to refer to something evil which affects everything it touches (e.g. Gal. 5:9). The exception is when Jesus uses it in two of his parables to describe the good effect of the kingdom of heaven (Matt. 13:33; Luke 13:20–21).

[12] Bruce, p. 90.

[13] Hodge writes (p. 87), 'As the blood of the lamb sprinkled on the doorposts secured exemption from the stroke of the destroying angel, so the blood of Christ secures exemption from the stroke of divine justice. Christ was slain "for us", in the same sense that the passover was slain for the Hebrews. It was a vicarious death. As Christ died to redeem us from all iniquity, it is not only contrary to the design of his death, but a proof that we are not interested in its benefits, if we live in sin.'

One persistent, flagrant sinner who remains accepted without discipline within the Christian fellowship taints the whole body. Just as the Jews had to celebrate their deliverance from bondage with no leaven, so Christians must continually celebrate their deliverance from sin without any compromise with the very things from which they have been set free. Otherwise, the whole worship and community life of the Christian church becomes a charade, full of insincerity and falsehood.[14] We note that Paul is talking of deliberate repeated sin within the fellowship. Godet calls it 'active connivance'[15] and Hodge describes it as doing evil 'with delight and persistency'.[16] We all commit sin, we all need cleansing: but we are all bound to be ruthless with anything that betrays our calling and taints our fellowship in Christ. Paul is not expecting perfect holiness or absolute purity: his plea is for *sincerity and truth* (8).

The first of these two words speaks of allowing the light of the sun to shine on and to test our motives, as well as our behaviour. That means the end of anything furtive, of play-acting and pretence. It means not closing up to one another as persons. It means freedom. The emphasis in this word, *eilikrineia*, is not on our perfection and sinlessness, but on our openness and honesty, walking in the light of God's presence and wanting God, by his light, to expose areas of darkness (cf. John 3:19–21), so that we come closer to one another as well as closer to him.[17]

It is in this atmosphere of openness, sincerity, truthfulness and integrity that our sins and failures can be properly dealt with in the body of Christ, not in a spirit of judgmentalism, but openly, courageously and with consistency. It is transparency of this kind that makes the Christian community distinctive. Paul is too much of a realist to think that any local congregation will be morally pure through and through. He *does* look for this kind of integrity and sincerity.

A powerful incentive for living this kind of corporate life is contained in the phrase *you really are unleavened* (7). That Paul should think of any

---

[14] 'The proverb, "a little leaven leavens the whole lump", symbolizes the notion that the continuing presence of a transgressor in the community renders the community guilty of the transgression' (G. Angel, *Dictionary of New Testament Theology*, Vol. 2 [Zondervan, 1982], p. 463).

[15] Godet, 1, p. 266.

[16] Hodge, p. 88.

[17] The word *eilikrineia* is used five times in the New Testament, four of which are directly applicable here. First, all our *speaking* should be honest and open (2 Cor. 2:17). Second, in the area of our *thinking*, we should be open to new truths, being prepared to penetrate with our minds into matters which might seem dangerous (2 Pet. 3:1). Third, our whole *behaviour* both in the church and in the world is to be thus radiant with the grace of God (2 Cor. 1:12). Fourth, this will serve to mould our very *character* over against the Day of Christ (Phil. 1:10).

congregation known to him as *unleavened* is remarkable; that he should so regard the church of Corinth is amazing; that he should address the church at Corinth in the midst of this particular obscenity as *really ... unleavened* is so arresting that it demands closer investigation. It clearly summarizes the essential conviction in Paul's mind about all Christians: 'You *are* unleavened, purified from the evil which is yours by nature; so *become* what you are.' This, in fact, is the kernel of Paul's theology and the essence of his incentive for holy living; 'Look at what God in Christ has done for you ... Now get on with becoming what he has made possible.'

That is the reason for his insistence on celebration: *Therefore, let us celebrate the festival* (8). It is possible that Paul is thinking explicitly of the special joy of celebrating Easter. If he was writing this letter around the time of Passover he was most concerned that the church at Corinth should not be prevented from the full joy of Easter celebration. This would then be the earliest mention we have of the Christian church treating Easter in this special way. Paul is probably reminding the Corinthians (in the words on a modern poster), 'We are an Easter people and "Hallelujah!" is our song' – in other words, we live on the other side of the cross and the resurrection, and therefore certain habits are simply out of place; so long as we cling on to them we cannot truly celebrate, either in public worship or in the tenor of our daily lives.

Celebration is a distinctive mark of the Christian community: hence Lightfoot's rendering, 'Let us keep perpetual feast.'[18] Some of the small ways in which today we can celebrate Easter more regularly are by using the well-known Easter hymns regularly through the year, by explicitly talking of sharing in the Lord's Supper as a reaffirmation of the promises made at baptism (dying and rising with Christ), and by constantly empha-sizing the completely new pattern of behaviour expected from and available to those raised to share the resurrection power of Jesus. In such ways we do justice to Godet's statement: 'The Christian's Paschal feast does not last a week, but all his life.'[19] Chrysostom put it like this: 'For the true Christian it is always Easter, always Pentecost, always Christmas.'

The world is waiting to see such a church, a church which takes sin seriously, which enjoys forgiveness fully, which in its time of gathering together combines joyful celebration with an awesome sense of God's

---

[18] The Greek verb is in the present continuous tense.
[19] Godet, 1, p. 266.

immediacy and authority. 'When we live in victory over the forces that destroy others, then people begin to see that there is meaning and purpose and reason for the salvation we profess to have' (Stedman). But that will never happen if we refuse to come into costly, compassionate contact with men and women of the world. Hence Paul's important warning in verses 9–13, where he puts right some false deductions made by the Corinthians in response to an earlier letter he had written (9).

c. Some words of warning (5:9–13)

The ease with which Christians can opt out of proper contact with unbelievers is epitomized in the corrective contained in verses 9–11. In a previous letter Paul had warned the Corinthians not to mix with immoral men and women. The confusion had probably arisen from the double nuance in the Greek word *synanamignysthai*. Its primary meaning would be to forbid all social *intimacy*, or it could mean all social *contact*. Perhaps with a measure of deliberate misrepresentation, the Corinthians had taken the second meaning and applied it to all and sundry. Paul had meant deliberate maintenance of close fellowship with professing Christians who were persisting in blatant sin.

It is certainly possible that the more legalistic members of the church at Corinth had decided to interpret the apostle's instruction as carte blanche for isolationism from the world. After all, Corinth was a very frightening scene for Christians, especially those rescued only recently from its uglier vices. In many Christians there is an almost subconscious switch-off mechanism when it comes to real involvement in the secular world. It seems too dangerous and too alluring. Paul actually alludes to this tendency in verse 10: *not at all* [Greek *ou pantōs*] *meaning the immoral of this world.*

Down the centuries Christians have often opted out of God's call to be fully involved on the pattern of his own incarnation. The first way is in the guise of the pietist, who cannot face the world and retreats into his or her personal relationship with God, seeing people simply as having souls to be saved. There is the monastic option which, since the third or fourth century AD, has at its best always been driven out into costly availability, particularly to the poor and needy. Perhaps the most subtle and common trend has been psychological: Christians cannot face the problems of the world; they are altogether too big and too bad, and therefore it is safer not to bother about them at all. The most telling index of this attitude is the way we fill our diaries with Christian meetings, rather than make ourselves available for genuinely meeting unbelievers in open-ended friendship.

The Corinthian Christians were, therefore, not unusual. Paul's principle is clear and unambiguous: 'strict discipline within: complete freedom of association outside'.[20] It is important to notice that, in spite of the particular challenge of *porneia* (fornication) mentioned in this chapter, Paul refused to allow any 'league table' of sins to appear in the minds of the Corinthians. In verses 10 and 11 he catalogues several sins which equally flout the standards of God, both outside and inside the church. Each must be taken with the same seriousness when it occurs persistently within the Christian community. It is worth noting each one carefully, both because of their timeless relevance and because it is easy to treat certain sins with less scruple than others.

Paul is talking about five areas of behaviour – sex, money, possessions, drink and the tongue – in which consistent transgression of Christian standards calls for discipline. It is obvious that the Christian church today is under a powerful obligation to be utterly distinctive in sexual behaviour.

i. Greed. No less is this true over the sin of *greed.* The Greek word *pleonexia*, normally translated 'covetousness', has the connotation of grasping more and more, being totally unsatisfied with what we already have. If we were to ask virtually any Christian from countries in the Global South what is the most common and destructive sin in the Western church, the answer would invariably be 'covetousness'. Martin Luther set an example in this matter:

> Luther threatened to excommunicate a man who intended to sell a house for 400 gulden, which he had purchased for thirty. Luther suggested 150 as a reasonable price. Inflation in this period had sent prices up, but the profit this man intended to rake off was exorbitant, and Luther, who was generally quite able to call a spade a spade, rightly labelled this piece of unbridled greed a sin that called for discipline.[21]

We could hardly have a clearer example (or one more apposite for the twenty-first century) of the comprehensive nature of true church discipline.

---

[20] Barrett, p. 132.
[21] Quoted by Marlin Jeschke in *Discipling the Brother* (Herald Press, 1972), p. 76.

ii. Idolatry. Paul's next example of sin in the Christian community is *idolatry*, something that is all-pervasive and very hard for Western Christians to recognize. René Padilla, from Argentina, has written:

> Today, the idols which enslave men are the idols of the consumer society. For example, the cult of increased production through the irreparable sacking of nature, blind faith in technology, private property seen as an inalienable right, ostentation, fashion, results, success. These are the idols of the consumer society.[22]

Because this is the character of the society in which we live, we cannot totally opt out of it, at least not without needing *to go out of the world* (10). This would be a complete denial of Jesus' own prayer for his disciples: 'I am not asking you to take them out of the world, but I ask you to protect them from the evil one' (John 17:15). Nevertheless we must ask ourselves whether our pattern of church life in general – and the integrity and transparency of relationships between fellow Christians in particular – is adequate to bring such matters as Padilla itemizes on to the agenda of what it means to live distinctively as the Christian community in today's world.

iii. Reviling. A further occasion for such church discipline, says Paul, is when a Christian is a *reviler* (Greek *loidoros*). Barrett talks of 'an abusive man',[23] Morris of 'a railer . . . one who abuses others',[24] and then quotes Jesus' own words of condemnation: 'if you insult a brother or sister, you will be liable to the council; and if you say, "You fool", you will be liable to the hell of fire' (Matt. 5:22). The word has the particular meaning of reviling those in leadership, a trend which is as blatant today in Western churches as in Western society at large. Disrespect for those entrusted with responsibility for others – whether as school teachers or university lecturers, police or politicians, parents or magistrates – is endemic. It is mainly violence with the tongue, and it is also directed at those entrusted with oversight in God's church. Such people are constantly critical, running down everything and everyone in the Christian community. They reveal a deeply seated rebelliousness against all authority and refuse to come into line over such behaviour.[25]

---

[22] R. Padilla, *The New Face of Evangelicalism* (Hodder & Stoughton, 1976), pp. 212–213.
[23] Barrett, p. 131.
[24] Morris, p. 92.
[25] Cf. 2 Pet. 2:9–22.

iv. Drunkenness. The Christian who is regularly guilty of being a *drunkard* is seen by Paul in the same light. Such people need to be disciplined as much as those who persist in sexual immorality, in rampant covetousness or in abusive contempt of authority. A casual approach to the sin of drunkenness can easily pervade a church fellowship. This attitude, which in many ways reflects a full swing of the pendulum away from the widespread teetotalism of immediate post-war evangelicalism, becomes more serious in view of the huge increase in the amount of alcoholic drink now being consumed in British households. In such a climate drunkenness is often regarded as a temporary lapse, the butt of party jokes, rather than the handing over of our bodily faculties to a force other than the Holy Spirit.

v. Violence. The word translated *robber* (*harpax*) has the clear connotation of violence. In the first list (10) covetousness and robbery (*the greedy and robbers*) are linked together. If people really want something, not much can prevent their obtaining it. Today violence is writ large across society: violence in the classroom, in the inner city, on the television screens, towards children, in the womb, towards the elderly and the terminally ill, on the sports field and on the roads. Such violence – without mentioning the more bloody violence of urban terrorism, civil war, international hostility and the nuclear menace – is very often in pursuit of personal gain. The sanity of humankind, as well as the glory of God, cries out for a church which is distinctive in all these areas, whatever the cost in terms of its reputation. That necessitates consistent, Christ-centred discipline.

It would be naive to imply that the two-edged principle of purity within the church and open-ended mixing with outsiders is not extremely difficult to maintain. Yet it contains the key to effective Christian witness. Salt and light, the two metaphors used by Jesus to describe the distinctiveness of the church (Matt. 5:13–14), both assume involvement in corruption and darkness. The example of Jesus also points in the same direction: he was entirely without sin, and yet he was accused of being 'a glutton and a drunkard, a friend of tax-collectors and sinners' (Luke 7:34). The tragedy of so much modern Christianity – and, incidentally, the basic reason for so much ineffective evangelization – is that the Christian community is both remote from unbelievers and lax with fellow believers who persist in sin of one kind or another. In a word, there is no distinctiveness.

The desperate need for Christians to excise innumerable church meetings, in order to free their diaries for proper meeting with unbelievers, was summed up with characteristic candour and pungency by Martin Luther:

> The kingdom is to be in the midst of your enemies. And he who will not accept this does not want to be of the kingdom of Christ. He wants to be amongst friends, to sit among roses and lilies, not with the bad people. Oh, you blasphemers and betrayers of Christ! If Christ had done what you are doing, who would ever have been spared?

The Corinthians were not merely failing to be distinctive; nor were they simply lax about Christian standards of behaviour. They were actually 'arrogant' about their tolerance and their broadmindedness. From the perspective of Christians in the Global South the church in the West today is equally guilty, not just of moral laxity, but of smugness. There is a culpable blindness about the seriousness of certain sins, coupled with a perverse refusal to recognize the close link between this sinful compromising and ineffectiveness with the gospel. In its turn this leads to a continued spirit of patronization towards Christians overseas. In virtually every area of behaviour mentioned in verses 10 and 11 by Paul, the church in the UK is manifestly guilty, so manifestly that visiting Christians from Africa, Latin America or Asia are deeply hurt and shocked by our apparent lack of concern. So far from the church not being out in the world, the world has thoroughly permeated the church.

Perhaps the most damaging result of being a church without any distinctiveness is that we resort to a hard judgmentalism towards unbelievers, thus adding a spoken parody of the gospel to our practical denial of its power to make our own lives at all different. We stand on one side of the yawning chasm between the church and the world, and we proclaim loud and clear, 'How wicked you are!' In later chapters Paul makes it plain that his own policy is to cross every barrier between Christians and unbelievers in order to win them to Christ.[26] *For what have I to do with judging those outside? . . . God will judge those outside* (12–13). The relevance of this to the corporate responsibility of the church in a nation is also worth stressing. In South Africa for several decades most

---

[26] Cf. 1 Cor. 9:19–23; 10:27.

Christians spoke out clearly, indeed stridently, against the injustice and evil of apartheid. Those criticisms were accurate and apposite, but the sad fact of the matter was that the Christian church revealed nothing different, let alone better, in its own community lifestyle. As a result, the emphasis among Christians in South Africa in the 1970s began to veer towards ensuring that specifically in the community life of the church there was more justice; no discrimination; truth, righteousness, love and compassion.

A prophetic ministry is essential in every nation along the lines demarcated by Old Testament prophets like Amos and Jeremiah: but its impact is muted to the extent to which the church is indistinguishable from the society in which it is placed. Purity in the church and penetration of the world: these are the two complementary responsibilities of Christians in Corinth, Cape Town, Coventry, anywhere. Paradoxical as it may seem, the two actually interact creatively with each other. Contrary to the conviction of legalists, ancient and modern, the more thoroughly Christians who are distinctive mix with unbelievers, the less danger there is of moral compromise, especially if such witness is a corporate, compassionate and clear testimony. Equally, unbelievers are drawn more effectively into Christian communities where there is an unmistakable and translucent distinctiveness in the things that really count: sex, money, possessions, drink and the tongue.

We need to underline the severe strictures passed by Paul on *judging those outside* (12). So much judging is nothing more than judgmentalism. The words of Jesus are categorical in their warning to us: 'Do not judge, so that you may not be judged' (Matt. 7:1). Indeed, the drift of that passage in the Sermon on the Mount indicates that we notice faults in others precisely because they are true of ourselves, and normally in greater measure. In other words, we are given the facility to notice failings in others, not to sit in judgment on them, but to examine and correct ourselves over these selfsame matters. They act as mirrors for us (cf. Rom. 2:1–11).

There is no contradiction between Paul's firm insistence on the need for discipline over blatant and continuous sin in the church fellowship, and Jesus' injunction that we should not judge one another. The former preserves Christian distinctiveness; the latter promotes it. We need, therefore, to apply our capacity for judging not to outsiders (for they are God's responsibility), nor to our brothers and sisters in Christ in daily fellowship (our responsibility to them is to encourage and build them up), but to anyone who *bears the name of brother or sister* (11) but is transgressing basic Christian standards, thus scandalizing the community of believers, evacuating the gospel of its power, handing over important territory to enemies of God and robbing the Lord of his glory.

So Paul's instructions in this situation are clear: 'he . . . [should be] removed from among you' (5:2); 'hand this man over to Satan for the destruction of the flesh' (5); 'Clean out the old yeast' (7); *not to associate with anyone who bears the name of brother or sister who is sexually immoral . . . Do not even eat with such a one* (11); *Drive out the wicked person from among you* (13).

This last instruction is, in fact, a quotation from the book of Deuteronomy. It comes on six different occasions: connected with a false prophet who purports to bring instructions (via dreams) to the people of God to follow other gods (13:5); with a man or a woman who has begun to serve other gods (17:7); with a man caught stealing (24:7); with a woman given in marriage on the assumption that she is a virgin when she is not (22:21); with a man who compels 'a betrothed virgin' to lie with him within the city walls where she could readily have called for help (22:24); and with any person who has maliciously brought false witness against another (19:19). Whether it is a matter of idolatry or immorality, the command of God is the same: 'purge the evil from your midst' (meaning the deaths of the guilty). Indeed, if we take these six examples from Deuteronomy, we find a remarkable parallel to the particular sins mentioned in 1 Corinthians 5:11 as requiring similarly firm discipline. The important single difference is that the instructions in Deuteronomy are all given in the second person *singular*, whereas Paul records it in the *plural*. In this simple way he endorses the truth that 'excommunication is not an apostolic prerogative: if it is to be exercised at all, it must be exercised by the whole community, in whose hands (under Christ) authority lies'.[27]

Throughout this section we have used the word 'excommunication' of the discipline required by Paul in the case of this Corinthian Christian. To modern ears this might beg the question; to his contemporaries it would have been much clearer. Whenever Christians met together as the Lord's people in the home of a believer, they would have 'broken bread' and

---

[27] Barrett, p. 133.

prayed – a combination of 'eucharist' (i.e. giving thanks) and *agapē* (i.e. sharing in a fellowship meal in love) which together expressed the fundamental unity of the body of Christ. Paul's discipline is to exclude the guilty party from such occasions; and this is the contemporary equivalent of what today is called 'excommunication'.[28] The initial pain involved in maintaining such a firm discipline is more than outweighed by the accentuated clarity of the church's corporate witness, not to mention the almost tangible relief felt by other members of the congregation whose lives have been affected, to a greater or lesser extent, by the situation. In general, more people are affected than we might think, and these are affected more profoundly than we might hope. The whole of the matter can be summed up in the clarion call from the Lord to his church to be different, to be holy, to be perfect. Pietism or monasticism is, for Paul, no viable option. For equally strong reasons, the church cannot afford to become so assimilated to its environment that it is impossible to tell the difference between believers and outsiders. The church is called to be a *tertium genus*, a third race, the alternative community in society: in the words of Peter,

> you are a chosen race, a royal priesthood, a holy nation, God's own
> people, in order that you may proclaim the mighty acts of him who
> called you out of darkness into his marvellous light.
> Once you were not a people,
>   but now you are God's people;
> once you had not received mercy,
>   but now you have received mercy.
> (1 Pet. 2:9–10)

3. The need for clear convictions (6:9–11)

The second part of chapter 6[29] follows on naturally from Paul's insistence on proper church discipline in chapter 5. The subject matter is still mainly sexual morality. It is plain that blasé arrogance about an unpleasant case

---

[28] Some think that the person described in this chapter was actually brought to repentance, restoration and readmission to full fellowship by the firm discipline Paul advocates here (cf. 2 Cor. 2:5ff.). A similar reference to this case is detected by some in 2 Cor. 7:6–13. But it is a moot point whether either of these passages refers to this one crisis at Corinth.

[29] The paragraph on going to law (6:1–8) is dealt with separately in chapter 6 of this book.

of incest in fact represents but the tip of a lethal iceberg in an ocean of highly dubious attitudes towards things physical and sexual.

For all their so-called knowledge, the Christians at Corinth had lost sight of the centrality of Jesus Christ, the controlling power of the Holy Spirit and the transforming experience of having been called and saved by God. They had come to boast in their broadmindedness, in their chosen gurus and in their independence of the apostle himself. So Paul takes them right back to the fundamentals, to basic convictions about the future and about the past.

a. Convictions about the future (6:9–10)

It has often been stated that Paul does not talk very often about *the kingdom of God*.[30] If we examine more closely the occasions on which Paul explicitly refers to the kingdom of God, we see rather an important emphasis.[31] These references make it clear that for Paul the reality of the kingdom of God was completely central to his own convictions and to his consistent teaching, which we know (from this letter, cf. 4:17; 7:17) to have been basically the same in each situation. We can add to these references Luke's own summary of Paul's teaching day after day in Rome: 'He lived there for two whole years at his own expense, and welcomed all who came to him, proclaiming the kingdom of God and teaching about the Lord Jesus Christ with all boldness and without hindrance' (Acts 28:30–31).

Although the New Testament clearly contains many different expressions of the gospel, each suitably relevant to its context, it seems important to stress that today careful, relevant exposition of the biblical teaching about the kingdom of God is crucial. Evangelicals have stressed the preaching of the gospel; others have stressed the importance of the kingdom; Jesus came proclaiming the gospel of the kingdom (cf. Luke 4:43). This balance is needed in every kind of situation today. It is needed whether the emphasis is Latin American 'liberation theology' or African 'black theology'. It is needed in the context both of oppression by military dictatorships and of threatened communist takeover. It is needed when the tension comes from the yawning chasm between creed and conduct or from the painful wrench between obedience to Christ and loyalty to

---

[30] E.g. Morris (p. 85) and Barrett (p. 140).
[31] I.e. Rom. 14:17; 1 Cor. 4:20; 6:9; 15:24, 50; Gal. 5:21; Eph. 5:5.

the nation. It is needed when our concern is with the oppression of the poor or the callousness of the wealthy. It is needed when the focus falls on ecclesiastical irrelevance and bureaucracy or on political self-interest and maintaining current standards of living at any cost. In each and every situation it is incumbent upon the church to proclaim the gospel of the kingdom: 'Jesus has come as King of kings; he has established the kingdom of God; he is supreme over all other rulers; his kingdom is eternal, total, impregnable; will you bow the knee to Jesus as king?' Paul spent his time thus 'proclaiming the kingdom of God and teaching about the Lord Jesus Christ' because he was absolutely convinced about the pre-eminence of Jesus.

This kingdom has a future application, however much it is to be entered and enjoyed now. This is summarized in the word *inherit* in verses 9 and 10: Greek *klēronomein*. On four occasions when he refers to the kingdom of God, Paul talks of inheriting (or not inheriting) it. Morris[32] says that *klēronomeō* means to 'enter into full possession of' something which has already been promised to us. Peter talks of the inheritance available to all those who have been 'born again' (the only means of entrance into God's kingdom – John 3:1–6) when he says,

> By his great mercy he has given us a new birth into a living hope through the resurrection of Jesus Christ from the dead, and into an inheritance [*klēronomian*] that is imperishable, undefiled, and unfading, kept in heaven for you.
> (1 Pet. 1:3–4)

This inheritance is here likened to (and contrasted with) the Promised Land which awaited God's people under the old covenant. That earthly inheritance was subject to natural disasters, invaded by hostile enemies, marauded by wild beasts, and generally something of a problem for the people of God to contain, let alone fully to enjoy.

In spite of all the difficulties facing the people of Israel in claiming their promised inheritance, they were under a divine obligation to exterminate every alien influence both in the land and in their own community life. The same summons comes to the people of God under the new covenant: our inheritance is imperishable, undefiled and unfading: there is nothing

---

[32] Morris, p. 97.

inherently corrupt or corrupting in the kingdom of God: nor will anything of that nature be allowed to enter it. The two cannot mix. The unrighteous cannot inherit the kingdom of God, because God is altogether righteous. The unrighteous actually exclude themselves from the kingdom of a righteous God. They exclude themselves by their own chosen behaviour. Because God's kingdom reflects his own character of righteousness and compassion, those who insist on living by different standards will not be there. Paul is not talking about isolated acts of unrighteousness, but about a whole way of life pursued persistently by those who thus indicate that they would be aliens in the kingdom of truth and light.

Now the church in Corinth – or anywhere at any time – was called to reflect the conditions which prevail in the kingdom of God. The church is a sign of the kingdom, a pointer to its true character. Church discipline is, therefore, not a matter of arbitrary decisions about sexual morality; it is based on firm convictions (rooted in and taken from the Scriptures) about the essential character of God's kingdom, both in the ways Jesus himself revealed its nature, and in the visionary portrait we are given (especially in the book of Revelation) of the quality of life it will one day fully manifest. '*Outside* are the dogs and sorcerers and fornicators and murderers and idolaters, and everyone who loves and practises falsehood' (Rev. 22:15, emphasis added). An old children's hymn puts it plainly:

There is a city bright;
    Closed are its gates to sin;
Nought that defileth,
Nought that defileth,
    Shall ever enter in.[33]

The significance of this conviction about who will, and who will not, inherit the kingdom of God effectively revolves round our belief about the judgment of God. If we are unable to accept the reality, the eternal reality, of judgment, we will not accept the urgent need for discipline in the church. It is not trivial that Paul warns the Corinthians, *Do not be deceived!* (9) – the word indicates a tendency to wander off course into a minefield of falsehood, both false teaching and false behaviour.[34]

---

[33] Mary A. S. Deck (1813–1903).
[34] Cf. Gal. 6:7ff.; Eph. 5:6; Col. 3:5–6.

When we look at the actual list of those excluded from full possession of the kingdom of God, there is little difference from those mentioned in 5:10–11. The extra words are *adulterers, male prostitutes, sodomites* and *thieves*. A generic word is used, *wrongdoers* (or 'the unrighteous'), and this is probably intended to anticipate the work of God in justifying the un-righteous, referred to in verse 11: 'you were justified in the name of the Lord Jesus Christ and in the Spirit of our God'. Adultery is, in effect, the main theme of verses 12–20 (see next section).

Thieves, says Morris,[35] are 'petty pilferers, sneak-thieves, rather than brigands'. Barclay[36] enables us to appreciate the seriousness of this evil:

> The ancient world was cursed with them. Houses were easy to break into. The robbers particularly haunted two places – the public baths and the public gymnasia, where they stole the clothes of those who were washing or exercising themselves. In particular, it was common to kidnap slaves who had special gifts. The state of the law shows how serious this problem was. There were three kinds of theft which were punishable by death: (i) Thefts to the value of more than 50 drachmae (about £20). (ii) Thefts from the baths, the gymnasia, the ports and harbours to the value of 20 drachmae. (iii) Theft of anything by night. The Christians lived in the middle of a pilfering population.

Today's acquisitive society has produced a situation where the need for all kinds of protection (for individuals, possessions, buildings, property, etc.) has resulted in security being big business.

The most important addition to Paul's list of those to be excluded from God's kingdom is contained in the one English word 'homosexuals'. This actually collates two Greek words, *malakoi* and *arsenokoitai*. Barrett sees these words as referring to 'the passive and active partners respectively in male homosexual relations',[37] but the New Revised Standard Version translates the first word as *male prostitutes* and the second as *sodomites*, or 'homosexual offenders', with the inference that Paul was referring, not to all homosexual practices, but only to those which were seen as deviant.

Paul's comments here have nothing to say about homosexual tenden-cies: those debarred from God's kingdom are those who are active in

---

[35] Morris, p. 97.
[36] Barclay, p. 59.
[37] Barrett, p. 140.

behaviour which flouts the commandments of the King of the kingdom. Today we probably understand far more about the factors which encourage, or perhaps even produce, homosexual tendencies. A person is significantly affected by his or her environment, heredity, circumstances, treatment by others (notably his or her parents) both as a child and as an adolescent. Some may be born with a homosexual inclination. God knows the truth about these things far more precisely than any psychiatrist, and any judgment he passes will be just judgment. Yet still it stands written, *wrongdoers will not inherit the kingdom of God.* We need the radical honesty which asks, 'Do we really think that the laws of God will be changed for our generation, just because we have been born into it?'

We concede too that it is difficult to affirm Paul's unambiguous words in these verses without running the risk of appearing prejudiced against those who practise homosexuality. To what extent can responsibility for such a way of life be laid at the door of such people? Are there not some practising homosexuals who are more sinned against than sinning?

Many of the evil practices outlined in these two chapters could similarly be traced to the social conditions imposed on the majority by those in authority. We have, therefore, to assert with equal firmness *both* the inherent responsibility of every human being (created in the image of God) for his or her actions, *and* the mitigating circumstances which God (who judges justly) will assuredly adduce when he determines the bona fide citizens of his kingdom. Again we need to remind ourselves that 'God will judge those outside', and 'The Father . . . has given all judgement to the Son . . . and he has given him authority to execute judgement, because he is the Son of Man' (cf. John 5:22–27).

These were Paul's cardinal convictions about the future. They represent the very core of his regular teaching 'in all the churches'. He believed that the kingdom of God had already been ushered into this world through the arrival on the scene of King Jesus. Citizens of such a kingdom were *called* to live in a special way: more than that, they were *able* to live in a distinctive way, and it was therefore doubly crucial for them to be different.

b. Convictions about the past (6:11)

There are few more exciting and energizing statements in the New Testament than this little phrase: *And this is what some of you used to be.* We have only to recall the moral cesspit of first-century Corinth to appreciate the wonder of Paul's assertion. No power on earth could have produced such a transformation in this motley collection of Christians, to whom he is so deeply devoted that he explicitly addresses them as 'brothers and sisters' twenty times in this single epistle. He had himself been terrified at the very prospect of bringing the gospel of the kingdom to such a city. Every single individual rescued from the tentacles of rampant vice was a glorious trophy of divine grace. Never had Paul been more convinced that God is able to save to the uttermost all who come to him through Jesus (cf. Heb. 7:25, AV). Every Corinthian Christian was living evidence that God's answer to sophisticated Greek wisdom was not clever arguments but changed lives.

One of the most vivid and moving Christian biographies describes the grace of God at work in the life of John Newton, the captain of ships engaged in the slave trade between Britain, Africa and the West Indies, whose life was so thoroughly (though painfully and turbulently) changed that he himself became friend and pastor to Wilberforce in his dedicated mission to abolish slavery. That is what the God of all grace can do to moral and spiritual wrecks like John Newton.[38]

This is what some of you used to be, and we need only to remind ourselves of Corinthian trendiness to appreciate something of the miracle of a Christian church existing at Corinth at all. 'This is what you *used to be*': something had happened; they were no longer inextricably caught up in this way of life. Paul is absolutely clear about this: *But you were washed, you were sanctified, you were justified*. All three verbs are in the aorist tense, indicating a once-for-all event which had completely transformed them. It is generally agreed that these three verbs, together with the phrases *in the name of the Lord Jesus Christ and in the Spirit of our God*, have a definite baptismal ring. While recognizing that the church at Corinth was already in danger of seeing the two sacraments of baptism and Holy Communion as semi-magical safeguards against divine judgment,[39] we can still appreciate both the theological and the psychological impact of these three statements: 'you have been washed; you have been sanctified; you have been justified'. Their baptism was a dramatic event they could all remember. 'Think of what it symbolized,' says Paul. Thus, he recalls these ambivalent Christians to the reality and the depth of the

---

[38] John Pollock, *Amazing Grace* (Hodder & Stoughton, 1981).
[39] Cf. chapter 10.

grace which rescued them from so disastrous a past. 'Such a fathomless depth of grace is not to be re-crossed.'[40]

The human and the divine elements in salvation, symbolized in water baptism, are also brought out in the three verbs in verse 11. The first is in the middle voice (literally 'you washed yourselves'), while the other two are passive. This would correspond to the decisive act of the Corinthians in making a clean break with their old way of life, interacting with the sovereign initiative of God in accepting them into his kingdom as fully justified royal subjects and in setting them apart for special service under his kingly rule.

The intensity of the change this achieved is underlined by the triple *alla* (= *But*) in the original, one before each verb: 'You were like that, but now you have washed yourselves; you were like that, but now you have been given different and special work to do; you were like that, but now it is all a thing of the past and you are the royal sons of a royal king!' Paul is totally convinced about what has happened to the Christians at Corinth. Whatever the problems in the church, whatever their personal failures and corporate worldliness, however much pain he personally feels about their attitude to himself – he remains established in his convictions about the past: they have been washed, sanctified, justified . . . and the whole weight of God the Holy Trinity lies behind that conviction: verse 11 has a clearly trinitarian sound to it.

However reminiscent of baptismal liturgy and practice, Paul's language is not placing confidence about the Corinthians' standing before God in the actual event of baptism. That much is plain from the double phrase *in the name of the Lord Jesus Christ and in the Spirit of our God.*

To have – and to be controlled by – such Christ-centred convictions both about the future and about the past is essential to a healthy body-life in the local church and to the individual believer's own spiritual health (cf. Titus 3:3–7).

4. The need for purity (6:12–20)

The theme remains sexual ethics, but Paul moves from aspects of church discipline and the immorality of certain behaviour into a masterly presentation of the beauty of sexual holiness. Negative injunctions about sexual

---

[40] Godet, 1, p. 297.

practices have their place; warnings about the consequences of disobedience are necessary. But the most attractive aspect of a truly biblical sexuality is its power to provide what Os Guinness[41] has called 'both the basis and the balance for human love – its height, its depth, its realism and its romanticism'.

Therefore, in a world which is largely obsessed with sex as the universal panacea for our emptiness and our needs, this passage in Paul's writings comes to us with topical pungency. One of the many graffiti in Berkeley, California, in the late 1960s was 'Sex makes free.' Many Corinthian Christians were looking in the same direction, perhaps under different pressures and for different reasons, but Paul was compelled to take them up on their own presuppositions. Their major premise was *All things are lawful for me* (12). It is even conceivable that they were mimicking Paul himself, because it could certainly have been one of his own catch-phrases.[42] Either way, whether a Corinthian password or a Pauline motto, it needed reinterpretation in rather the same way as Augustine's oft-quoted dictum, 'Love God and do what you like.'

Paul's dilemma was accentuated by the presence in the church at Corinth of both antinomians and legalists. He was bound to fight the battle on both points: if he conceded too much in one direction, he would give too much leeway to those at the opposite extreme. Walking in the Spirit is always a matter of steering the middle and narrow course between too much licence and too many rules and regulations.

Another influential sentiment in the Greek thought-world of Paul's time was the Stoic attitude towards the body as being the prison-house of the soul. One Greek proverb went thus: 'The body is a tomb.' Epictetus had said: 'I am a poor soul shackled to a corpse.' If the human body is thus denigrated and trivialized, it is logically possible to adopt one of two mutually contradictory attitudes to it: either batter it into total subjection and ruthlessly control all your physical appetites;[43] or let the body have its full scope and satisfy every whim and fancy, because it is of no moral significance anyway, and certainly does not affect soul or spirit.

Before Paul gives a fully Christian perspective on the body, he deals with the general principle raised by the slogan 'All things are lawful for me.' Paul sees the necessity of qualifying what could look like blanket

---

[41] In a sermon in St Aldate's Church, Oxford, in December 1979.
[42] He virtually admits this both here and in 10:23.
[43] Cf. Paul's own concession to this in 9:27.

approval for anything a Christian might feel like doing. Indeed, taken on its own, it sounds very similar to a strong Western trend which has infiltrated the church since the beginning of the 1970s: 'Do what you feel like doing, and if you don't feel like doing it, don't do it.' Such an attitude demonstrably needs some stronger theological undergirding.

If we put together 6:12 and 10:23, we have three crucial qualifications on this apparent carte blanche. It is worth looking at each in turn, because Paul is enunciating principles for the whole of our daily behaviour in the world, before applying it specifically in the area of sexuality. First, he maintains, *not all things are beneficial*. It is certainly true that the Christian gospel is a message of freedom (cf. Gal. 5:1ff.); but that does not mean that anything and everything is helpful or advisable. As Morris says, 'There are some things which are not expressly forbidden, but whose results are such as to rule them out for the believer.'[44] Paul is not satisfied with a 'lowest common denominator' approach to his daily behaviour; he wants to ensure that what he does is genuinely helpful for his daily witness to unbelievers, for his work in the church and for his walk with Christ. Paul thus wants everything we do to have a positive result on our own lives and on the lives we touch day by day. That principle could most profitably be applied in the whole arena of interpersonal relationships, especially between the sexes.

Paul's second qualification on the 'All things are lawful' slogan contains an interesting play on words, best captured by Barclay's own paraphrase: 'All things are lawful for me, but I will not be dominated by anything.' In chapters 8–10 we shall see Paul arguing passionately and persuasively that the essential Christian freedom is the freedom *not* to be free – that is, a deliberate choice to restrain my freedom for the sake of the gospel. People who have to express their freedom are actually in bondage to the need to show they are free. Genuinely free people have nothing to prove. It is, in fact, very likely that Paul's word-play here pinpoints a major area of debate between the apostle and the Corinthians. Between 6:12 and 11:10 there are sixteen uses of the root word, variously used in the Greek either as a verb (in two forms – *exestin* and *exousiazein*) or as a noun (*exousia*).[45] It would appear that Paul is having a head-on confrontation with the

---

[44] Morris, p. 99.
[45] The English translations reflect the variety of the Greek: lawful/rule/be ruled or enslaved by/have under control/liberty/right(s)/rightful claim/authority. The references are 6:12; 7:4, 37; 8:9; 9:4–6, 12, 18; 10:23; 11:10.

Corinthians on the ageless question of a person's 'rights'. The Christians at Corinth were very conscious of and insistent upon their rights, and they were less than happy if ever Paul reacted in kind, even if he was a fully fledged apostle. In fact, as we shall discover, the reality of Paul's inner freedom in Christ enabled him to sit very loose to whatever rights he might have claimed (cf. especially 9:2).

In the specific issue at stake in 6:12, Paul seems to be saying that rights of any kind are of no determinative value in his daily life. That is an extremely revolutionary statement and denotes a measure of freedom unfamiliar to most Christians, let alone the unbelieving world in general. The constant stress, in any dispute, is on the 'rights' of those concerned, whether it is the rights of workers or management, of single parents or large families, of black people or white people, of women or men, of the poor or the property-owners. It is commonly – and usually without a murmur of dissent – asserted that we all have a right to food, clothing, housing, education, health services, holidays, and particularly to a standard of living which continually rises, or at least to wage increases which keep pace with the cost of living. The Christian often adopts this claim to personal rights without question. But is Paul not refusing to allow even his so-called legitimate rights to infringe his true liberty in Christ? If I am constantly concerned about my rights, like the Christians at Corinth, how can I be genuinely free to respond to what my *Lord* wants me to do?[46]

Paul's 'rights' cover the whole of life,[47] but he is not going to allow those universal 'rights' to dictate to him. Only Jesus Christ can do that, and he has total rights over every part of Paul's life.

Once we have been liberated from the need to receive, let alone to assert, our rights, we can then see clearly the habits and the things which tend to enslave us. If there is anything I find I cannot give up, that has become an infringement of my freedom in Christ: 'people are slaves to whatever masters them' (2 Pet. 2:19). Several such things have no moral value at all; they are, at best, morally neutral. Many are simply occupations, pastimes, sporting activities, hobbies, leisure pursuits, and the like. When we hold these in their proper place and proportion, they contribute to our

---

[46] A perfect example of this need to preserve my freedom to respond to the Lordship of Jesus in every situation is given in 7:3–5, where the husband's 'conjugal rights' over his wife's body (and vice versa) are specifically subjugated to an occasional call from God to special prayer.

[47] Cf. 3:21–22, 'all things are yours, whether . . . the world or life or death or the present or the future'.

wholeness as individuals in Christ and therefore to the way we reflect the image of God. But Paul is adamant that he will not surrender the control of his life to anyone or anything but 'the Lord Jesus Christ and . . . the Spirit of our God'. He regards himself as a bondslave of Jesus Christ, and there is no way in which he will allow his person or his behaviour to be controlled by another force. Indeed, the last phrase in verse 12 could equally be translated, 'I will not be enslaved by *anyone*.'

Paul's third qualification of 'All things are lawful' comes at 10:23: 'but not all things build up'. The specific context of that statement will be more fully examined in due course, but even a cursory reading of 1 Corinthians as a whole makes it very clear that Paul's major preoccupation is that the body of Christ in Corinth should be built up, not just on the right foundation, but by the wise use of sound materials (cf. 3:11–15). The leading question which Paul wants all Christians to ask themselves constantly is this: 'Will this or that proposed course of action prove constructive?' This whole section (6:12–20) is as constructive a contribution to Christian sexual ethics as we can find inside or outside the New Testament.

Before giving his rich exposition of a truly Christ-centred attitude to the body (*sōma*), Paul dismisses a diversionary tactic about *the stomach* (*koilia*) – probably presented in the form of another catchphrase bandied about by those who were attempting to justify each and every physical indulgence.[48] He deals abruptly with their slogan by making it plain that he is not thinking about stomachs or bellies at all. There is all the difference in the world between food, which is digested by the stomach and passed out through the bowels, and sexual intercourse, which affects the whole person and cannot be dismissed flippantly as a purely physiological phenomenon. He finishes that non-argument with a sentence which either quotes their own saying or conveys his own judgment: *God will destroy both one and the other* (i.e. food and belly). He might equally have quoted his unequivocal statement to the Romans: 'the kingdom of God is not

---

[48] Bruce (p. 63): 'This too may have been part of the libertine argument: since food and stomach alike will pass away, why attach religious importance to either – or, for that matter, to sexual relations? Paul agreed that food and drink and the like were "things which all perish as they are used" (Col. 2:22); in respect of them the conscience of the Christian was subject to no man's judgment (Rom. 14:3; Col. 2:16). But sexual relations were on a completely different footing: they affected the personality of the parties involved as food did not. Jesus had contrasted food, which "goes into a man from outside and cannot defile him, since it enters, not his heart, but his stomach," with those "evil things which come out from a man, from within, out of the heart, which defile a man" (Mark 7:18–23).'

food and drink but righteousness and peace and joy in the Holy Spirit' (Rom. 14:17).[49]

The stage is now set for Paul to unfold his view of the body, in contrast with prevailing views held by both pagan philosophers and untaught Corinthian Christians. When we pause to recall that the language of the body is fundamental to several chapters in 1 Corinthians (e.g. 6, 10 and 11, 12 and 15) – each with a different emphasis in application – we are in a better position to appreciate Paul's theology. The chapters tackle the practical purpose of the body (6), the body of Christ in the Eucharist (10 and 11), gifts and variety in the body of Christ (12) and the eventual resurrection of the body (15). No wonder it is commonly asserted that no other major religion in the world holds such a high view of the body, and the most obvious perspective on this truth is the very fact of the incarnation. That is the measure of God's commitment to the body.

Paul makes five powerful statements about the body and then concludes with his tour de force: *you are not your own . . . you were bought with a price; therefore glorify God in your body* (6:19–20). Let us remind ourselves that Paul is talking about our own physical bodies, bodies which 'grow tired and wear out, which sweat, bleed and vomit, which grow pot-bellied and run out of breath' (Os Guinness). 'It is our bodies', Guinness continues,

> which are instruments either for evil or for good. It is our bodies that Paul urges us to present to God as a living sacrifice. Obedience or disobedience are expressed in our bodies or they are expressed nowhere. Obedience for the Christian is a body activity. God does not address us purely as minds or emotions or wills, but as people with bodies. His concern is not for abstract acts, like adultery in theory, or immorality in theory, but his concern is for the whole person who does these actions.

Paul's five truths about the body can be summarized as follows:

---

[49] At the same time we need to remember Paul's own sadness, in writing to the Philippians (3:18–21), that there were many Christians living as 'enemies of the cross of Christ' – for the very basic reason that 'their god is the belly' (Greek *koilia*, as in 1 Cor. 6:13). Such Christians could well have been similar to those arousing Paul's passionate outburst in this letter. Paul's answer to the Philippian miscreants effectively makes the same distinction between the belly and the body of the Christian. It is all too possible, by gluttony or drunkenness, to worship food and drink; but the most important result of such disobedience is that overindulgence totally ignores our ultimate calling, which Paul describes like this: 'the Lord Jesus Christ . . . will transform the body of our humiliation so that it may be conformed to the body of his glory'.

    i. The purpose of the body in the Lord (13).

   ii. The resurrection of the body in the Lord (14).

  iii. The interaction of the body with the Lord (15–17).

  iv. The habitation of the body by the Lord (19).

   v. The redemption of the body by the Lord (19–20).

Each truth contradicts the mood of his contemporaries and is worth examining more fully.

a. The purpose of the body in the Lord (6:13)

God has a purpose for our bodies, and it is certainly not for us to indulge them with sexual immorality of any kind, let alone the specialist kind rampant in the licensed prostitution of contemporary Corinth. The fact that Jesus himself took human flesh and blood shows that *the Lord is for the body*. This is underlined by the further fact that God did not allow his 'Holy One [to] experience corruption', but raised him from the dead.[50] This shows also that death does not terminate God's purpose for our bodies. More than that, 'the Lord is for the body', that is, the Lord is necessary for the body to function. Godet summarizes: 'The body is for Christ, to belong to him and to serve him, and Christ is for the body, to inhabit and to glorify it.'[51] The remainder of 6:12–20 spells this out more fully.

b. The resurrection of the body in the Lord (6:14)

The purpose which God has for our bodies is in no sense thwarted by death and dissolution. This theme Paul takes up more thoroughly in chapter 15, but he summarizes the supremely relevant truth in 6:14: *God raised the Lord and will also raise us by his power.*[52] Allo makes the important point that in verse 14 Paul endorses the Jewish belief about the after-life, but expressly contradicts the Greek view expressed by Plato: in talking of our bodies as an integral part of our entire and indestructible personality, he says 'God will raise *us* up', when he has essentially in mind the raising of our bodies. That is the eternal dimension of God's purpose for the body.[53]

---

[50] Cf. Acts 2:22–32; 13:27–37.

[51] Godet, 1, p. 307.

[52] Cf. Rom. 8:11; 2 Cor. 4:14.

[53] Allo, p. 145.

Paul preserves the consistent teaching of the New Testament in attributing the resurrection of Jesus to the dynamic agency of God the Father.[54] Whatever is true of Jesus is true of all in Jesus (cf. 1 Cor. 15:20ff.). Our bodies are not dispensable, in the ultimate sense; they are the raw material of a more glorious creation. We note that it is the dynamic power (*dynameōs*) of the Lord which will guarantee the resurrection of our bodies; no other power on earth could possibly achieve that result, however much 'morticians' make a lucrative living out of deep-freezing human corpses for later resuscitation. It is, incidentally, most striking that Paul is confident about the bodily resurrection both of these arrogant, divided Corinthians and of his own weather-beaten, whip-lashed, fever-wracked, stoned and exposed fragile human frame. If we can look at our own feeble mortal bodies and say with equal assurance, 'I believe in the resurrection of the body', we are indeed children of the resurrection.

c. The interaction of the body with the Lord (6:15–17)

The extent to which the human body of Christians and the Lord himself are intertwined is eloquently described in the phrase in verse 15: *Do you not know that your bodies are members of Christ?* This is extraordinarily bold language: our physical bodies are limbs of Christ, and Paul's rhetorical question ('Do you not know this?') reveals how fundamental is this union with the risen Lord. This is the measure of our oneness with Christ: *anyone united to the Lord becomes one spirit with him* (17). The two personalities become one, so merged that Paul uses the same phrases (*kollōmenos* = 'glued together') to describe the Christian's integration with Christ and a man's action in joining himself to a prostitute (16).[55]

Jesus himself taught this perfect oneness between himself and those who believe in him (cf. John 17:20ff.). This language, though often described as mystical, also has clear overtones of physical/spiritual union. This is why Paul uses the same vocabulary, explicitly in connection with marriage, to describe the relationship between Christ (the Bridegroom) and the church (his Bride – Eph. 5:19ff.). The complete and permanent oneness between husband and wife is a powerful pointer to the relationship, for time and for eternity, between Christ and his church. In God's ideal purpose for marriage, two believers should be so united as persons

---

54 Cf. Acts 2:24, 32; 3:15, 26; 4:10; 5:30, etc.
55 The compound word *proskollaōmai* is used in the Septuagint of Gen. 2:24 to describe the man's 'cleaving' to his wife.

that 'two become one', expressed in the physical oneness of sexual intercourse. Yet even that approximation to the ideal plan of God is, at its very best, only a pointer (and in that sense a 'sacrament') to the perfect union/marriage between Christ and his church.

If each individual believer's bodily members are actually limbs of Christ, it is inconceivable (as well as immoral) for a believer to abuse that body by resorting to sexual intercourse with prostitutes. This is also the strongest reason why believers ought not to marry unbelievers (cf. 2 Cor. 6:14ff.). The physical limbs of a Christian are members of Christ; those of the non-Christian are not. If a Christian, therefore, chooses to have sexual intercourse with an unbeliever, that Christian *becomes one body with* the unbeliever (16), according to the foundational truth expressed in the phrase *The two shall be one flesh* (cf. Gen. 2:24). But it is impossible for that 'one-flesh' relationship to be integrated with the 'one-spirit' relationship between that believer and the Lord (17). Such a believer is from that point onwards living a disintegrated life.[56]

Some further comments of Os Guinness explain the implications of this fundamental truth:

> This is the ideal that judges all the rest of Christian sexual ethics in the Scriptures. That is what is behind every prohibition in this area. Why should not men sleep with animals? Why is adultery wrong? Why are homosexual practices wrong? Why is pre-marital intercourse wrong? Simply because there is no true oneness and therefore there should be no one-flesh either. And that is precisely what Paul is arguing here. The point is not that some Corinthian Christian was sleeping with a prostitute; Paul could just as easily have said, 'He who joins himself to the good-looking housewife down the street' or 'She who joins herself to the good-looking athlete down the stairs.' He says 'he' because in Corinth it was men who tended to have double standards; and he says 'prostitute' because in Corinth that was the particular problem. But the

---

[56] C. F. D. Moule (*An Idiom Book of New Testament Greek* [1953], p. 196) suggests that the phrase 'Every sin that a person commits is outside the body' (18) was another Corinthian slogan, with the claim that physical lust cannot touch the real personality of the 'initiated'. On the contrary, says Paul, if a Christian commits fornication, it is precisely his or her personality that is being damaged. Godet says, 'the immoral man sins against his body as it will become in eternity'. We presume that he means that there is some indescribable way in which the Christian who fornicates somehow imperils or damages the person he or she is destined to be after resurrection. As Allo (p. 149) explains: 'Our body is called to eternal glory as a member of Christ; there is nothing which so directly wounds the personal dignity, the honour, the nobility of our body than for it to be made a member of a prostitute, to be thus reduced to slavery, to the condition where it is given over to pleasures which are both fleeting and vulgar.'

true problem was that there was intimacy without intention, and there was communion without commitment.

It should be positively affirmed that virginity is one of the most creative, releasing, purifying and beautiful gifts which can be brought to Christian marriage. If either partner is unable to bring such a contribution, his or her whole personhood is impaired – though not irretrievably, because the redemptive power of Christ himself is able to make all things new.

d. The habitation of the body by the Lord (6:19)
Paul's fourth plea for Christ-centred purity is the habitation of our bodies by the Lord, by the Holy Spirit. Our bodies are not simply physical shells of remarkable composition: they are *a temple of the Holy Spirit*. Earlier Paul affirmed that the whole church of God at Corinth was God's temple, with stern warnings against any who might destroy that temple (3:16–17). Now he uses the same metaphor to remind individual Christians at Corinth that God has given to each the gift of his indwelling Holy Spirit, *which you have from God*. In the earlier passage the reference was simply to 'God's Spirit'. Here he feels compelled to emphasize the call to holiness: 'your body is a temple of the *Holy* Spirit' (19).

e. The redemption of the body by the Lord (6:19–20)
Paul's final plea for purity is based on the cost of redeeming our bodies: *you are not your own . . . you were bought with a price; therefore glorify God in your body*. Before they began to experience the freedom for which Christ had set them free, the Corinthians were in the most servile bondage. They were slaves to themselves, their self-centred desires, self-indulgence and bodily passions.[57] Then came a master with the resources to set them completely free. He paid the necessary ransom. They had been set free from the futility and servitude of their previous manner of life. Their bodies were no longer like chunks of flesh up for sale to the highest bidder in the slave market, or available to a cult-prostitute for a fee.[58]

---

[57] Cf. Eph. 2:3; Rom. 6:20; John 8:34.

[58] It has been suggested (by Héring, followed by Ruef, p. 51) that Paul has in mind the price paid to the prostitute in return for her services. The price would then be worship of the temple deity (Aphrodite), and the devastating results of such behaviour with cult-prostitutes would reach into idolatry as much as immorality. Ruef argues that Paul is remonstrating with the Corinthians like this: 'You are the one who has been bought (by God), therefore you owe your body to him and the service which he requires is his glorification.' As Ruef himself admits, 'this is not a very delicate way of putting it, but the Corinthians were probably not very delicate people'.

They had been bought with a price and they now belonged to a new master. His orders now mattered, not their own fancies or foibles. He now intended every physical faculty they had within them to express the glory of God. So far from despising their bodies, marked as they were by all the degradation and indiscipline of sin, he was committed to working out from within 'the redemption of [their] bodies' (Rom. 8:23). Flesh and blood, particularly such dissolute flesh and blood, could never inherit the kingdom of God (1 Cor. 15:50); but the power of his redeeming love could – and would – complete what the Holy Spirit had already begun.

So we are urged to learn from the Spirit of God what it means to glorify God in our bodies: not to pander to them, make excuses for them or be flippant about the many powerful temptations to abuse them. Paul forthrightly commands the Corinthians to flee two sins: immorality (6:18) and idolatry (10:14). Joseph had to run from the sexual advances of Potiphar's wife (cf. Gen. 39:6ff.). Christians today do not have to be citizens of Corinth, or handsome visitors in the opulent courts of amoral Egyptian rulers, to discover the practical wisdom of running away from temptation when the odds are stacked too high against them.

This, however, is the negative (though necessary) aspect of Christ-centred purity. Paul's last word on the subject is far more challenging and positive: *glorify God in your body*. Let Godet have the final comment on this call to purity: 'Display positively in the use of our body the glory and especially the holiness of the heavenly Master who has taken possession of our person.'[59] The poetic vision of the psalmist is the perfect epilogue:

> For it was you who formed my inward parts;
>> you knit me together in my mother's womb.
> I praise you, for I am fearfully and wonderfully made.
>> Wonderful are your works;
> that I know very well.
> My frame was not hidden from you,
> when I was being made in secret,
>> intricately woven in the depths of the earth.
> Your eyes beheld my unformed substance.

---

[59] Godet, 1, p. 314.

In your book were written
    all the days that were formed for me,
    when none of them as yet existed.
(Ps. 139:13–16)

1 Corinthians 6:1–8

6. Settled out of court

At first sight these verses appear to be an intrusion into Paul's incisive comments on sexual morality, which actually continue from a different perspective in chapter 7. There is, however, an important thread which explains the switch to litigation between Christians.[1] We have already seen that the Corinthians were proud, competitive and assertive people. They were concerned most of the time for their *rights*. Their rights had virtually taken over from their redemption as the mainspring of their life together. As a result, they were extremely touchy if anyone infringed their rights or inhibited their freedom. This inevitably led to grievances between fellow Christians, and such grievances could be harboured unendingly. To take them into the law courts was, then as now, a protracted and an expensive business, not calculated at all to improve relationships in the body of Christ. But once a group of Christians becomes obsessed with its rights instead of its responsibilities, there will be untold trouble until they find the way to true repentance.

The way of the 'freedom' lobby at Corinth was to lay claim to rights here, there and everywhere – in marriage, over food laws, in business ethics, in casual relationships, in public worship, in exercising their spiritual gifts, even in specific areas of fundamental Christian doctrine. 'Why shouldn't I do what I feel like?' was their defiant cry.

---

[1] Allo (p. 132) sees the old sin of covetousness (*pleonexia*) as the root cause of all the litigation prevalent in the church at Corinth. Wanting to grab as much as we possibly can is such an ingrained desire in our fallen natures that he could well be right. Instead of being prepared to let fall any claims they might have to this piece of property or that article, the Christians were hanging on for all they were worth to anything remotely within their rights.

The ascetic, legalist group in the church held adamantly to the safe, predictable way without risks. Over the matter of taking quarrels into the secular law courts, their links with Jewish custom would have pre-conditioned a sense of abhorrence at the very thought: 'It was the Jewish custom to settle disputes within the Jewish community, and there were also Greek and Roman social and religious groups who followed the same practice.'[2] Barclay has a fascinating description of Greek love for litigation.[3] The following quotations catch the spirit of the age:

> The Greeks were naturally and characteristically a litigious people. The law-courts were in fact one of their chief amusements and entertainments . . . In a Greek city every man was more or less a lawyer and spent a very great part of his time either deciding or listening to law cases. The Greeks were in fact famous, or notorious, for their love of going to law. Not unnaturally, certain of the Greeks had brought their litigious tendencies into the Christian church; and Paul was shocked.

In other words, the habit of the Christians in Corinth over litigation was in essence no different from their assimilation to Corinthian sexual laxity: the world was once again invading the church.

This practice of Christians taking one another to court had probably become a regular habit in Corinth. One or two examples would hardly have aroused Paul's ire so forcefully. It is conceivable that the notorious case of incest recorded in chapter 5 had itself been taken into the law courts.

There may well be another reason for Paul spending time at this stage trying to kill off the litigious spirit in the church at Corinth. If *rights* was one obsession of the Corinthians, the other was *judgment* – the root Greek word *krinein* comes in its cognates over forty times in the letter, and eight times in the first eight verses of this chapter. The combination of asserting my rights and passing judgment on everyone else is one of the most insidious tendencies in the church of God. Both evils should have been transcended through the redemption which is ours in Jesus Christ. Rights have given way to reconciliation and mutual responsibility: passing judgment has been buried with Christ as one of the most destructive and loathsome characteristics of our unredeemed lower nature. Whatever

---

[2] Barrett, pp. 135–136.
[3] Barclay, pp. 55–56.

Paul had preached at Corinth about Jesus Christ and him crucified, these two cardinal lessons simply had not been received. The same litigious spirit has often pervaded the church in the twenty-first century.

A further general comment about Paul's attitude to contemporary legal authority must certainly be made before we look at the details of his teaching. However adamant he is here about the obscenity of Christians taking one another to court, it is clear from the Acts of the Apostles that he believed it to be totally correct – and important for him (and his colleagues) – to insist on the responsibility of those in authority to administer justice with integrity and consistency.[4]

Paul appealed to Roman justice, but never in matters between fellow Christians, nor with the purpose of accusing his fellow Jews (cf. Acts 20:19); only in defence of his work as a minister of the gospel. He basically believed in the God-given rights and responsibilities of those in authority (cf. Rom. 13:1–7): but he also believed that, as a citizen, he was under a divine obligation to insist that the authorities acted within the limits of their office, that justice was both done and seen to be done.[5] It is, therefore, important to say that Paul's outburst against the Corinthians taking their disputes into the law courts has nothing whatever to do with any mistrust in the integrity or the propriety of law courts. There is a time and a place for everything, but (as far as Paul is concerned) no time is right for Christians to go to court with one another. To call secular judges 'the unrighteous' (*adikoi*, 1), 'those who have no standing in the church' (4) and 'unbelievers' (6) in the space of a few verses might seem excessive, almost prejudiced. But in each case he is pointing out that the Christian community actually possesses within its own number the resources needed to sort out any problems of this kind. The Corinthians had an entirely wrong attitude to their failures, their destiny, their resources and their calling. Paul, therefore, calls them to account.

1. You are flaunting your failures (6:1)

'You are washing your dirty linen in public.' Outsiders are quick enough to pounce on the slightest inconsistency in a Christian or in a church: why

---

[4] Morgan says: 'The man who wrote this letter appealed to earthly courts. He appealed to Caesar, and claimed his Roman citizenship under certain conditions; and at the last, when secondary officers were trafficking with his liberty, he used the great talismanic word, "I appeal to Caesar." As to whether he got justice, that is another matter. I do not press that, but he used his right in the interest of his earthly citizenship' (p. 61).

[5] Cf. Acts 16:37; 24:24.

else are scandals about clergymen such good 'copy' in the newspapers? Of course, this is no reason to sweep everything under the carpet and to pretend that Christians are all wonderfully holy. But there is a very proper place for a godly discretion and a due sense of shame when it comes to our failures as brothers and sisters in Christ. Hence Paul's expostulation, 'Does he *dare* go to law . . . ?' – the Greek word comes right at the beginning of the sentence (and of the paragraph) and accentuates Paul's own sense of indignation that a fellow Christian should be so presumptuous. Both terms *the unrighteous* (*tōn adikōn*) and *the saints* (*tōn hagiōn*) have no moral or professional connotation.

2. You are forgetting your destiny (6:2–4)

In one of the several instances (six in this chapter alone) where Paul asks the rhetorical question 'Do you not know . . . ?', he challenges the Christians to remember the responsibilities which will come their way when the kingdom of God is fully established. The fact that he should make the point in this way reveals the basic nature of this doctrine. With all that Paul had been *unable* to teach the Corinthians because of their rampant immaturity (cf. 3:1ff.), he had been able to tell them about basic matters to do with the coming and the fulfilment of God's kingdom.

No doubt the accepted teachings of Jesus himself formed the backbone of this catechesis.[6] It is not difficult to see passages in the Gospels from which he would have formulated this eschatological perspective on the future role of *the saints* in the new age. For example, when Simon Peter was beginning to feel the pinch of discipleship after the rather abrupt dismissal by Jesus of the rich young ruler, he asks: 'Look, we have left everything and followed you. What then will we have?' Jesus said to them,

> Truly I tell you, at the renewal of all things, when the Son of Man is
> seated on the throne of his glory, you who have followed me will also
> sit on twelve thrones, judging the twelve tribes of Israel.
> (Matt. 19:27–28)

Throughout the New Testament the message is consistently conveyed that Christians are raised to share with Christ in all the reality of his

---

6 Paul refers to these handed-down 'traditions' in 11:2, 23; 15:3.

resurrection life.[7] It is probable, however, that the major source of Paul's teaching is a passage from the book of Daniel, which describes a particularly vivid dream. It is worth quoting several verses from the whole chapter, in order to give substance to Paul's own perception of the kingdom of God.

As I watched,
thrones were set in place,
  and an Ancient One took his throne;
his clothing was white as snow,
  and the hair of his head like pure wool;
his throne was fiery flames,
  and its wheels were burning fire.
A stream of fire issued
  and flowed out from his presence.
A thousand thousand served him,
  and ten thousand times ten thousand stood attending him.
The court sat in judgement,
  and the books were opened . . .

As I watched . . .
I saw one like a human being [a son of man]
  coming with the clouds of heaven.
And he came to the Ancient One
  and was presented before him.
To him was given dominion
  and glory and kingship,
that all peoples, nations, and languages
  should serve him.
His dominion is an everlasting dominion,
  that shall not pass away,
and his kingship is one
  that shall never be destroyed . . .

'the holy ones of the Most High shall receive the kingdom, and possess the kingdom for ever – for ever and ever . . .

---

[7] Cf. Rom. 6:4ff.; Eph. 2:4ff.; Rev. 20:4–6.

'Then the court shall sit in judgement . . .
The kingship and dominion
    and the greatness of the kingdoms under the whole heaven
    shall be given to the people of the holy ones of the Most High;
their kingdom shall be an everlasting kingdom,
    and all dominions shall serve and obey them.'
(Dan. 7:9–27)

The sheer grandeur of this perspective on the consummation of the kingdom of God, and the part to be played in it by 'saints' like these Corinthian bickerers, must have made Paul wince whenever he thought about the scene in Corinth: like Daniel, he might have declared, 'Here the account ends' (Dan. 7:28). How, in the name of the Most High God, could these folk at Corinth sink that low? *Do you not know that the saints will judge the world?* It all becomes farcical, if not blasphemous, to go to court about *trivial cases* (a phrase parallel to the English legal institution called 'petty sessions').

Paul is still not finished. So far are the Christians at Corinth from forgetting their destiny in the kingdom of God that they have not registered that even angels are to be in the dock. Where does that leave squabbling about *ordinary matters* (RSV: 'matters pertaining to this life')? Angels have a difficult role to play at the best of times. They give the best of their energies to the worship of heaven (Rev. 5:11–12) and the service of the saints (Heb. 1:14), but they have immense difficulties understanding the glories of salvation. Indeed, Peter imagines them peering down from heaven trying to penetrate the mysteries of what it means to be redeemed (1 Pet. 1:12). But, by and large, 'the wisdom of God in its rich variety', seen in 'the boundless riches of Christ', is beyond the ken of 'the rulers and authorities' (Eph. 3:8–10). It is the task of the redeemed people of God, including the church of Corinth, to communicate this divine wisdom to these angelic beings.

As Paul has already explained (1 Cor. 2:1–2), this wisdom is in 'Jesus Christ, and him crucified', and there are fallen angels who cannot stomach that fact. It was their pride which had them originally cast out of the kingdom of God, and they still await divine judgment for that rebellion.[8] 'Corinthian Christians, do you not know that we are to judge those angels?

---

[8] Cf. 2 Pet. 2:4; Jude 6.

How could you have forgotten such basic Christian teaching and plummeted to the depths of sitting in judgment on one another?'[9]

This double perspective on the co-responsibility of Christ and Christians for judging both human beings and angels over matters of eternal significance throws an entirely new light on the Corinthians' zest for their rights and for judging one another in an arrogant and rapacious spirit. To us it may look a bit like Paul taking a sledgehammer to crack a nut, but his method is undeniably impressive.

In describing magistrates at Corinth as *those who have no standing in the church* (4), Paul is telling the Christians, 'If all this is to be so, in terms of the spiritual destinies of men and women for eternity, surely you can look after your own earthly affairs and settle any internal disputes, without resorting to men over whom you yourselves will, one great Day, sit in judgment. Yes, you are forgetting your destiny.' Perhaps Paul is even allowing himself a quiet chuckle at the remarkable change-around which will happen at the revelation of Jesus as King and the full consummation of the kingdom of God.

Some commentators have suggested that Paul wanted the least-equipped and most obtuse members of the Christian community to be assigned to this duty: 'Why do you *not* lay them before the least esteemed in the church?' (a possible rendering). Possibly he is deliberately turning upside down the Corinthians' assessment of who really matters in the community, Christian and secular. The word translated *have no standing* was used earlier (1:28) with the very powerful sense of 'despised', or 'reckoned as nonentities'. With a quick half-reference Paul could be condemning Corinthian – and much modern – thinking about those who matter to God. One of the most insidious and pervasive attitudes among evangelical Christians is the importance attached to 'top people'. There has been proportionately too much time, energy, imagination, money, personnel, prayer and enterprise devoted to winning to Christ people of influence, natural leadership and success – almost to the point where we have reversed the pattern and the priority of Jesus' own ministry.

---

[9] Hodge (p. 95) thinks that the use of the word 'judge' throughout this paragraph carries the wider sense of 'preside', i.e. not necessarily convicting people (and angels) of wrong, but generally demonstrating who is in charge. He says of Old Testament instances: 'As kings were always judges, and as the administration of justice was one of the principal functions of their office, hence to rule and to judge are in Scripture often convertible terms.'

The Christians at Corinth probably regarded the local magistrates as men of consequence, to be cultivated for selfish motives. Paul rejects this attitude: 'in accepting the standards of Christ Christians have deliberately set aside the standards of the world'.[10] One of the tightest straitjackets confining most evangelical Christianity in the Western world today is its middle-class, suburban nature. The fascinating counter-truth, from a global perspective, is that biblical Christianity today flourishes most obviously in countries, continents and cultures least affected by the 'top people' syndrome.

3. You are bypassing your resources (6:5–6)

Paul's sense of indignation now assumes a trace of mocking irony. The Corinthians were so proud of their wisdom, and yet it was apparently impossible to discover just one Christian *wise enough to decide between one believer and another*. Paul believed that in every church resided everything needed to express the love of Christ. He has reminded them that, as a church, they were 'enriched in him, in speech and knowledge of every kind' (1:5). Christ lives in his church and Christ is the very wisdom of God, whom God has made the source of our life (1:24, 30). If such wisdom, resident in the church at Corinth, could not be mobilized to sort out a few personal squabbles, then the Christians certainly needed to go back to the drawing board.

Whenever personal relationships become strained within the body of Christ, it is important to identify and use specially gifted members of the congregation to bring the wisdom of God into the situation. Few things impair the witness of a church more than broken relationships. There will always be disagreements among Christians, but the disciplined approach of Jesus to such matters needs more uninhibited obedience (cf. Matt. 18:15–17). The best catalysts for healing fractured relationships are usually those with listening hearts and the patience to hear both sides out to the end. To such a one 'is given through the Spirit the utterance of wisdom' (1 Cor. 12:8).

4. You are betraying your calling (6:7–8)

Such betrayal is implicit in the way the Corinthians were treating one another. They had been called to be saints (1:2), called to share in Christ

---

[10] Morris, p. 95.

himself (1:9), called to know in Christ the power and the wisdom of God (1:24), called to shame the wise and the strong by the sheer quality of their community life (1:27) – and here they were, living defeated lives, behaving like any unconverted pagan, and giving in to such basic temptations as resentment and covetousness. Some Christians were, no doubt, winning law cases at the expense of others, but *to have lawsuits at all with one another is already a defeat for you.* As Morris puts it, 'To go to law with a brother is already to incur defeat, whatever the result of the legal process.'[11]

There is a much better way, which represents the true calling of the Christian church: those who genuinely have been defrauded or suffered some wrong are to accept it without bitterness. That was the clear teaching of Jesus:

> You have heard that it was said, 'An eye for an eye and a tooth for a tooth.' But I say to you, Do not resist an evildoer. But if anyone strikes you on the right cheek, turn the other also; and if anyone wants to sue you and take your coat, give your cloak as well.
> (Matt. 5:38–40)

The feel of this teaching is applied specifically to disputes between brothers and sisters in Christ:

> Be on your guard! If another disciple sins, you must rebuke the offender, and if there is repentance, you must forgive. And if the same person sins against you seven times a day, and turns back to you seven times and says, 'I repent', you must forgive.
> (Luke 17:3)

No wonder the apostles immediately reacted with the plea, 'Increase our faith!' (Luke 17:5).

So far had the Christians at Corinth strayed from the way of forgiveness and acceptance of wrongs at the hands of fellow believers that they were now actually wronging and defrauding one another. The word *wrong* refers to general injustices: *defraud* to wrongs in regard to property. So reputations and personal possessions were no longer sacrosanct in the

---

[11] Ibid., p. 96.

Christian community. They had moved so far from the supernatural reality of mutual love with the love of Christ that they were deliberately flouting normal standards of business and social ethics. Allo reckons that Paul's language indicates that such flagrant misdemeanours had now become unexceptional in the church at Corinth.[12] No wonder we can, behind all the legal language and the factual statements of this short paragraph, 'sense the sadness of Paul'.[13]

---

[12] Allo, p. 137.
[13] Ibid., p. 136.

1 Corinthians 7:1–40

7. Marriage and singleness – two gifts from God

Paul begins to deal with the specific matters raised in the letter from Corinth. He probably has the letter open in front of him as he dictates his reply. The phrase *Now concerning* seems to indicate the specifics: marriage and divorce (7:1), virginity (7:25), food offered to idols (8:1), spiritual gifts (12:1), the collection for the church at Jerusalem (16:1) and Apollos (16:12). Bruce thinks that other questions in their letter are also answered in chapters 7–16, 'although their treatment is not introduced with the same formula'.[1]

In these chapters Paul steers skilfully between the twin excesses of licence and legalism, libertinism and asceticism. The most pronounced version of the second option is probably summed up in the catchphrase in 7:1, *It is well for a man not to touch a woman*. Barrett[2] adds the comment that Paul's own Jewish environment would have immediately brought to mind the verbal counterpart from Genesis, 'It is not good that the man should be alone' (Gen. 2:18). Whatever the origin of the phrase, Paul tackles the different relationship situations within the church at Corinth in the context of the internal controversy between the two parties.

1. Married couples (7:2–5)

Paul's approach to all the situations mentioned in the letter he received from Corinth undermines some popular views that he was a misogynist,

---

[1] Bruce, p. 66.
[2] Barrett, p. 154.

let alone a slavish adherent of contemporary shibboleths. The Corinthian rigorists had reacted so strongly against the sexual licence of the city that they had swung over completely to the other side, forbidding what God had created for us richly to enjoy. Marriage, says Paul, is the gift and plan of God. Sex is the gift and plan of God. To reject both as though they were evil is as much a deviation from the will of God as to indulge in sexual intercourse outside marriage.

In verses 2–5, Paul makes four statements about marriage which fundamentally challenge the contemporary view prevalent in Corinth.

a. He prohibits polygamy (7:2)

This is an oblique, but clear, prohibition: *each man should have his own wife and each woman her own husband.* His reasoning is exceedingly pragmatic and was probably at the back of the minds of those responsible for the preamble to the 1662 Prayer Book marriage service, where one of the three purposes for marriage is as 'a remedy against sin, and to avoid fornication'.[3] The Greek phrase rendered *because of cases of sexual immorality* means literally, 'owing to fornications', referring to 'the numerous acts and varied temptations which abounded at Corinth'.[4] This plethora of sexual temptation inevitably produced a general opposition to marriage as 'a reaction against the licentious manners which reigned in that city'.[5] It is also possible that people converted out of a virtually amoral lifestyle would have regarded Paul's insistence on monogamy as unrealistic: one certainly hears similar arguments today in so-called enlightened circles. From several sides, therefore, Paul would have been under fire for this firm statement of God's purpose for marriage.

b. He stresses complete mutuality of conjugal rights between husband and wife (7:3–4)

The underlying basis for Paul's insistence on husband and wife giving each other their due is his conviction about the responsibilities, rather than the rights, of married couples. The husband has no right over his own body, and neither does the wife over hers. 'By the marriage vow each relinquishes

---

[3] 'Paul does not say that marriage serves no purpose but that of acting as a prophylactic against fornication, but it does serve that purpose. Men and women have sexual urges, and if they are expressed within the institution that God himself has appointed they are less likely to be expressed in ways that God has forbidden. Marriage moreover must be real, and not "spiritual" marriage' (Barrett, p. 156).

[4] Godet, 1, p. 322.

[5] Ibid., p. 317.

the exclusive right to his or her own body, and gives the other a claim to it.'[6] 'By the conjugal bond, each spouse acquires a right over the person of the other. Consequently, each alienates a portion of personal independence.'[7] Partners deprive each other in marriage by failing to *give*, especially to give what God wants us to give. Paul here nails any selfishness or inconsiderate excess in the physical aspects of marriage. This whole approach to equality and mutuality in the marriage relationship was completely revolutionary in Paul's day, remained so for many centuries afterwards, and continues to be so in virtually every modern culture.

Husband and wife belong to each other, and the question of sexual activity, including intercourse, is a matter of sensitivity to the desires of one's partner. In fact, 7:4 is one of the several passages where Paul explicitly talks of rights; and, so far from being any kind of male chauvinist, he accords to the wife precisely the same rights to enjoy her husband's body as he accords to the husband. As Morris puts it: 'Paul does not stress the duty of either partner at the expense of the other, but puts them on a level. The present imperative, *render* [*give*], indicates the habitual duty.'[8] At the practical level this is a very challenging word to all Christian couples. Many reasons are given for withholding what is due to the other: tiredness, resentment, lack of interest, boredom, and so on. For Corinthian husbands, so wedded to their own rights, this very earthy instruction must have been something of a body blow.

Indeed, the command in verse 5 that partners must not 'defraud' or 'deprive' one another over sexual intercourse is probably a deliberate echo of the litigation issue in 6:1–8. The Corinthians had grown accustomed to asserting their rights with such tenacity that they were constantly parading their sense of being defrauded in the public courts. To have Paul talk to them bluntly about not defrauding their marriage partners about conjugal rights must have really cut them down to size, or, to use a metaphor more apt for Corinthians, pricked the balloon of their arrogance.

Throughout this passage Paul talks in terms of absolute equality within Christian marriage, which was not at all normal in his day. Furthermore, when we take into account 'the widespread exaltation of celibacy',[9] Paul's stress on the indispensability of sexual intercourse for the success of a

---

[6] Bruce, p. 67.
[7] Godet, 1, p. 324.
[8] Morris, p. 106.
[9] Ibid., p. 107.

Christian marriage is all the more striking. In view of current debates with Roman Catholic moral theologians on the purpose of sexual intercourse within marriage, it is worth noting that this discussion of married responsibilities has no hint of any procreative function being necessarily linked to intercourse.

c. He asserts both the ability and the need in Christian couples to abstain temporarily from sexual relations (7:5)

For certain Christians at Corinth, the very thought of abstaining from sexual intercourse would have been faintly ridiculous, if not totally idealistic. Their former trend to sexual licentiousness, prior to conversion, would not have disappeared with baptism, however powerful their experience of the power of God's Spirit. To such people Paul's one exception to the mutual self-giving of a Christian couple would have come as something of a challenge.

Paul's instruction is hedged about by four important provisos. First, both husband and wife must be acting, not simply *by agreement*, but 'in symphony' (literal translation).[10] This alone would prevent the all-too-common habit of an 'over-spiritual' partner seeing anything but prayer as somehow not pure enough for a God-centred marriage. If other Corinthian spiritualizations common today need to be exposed in their true colours, this form of conjugal bribery also calls for exposure.[11]

Paul's second proviso is that such harmonious agreement about sexual abstinence should be only *for a set time* (Greek *pros kairon*), that is, because this is precisely the right time to do this, not because (for example) 'we haven't done it for months or even years'. The Greek word *kairos* always refers to a key period in the timing of God, and that is exactly what Paul has in mind: a special need (perhaps in the family, in the local church, in the nation or on the mission field) demands that husband and wife drop everything in order to give themselves to special prayer.

This brings us to Paul's third proviso, that the abstinence should be with the express intention that they *devote [themselves] to prayer*. This deserves closer study, because the Scriptures consistently see marriage as a unique opportunity for prayer in pairs: and this kind of prayer is attended with special promises and special power, according to Jesus (see

---

[10] NB This 'symphony' should be the perpetual characteristic of Christian marriage.
[11] 'Marriage is to be real marriage, and any attempt to spiritualise it by one partner means that the other is being robbed' (Barrett, p. 156).

Matt 18:19). In Peter's penetrating teaching to Christian couples (1 Pet. 3:1–7), he concludes with the statement:

> Husbands . . . show consideration for your wives in your life together, paying honour to the woman as the weaker sex, since they too are also heirs of the gracious gift of life – so that nothing may hinder your prayers.

Peter is thus suggesting that the most profound purpose in Christian marriage is to release the power of God through a truly united prayer partnership. To be constantly deepening that will involve special times devoted to prayer, to the exclusion of any joyful expression of the one-flesh relationship which is also so vital to God's plan for marriage.[12]

Most helpful comments on this devotion by both partners to prayer come from Morris:

> Normally each belongs to the other so fully that Paul can call the withholding of the body an act of 'fraud'. *That ye may give yourselves* (*hina scholasēte*; we get our word 'school' from this verb) is literally 'that you may have leisure for'. Prayer must be unhurried. In the rush of life it may be necessary sometimes to take exceptional measures to secure a quiet, leisurely intercourse with God.[13]

Paul's fourth limitation on this kind of abstinence may seem obvious, but needs to be spelt out: there must be the deliberate intention of resuming sexual relations again, once the *kairos* is passed. Paul is not naive in talking at this stage of the scheming of Satan, and we shall look at this in more detail below. A couple called to be one flesh in the Lord lay themselves open to all kinds of *akrasia*, or *lack of self-control*, if they continue to abstain from sexual intercourse beyond the limits of the *kairos* impressed upon them by the Holy Spirit. In the context of contemporary Corinth, such *akrasia* could well have been the temptation to revert to *porneia*, that is, fornication.[14]

---

[12] It is intriguing to discover that in Judaism the newly married man was excused from the obligation of saying the 'Shema' – 'for the evident reason that his mind would be otherwise occupied, so that he could not give proper attention to prayer' (Barrett, p. 156).

[13] Morris, p. 107.

[14] Allo (p. 158): 'The Apostle, with his good sense, his moderation and the accuracy of his psychological insight, here fears that the unrestrained zeal of one of the partners would impose on the other, who is less self-denying or less disciplined, a moral pressure which he would be unable to bear and which would expose him to unfaithfulness or other temptations.'

d. He delineates the activity of Satan in the area of sex (7:5)

In Corinth, as today, sexual activity was (in the popular mind) 'doing what comes naturally'. We have already seen the powerful reasons adduced by Paul for honouring the sanctity of sex and the call to glorify God with our bodies (6:9–20). It is clear that Satan deliberately concentrates much of his subtlety in sexual temptation.

Such a perspective would certainly have been rejected out of hand by the libertines in the church at Corinth. For them the body (and therefore sexual activity) was morally neutral: it had no relevance for the activity of the Holy Spirit; it had no relevance for the activity of Satan. At the other end of the scale, the rigorists would have seen Satan everywhere in sex-ridden Corinth; for them the only way to avoid contamination (or worse) was to avoid all sexual activity completely. For such it would have been almost shocking to hear Paul's uninhibited instruction to Christian couples, having had a special period devoted to prayer, to *avoid* Satan's temptations by enjoying sexual intercourse once again.

If shared prayer is fundamental to Christian marriage, then Satan will do his worst in undermining it. Any honest survey of the prayer life of Christian couples would establish two common factors: one, that couples often find praying together the most difficult part of their whole relationship; two, that it is the husband particularly who encounters the greater problems in getting down to prayer with his wife. The reasons for this are not obvious, and are complicated at best. Equally, if true giving to each other in sexual intercourse is the essence of a union where God has joined two individuals together, then Satan will do his worst in inhibiting, spoiling, and robbing it of its purity and its fulfilling potential. Satan is always active in a Christian marriage, to quench shared prayer and to reduce the joys of sex to his own, debased, level.

2. Paul's personal remarks (7:6–9)

Now that he has reinstated Christian marriage along proper guidelines, Paul makes two rather more personal remarks. First (6) he admits that his advice (*This* probably refers to what he has said in verse 5) to married couples has no apostolic authority behind it: *I say this by way of concession, not of command.*[15]

---

[15] The word has the connotation of having a sympathetic appreciation of their situation.

Second, he affirms that he is far happier remaining unmarried: *I wish that all were as I myself am* (7). We can see many reasons for this, practical and vocational, personal and psychological. Paul was 'the apostle to the Gentiles' and that unique vocation required complete freedom to move unimpeded by interpersonal considerations, let alone responsibilities for a wife and family. He was also not the easiest of people to have as a colleague; he was impatient with those who could not work at his pace or failed to come up to his high expectations. He was a Christian who had learnt to rely on his own inner God-given resources, and to exercise the power of inner self-control (the full meaning of *enkrateuesthai* in 7:9). He did not need the companionship of a 'helper suited to him', however much he valued the partnership of trusted colleagues. Clearly, Paul had the *gift* of singleness – and that is precisely what he calls it in verse 7. It is as much a *charisma* as evangelism or speaking in tongues or the working of miracles.[16] Paul says exactly the same about marriage: that too is a *charisma*, because *each has a particular gift from God, one having one kind and another a different kind.*[17]

Paul is thus rehabilitating both celibacy and marriage as manifestations of the grace of God, to be undertaken and to be sustained purely in the strength which the Lord daily supplies. As Godet declares, both are gifts 'for the kingdom of God'.[18]

It is by no means certain precisely what Paul's marital status was. It has been normally assumed that he was never married, but this would have been extremely unusual for a Jewish rabbi.[19] It is conceivable that, on his conversion to Christ, his wife decided to leave him and return to her parental home (a very personal example of what Paul mentions in 7:15). Of course, it is possible that Paul was a widower and that his judgment about remaining in that condition rather than remarrying (7:40) is again a very personal judgment – as he intimates himself.

---

[16] Cf. Jesus' own teaching in Matt. 19:10ff., where he is responding to his disciples' own growing sense of alienation from a truly God-centred, God-honouring commitment to marriage. He had just said, 'whoever divorces his wife, except for unchastity, and marries another commits adultery' (9). 'Not everyone can accept this teaching, but only those to whom it is given. For there are eunuchs who have been so from birth, and there are eunuchs who have been made eunuchs by others, and there are eunuchs who have made themselves eunuchs for the sake of the kingdom of heaven. Let anyone accept this who can.' Paul was one of those able to receive it.

[17] 'There is no less need of a gift of grace to use marriage Christianly than to live Christianly in celibacy' (Godet, 1, p. 328).

[18] Ibid., p. 328.

[19] In Acts 26:10, in his defence before Agrippa in Jerusalem, Paul refers to exercising his right to vote in the proceedings of the Sanhedrin. As a member of that body he would have been a married man.

If Paul was unmarried, and had never been married, his advice to the unmarried[20] in verses 8 and 9 is unequivocal: *it is well for them to remain unmarried as I am.* The word *unmarried* here is gratuitous, but the thrust of his advice is not thereby misconstrued. He is arguing like this:[21] the best situation (his own) is that of the unmarried person who is under no pressure to marry. The next best is the person who must physically express his or her sexuality and does so within marriage. The least desirable is the person who needs marriage as a means of expressing his or her sexuality, but is compelled (or tries very hard) to do without it: *it is better to marry than to be aflame with passion* (9).[22] Incidentally, that last phrase (AV = 'burn') cannot mean to burst out into lustful acts, but rather means to be so consumed with inward desire that scarcely anything else either matters or can be coolly considered. Paul deals more fully with the situation of engaged couples in 7:36–38.

3. Marriage and divorce (7:10–16)

There is another vital question in Paul's mind, without its ever actually getting into the text: what about those who, being married 'for better, for worse', now feel that they do not need marriage or that they have made a mistake in getting married, or that they would actually be far more effective in the service of the Lord without the responsibilities of marriage? There are many examples of this kind in the church today. The question, therefore, needs a clear answer, not least because, in an age of easy divorce, it is very tempting to opt for a laissez-faire approach to a difficult marriage relationship, instead of working at it in the strength which God supplies, in the conviction that he is able to make something rich and good out of an empty shell.

Paul gives an unequivocal charge to couples who see little hope for their marriage: *To the married I give this command – not I but the Lord – that the wife should not separate from her husband (but if she does separate, let her remain unmarried or else be reconciled to her husband), and that the husband should not divorce his wife* (10–11).

---

[20] On his reference to 'widows', see later comments on 7:39–40.
[21] So Barrett, p. 161.
[22] For an entirely different interpretation of this phrase (which basically equates to 'burn' with enduring the torments of Gehenna), cf. Bruce, p. 68.

Paul's phrase *not I but the Lord* is naturally crucial. Does he mean that he has received direct personal communication from the Lord at this point? If so, how did it come – by a vision, a message, a dream, or by what means? Is he drawing some less-radical contrast between his own considered (and no doubt prayerfully achieved) decisions and unmistakable divine authority? The fact that he reverses the language in verse 12, where he says *I say – I and not the Lord*, adds to the debate. There are other phrases, simply within chapter 7, which could be (and have been) taken to indicate some ambivalence in Paul's own mind about the status of his teaching at different stages: for example, 7:6, 'This I say by way of concession, not of command'; 7:25, 'Now concerning virgins, I have no command of the Lord, but I give my opinion as one who by the Lord's mercy is trustworthy'; 7:40, 'But in my judgement she is more blessed if she remains as she is. And I think that I too have the Spirit of God.'

There is obviously scope for several opinions over these phrases. All in all, the comments of Barrett[23] seem balanced and helpful: where Paul had to hand actual sayings of Jesus, he explicitly quoted them. Barrett points out that 1 Corinthians was written before any of the Gospels and Paul would not necessarily have known more than a few of the sayings of Jesus. He certainly appears actually to quote very few; if he knew any more than he quotes, it might be because he quotes only where the teaching of Jesus varied considerably from prevalent Jewish teaching; and on this particular matter of divorce, we know that the teaching of Jesus was utterly different from the rabbinic schools of Hillel and Shammai (the two most influential) and from the text of the Old Testament itself (cf. Deut. 24:1–4).

There is certainly no need, or justification, to drive a wedge between Paul's own advice and the actual teaching of Jesus, as has been the habit of some writers. The phrase in verse 12, *not the Lord*, is not intended to signify that Paul is saying anything unsympathetic, let alone contrary, to what the Lord himself would have said. He would certainly not regard his own words as unauthoritative and, whatever the flavour of the statement in verse 40 ('I think that I too have the Spirit of God'), he is surely expecting to be received with more than mere respect. He was an

---

[23] Especially pp. 162–163.

apostle, whatever the Corinthians might have thought about his apostolic credentials.[24]

To return directly to the couple whose marriage is shaky, Paul categorically repeats the words of Jesus: 'Whoever divorces his wife and marries another commits adultery against her; and if she divorces her husband and marries another, she commits adultery.' The commitment to marriage by a man and a woman is lifelong, underwritten by God himself and not to be loosened, let alone destroyed, by mere humans. 'What God has joined together, let no one separate.'[25]

In Matthew's Gospel[26] there is one – and one only – basis for such divorce between two Christian partners: adultery, fornication, *porneia*. Why Paul does not mention this here we cannot tell. It might simply be that, Mark being generally accepted as the earliest Gospel to be written down, Paul knew only the Marcan version of the Lord's teaching. On the other hand, the rampant *porneia* in Corinth would have introduced this factor into so many marriages in the church, because of the past history of countless Christian couples, that to mention *porneia* without the opportunity for pastoral counsel face to face with each couple might well have imperilled many good marriages. The Christians at Corinth were not so firmly rooted in the reality of regeneration and renewal in the Holy Spirit as to give them the stability required to deal with a partner who raked up a murky past after a bitter domestic feud one difficult evening after a bad week at the office.

Paul's fundamental approach to the question of Christians getting divorced is, therefore, very simple: 'Don't. The Lord has expressly forbidden it; so do not even allow yourselves the luxury of entertaining it as a possibility.' If this is the express command of the Lord, it does no good whatsoever mentally to flirt with what is so clearly beyond limits. If, as not infrequently happens, a Christian couple think they have made a mistake in getting married, then it is important for them to accept the authority of the Lord's teaching and to apply themselves to their relationship, in the conviction that, if they work at it, God can make it new and vital.

---

[24] Several scholars, including Bruce (p. 69) and Moffatt (quoted by Morris, p. 109), emphasize that Paul's scrupulousness about quoting the actual sayings of Jesus underlines both the historical accuracy of such recorded words as we do possess, and the integrity of the primitive church in not 'inventing' such sayings to solve current disputes in the Christian community.

[25] Mark 10:9, 11–12. Cf. Mal. 2:13ff., culminating with 'I hate divorce, says the LORD'.

[26] Matt. 5:32; 19:9.

We need also to do justice to Paul's own parenthesis in verse 11: *but if she does separate, let her remain unmarried or else be reconciled to her husband.* In other words, Paul recognizes that a marriage between two committed Christians can reach an impasse. When it is on the rocks, two courses of action can be considered: the first option is to separate and remain single. Paul's advice in 7:40, in a rather different situation, would indicate that this might well be the better course to follow. The other option, when they have gone their different ways for a sensible period – presumably to afford each other a bit of breathing space to sort out the dynamics of their relationship – is to effect a proper reconciliation, on which to build a better and a stronger marriage. Either option, the former being a realistic recognition of the inevitable and the latter being a genuine commitment to real improvement, has the blessing of Paul. But on no account will he countenance the option of divorce.[27]

Paul then tackles a problem which must have been very common in Corinth: a newly converted Christian married to an unbeliever. It is always common where the gospel is being proclaimed with power. As one partner is converted, this leads to immense, and at times intolerable, strain being placed on both. The Christian partner has now discovered a totally new way of life and is committed to new standards, new loyalties, new priorities, new desires: he or she is 'a new creation' (2 Cor. 5:17). The necessary adjustments are immense. There will be many false starts, much inconsistency, great misunderstanding. At times the new Christian will feel torn in two.

Equally, the unbeliever will hardly know what has hit him; and it seems (statistically at least) to be the husband who finds himself living with some new kind of holy woman. The devastating impact of such an event, not least in what can genuinely be called a very good marriage, cannot be overestimated. A Cape Town brain surgeon put it most movingly. When asked what he found so difficult about his wife's new-found faith in Christ, he stressed two things: first, she was no longer the person with whom he had originally fallen in love and whom he had decided to marry; second, there was another Man about the house, to whom she was all the time

---

[27] NB The command to the wife not to 'separate' (*chōristhēnai*), but to the husband not to 'divorce' (*aphienai*), 'may reflect the fact that in Judaism only the husband had the right to divorce' (Barrett, p. 161). Actually Godet's comment here has the merit of prosaic common sense: 'The reason [for the two different words] perhaps is because the man is in his own home, and remains there, whereas the woman leaves the domicile' (1, p. 334).

referring her every decision and whom she chose to consult for his advice and instructions. He was no longer the boss in his own house: Jesus gave the orders and set the pace.

Paul was very acutely aware of these strains in many homes at Corinth. He also recognized that several external factors, not least his own admitted preference for the single life, put very strong pressure on the believing partner to call it a day and to start a new life without all the chafing and heavy burden of an unequal yoke (cf. 2 Cor. 6:14). It was more than likely that the Christian partner was tending to look down on, even to write off, the unconverted spouse. Peter found it necessary to have special words for Christian wives with unconverted husbands: 'Wives . . . accept the authority of your husbands, so that, even if some of them do not obey the word, they may be won over without a word by their wives' conduct, when they see the purity and reverence of your lives' (1 Pet. 3:1–2). Peter's emphasis on behaviour rather than conversation is fundamental in this connection.

Having recognized the reality of the scene at Corinth, Paul stresses the need to work at the marriage, just as Christian couples facing problems need to work at their marriages. He then gives four reasons for his advice: the fact of consecration, the status of the children, the possibility of conversion and the sanctity of marriage.

a. The fact of consecration (7:14)

The unbelieving husband is made holy through his wife, and the unbelieving wife is made holy through her husband. The tense of the word translated *is made holy* is perfect, and that indicates a relationship established in the past and still obtaining now.[28] Thus, when the one was converted to Christ and was born again, the other 'was made holy', or 'became consecrated', in a special way. The Corinthians probably felt that the unbelief of the one cancelled out the belief of the other. Paul insists the exact opposite: the belief of the one has led to a distinctive relationship between the unbelieving partner and the Lord. Precisely what this relationship might be is virtually impossible to define, but it probably has some hint of being specially marked out by God. It clearly falls short of

---

[28] The Greek preposition translated 'through' is *en* = 'in'. It is conceivable that Paul is arguing along the lines of the 'one-flesh' reality in 6:16ff., and saying that God regards two individuals who are joined together in marriage to be one, and that this oneness is the fundamental truth which brings about the consecration of the unbelieving partner *in* (meant literally and physically) the believer.

being 'saved', because the possibility of that happening (16) is another, distinctive inducement to working at the marriage.

Whatever vagueness we necessarily have to maintain, we must also do justice to the actual word translated *made holy, hēgiastai,* which is the perfect passive of the word 'sanctify' in 6:11, where Paul says to the Corinthians: 'you were sanctified'. It is also the root from which we get Paul's status word for every Christian: *hagios* = 'saint'. If he had wanted to find a Greek word with less theological significance, Paul's fertile mind would surely have discovered it. Perhaps the clearest route to interpreting the word is by recalling the actual context at Corinth: Paul is dealing with a group of rigorists who saw sin in sex wherever they could; he is probably defending sexual relations and also the birth of children in a marriage between a Christian and a non-Christian as being 'holy'. Calvin comments: 'The godliness of the one does more to "sanctify" the marriage than the ungodliness of the other to make it unclean.'[29]

b. The status of the children (7:14)

We have already noted that Paul uses the same root word (*hagia*) to describe the state of the children of a couple, only one of whom is a believer. For Paul this argument clinches the matter, because he takes it as self-evident. He appears to be relying on Jewish convictions and custom, which regards the children as being within the covenant. 'Until he is old enough to take the responsibility upon himself, the child of a believing parent is to be regarded as Christian. The parent's "holiness" extends to the child.'[30]

Incidentally, Jews trace their descent as Jews through the mother, on the prudential grounds that it is normally plain who is the mother of a child, but not always certain who is the father. If the children of a Jewish mother are within the covenant of God's special people, Paul argues that the children of one Christian parent (mother or father) are *holy*. Paul also posits the alternative to such children being regarded as 'holy' when he says, *Otherwise, your children would be unclean* (14). That last word (*akatharta*) speaks not simply of a non-relationship with the Lord, but of an actual uncleanness which Paul himself clearly does not believe to be an accurate description of the condition of children being brought up in

---

[29] Quoted in Barrett, p. 165.
[30] Morris. p. 110.

the Christian community. Paul does, in fact, work the logic of this conviction through with consistency in his instructions to Christian families in Ephesians 5 and 6 and Colossians 3, where he treats the children of believers as 'in the Lord' and takes that status as the foundation for their Christian upbringing.

c. The possibility of conversion (7:16)

Whatever the trials and the delays inherent in pursuing such an unequal partnership, Paul insists on holding out the real possibility that the miracle of conversion will eventually bring the family into true oneness in Christ.[31] The fact that this does happen, and happens on numerous occasions, is the greatest possible incentive to work at the marriage, even during lengthy periods of apparent obduracy.

The way Paul puts his question does, of course, leave the matter completely open: *Wife, for all you know, you might save your husband. Husband, for all you know, you might save your wife.* The simple answer is that neither does know, but we have every encouragement to press on in hope. Perhaps the very openness of the questions to wife and to husband is intended to safeguard the sovereignty of God in saving men and women. Yet even Paul slips into the same language later: 'I have become all things to all people, so that I might by any means save some' (9:22). The sentiment behind this verse has been well expressed by Michael Green:

> If one of you has been converted since marriage, then there is reason to suppose that the good Lord is at work in your family. And you pray, and you try to live a consistent life, so that if your partner is not won by your word, he/she may be won without a word having been said by the godliness of your life.[32]

d. The sanctity of marriage (7:15)

There is another incentive to work at such a partnership in spite of all its inherent problems. This is implicit in Paul's instruction that the Christian partner should never take the initiative to end the marriage. However

---

[31] It needs to be said that some commentators take exactly the opposite view of Paul's questions in verse 16, i.e. 'how can you possibly tell whether you will win your husband?' Cf. Morris (p. 111): 'To others Paul's meaning is that marriage is not to be regarded simply as an instrument of evangelism. To cling to a marriage which the heathen is determined to end would lead to nothing but frustration and tension. The certain strain is not justified by the uncertain result.'

[32] In a sermon preached in St Aldate's Church, Oxford, in December 1979.

uncommitted both to the marriage vows and to the very institution of marriage the unbeliever may be, the Christian partner upholds its sanctity and its lifelong permanence.

It is only after making these four points with some vehemence that Paul allows the possibility of separation. He always wants the Christian to take the way of faith and expectation before the situation is given up. It must be the unbelieving partner who concludes that any continuation of the marriage is impossible, and the implication throughout the passage is that the grounds for such incompatibility lie in the faith of the Christian. It is precisely here that the rationalizations can begin to creep in and to determine the decision to part.

Having said that, we must give proper weight to Paul's words *It is to peace that God has called you* (15). For him this appears to be the overriding principle. We have seen many times the paramount importance in this letter of the calling of God, and the next major paragraph (7:17–24) picks up the same theme. Here Paul reminds Corinthians experiencing real stress and distress at home that the essential nature of God's calling to each of them is an invitation, indeed a summons, into a peace in which he wants them to dwell daily. This peace is not mere absence of strife or the end of bickering: it extends to cover the wholeness and the healing of all our relationships. Tragically, there are certain intractable relationships where a Christian's peace in God can never be realized: *in such a case the brother or sister is not bound*. For God's children to know the creative peace of the Lord is a more final and absolute priority for Paul than for two people to continue chafing under an unequal yoke: let them separate.

The dilemma still remains about the precise meaning of the phrase *is not bound* (literally 'has not become a slave'). Few Christians would quibble with the rightness, in such extreme circumstances and after every conceivable avenue has been explored, of permanent separation between two incompatibles. But does the phrase countenance divorce, as distinct from separation (i.e. is the person freed from the marriage vows)? And if divorce is a valid option, is remarriage (obviously to a believer; cf. 7:39) also a possibility? What precisely is the lack of bondage which Paul is envisaging? It seems clear that the Christian partner is not bound to 'a mechanical retention of a relationship the other partner wishes to abandon'.[33] But is he

---

[33] Barrett, p. 166.

or she 'bound' or 'enslaved' to living as a divorced person with no prospect of remarriage? That is the question over which Christians of every persuasion will probably have to agree to disagree. The one consideration which, above all others, prevents the whole discussion from degenerating into ivory-tower theological ethics is the real possibility that Paul is actually writing out of the trauma of his own experience.

4. Christian vocation (7:17–24)

This next paragraph comes as a digression into Paul's teaching about different relationships within the family of God. He is, in effect, urging a basic attitude of contentment with whatever lot God gives to us, even if this includes circumstances which cause friction and frustration. To that extent he is urging the same approach to life's other tensions as to marriage. There are three basic priorities in the apostle's mind, all of which permeate his teaching in the rest of the chapter: the need to be firm in our situation; the need to be flexible about material things; and the need to be free from any distractions from our single purpose of pleasing the Lord. In this paragraph he applies these three priorities to *each of you* (17). He takes two particular examples, circumcision and slavery, and he argues for a radical Christian approach to both. Circumcision and slavery represented the two most divisive phenomena in the world of the New Testament. Circumcision constituted the greatest religious barrier, slavery the biggest social barrier. In each case, Paul is bold enough to assert, the salvation of God in Christ has rendered them null and void. Any man or woman in Christ has been so remade that earthly status, or lack of it, is irrelevant. It is, therefore, a distraction for Christians to become obsessed with either issue.

We need, of course, to say that the inspiration of God's Spirit in the later centuries of his church has produced different priorities at different periods: victims of the slave trade in the eighteenth century or of the Jewish Holocaust in the twentieth century would not readily dismiss these two issues as distractions. Having said this, we can see the thrust of Paul's reasoning. He is facing an unsettled community in a very cosmopolitan seaport, for whom steady application to the routine of the humdrum was at a premium. Paul wants to encourage stability, and he therefore makes the same point three times; *Let each of you lead the life that the Lord has assigned, to which God called you* (17); *Let each of you remain in the condition in which you were called* (20); *In whatever condition you were called, brothers and sisters, there remain with God* (24).

Paul is telling the Corinthians that the key to making their present situation count is to let God change *them* daily, right there where he has placed them. Circumcision does indeed present immense barriers between Jew and Gentile: but God can overcome those barriers by going to work within both Jewish Christians and Gentile Christians (18–19). The gulf between slave and free yawns far and wide: but God can bridge even that gap by going to work within both Christian slaves and free Christians (21–23). That means a heart-commitment to stay firmly where they were when God first called them into fellowship with his Son, Jesus Christ (1:9).

There are conceivably three or four occupations which a new believer would immediately need to renounce (e.g. gambling, organized crime, prostitution); but normally 'a man is not called to a new occupation; his old occupation is given new significance'.[34] As Paul says in verse 24, 'there remain *with God*' (emphasis added); the two are partners now, which was not true before. This will actually have transforming influence on the whole way we 'walk' (17),[35] and it will become an absorbing challenge to work out in practice the implications of what God has *assigned* uniquely to us. When God's time to move on arrives, he will give us the necessary restlessness to get up and go.

There was, in fact, another pressure towards such perpetual restlessness at Corinth. Paul had faced it in a particularly destructive form at Thessalonica.[36] Christians were convinced that the end of the world and the return of Jesus in glory were about to take place. Secular pursuits and steady routine were thus 'unspiritual'. This produced, on the one hand, a frenzied brand of evangelism (because that was the only Christian service worth the name at such a critical moment); on the other hand, there were those who simply opted out of everything and did not even do an honest day's work – after all, what was the point of 'filthy lucre' with the end of the world about to engulf you? Paul had to be very firm with Macedonian Christians, especially breadwinners in the family, who acted with that measure of irresponsibility.

---

[34] Ibid., p. 170.
[35] *Peripatein* is a favourite word of Paul to describe the Christian's daily behaviour: cf. Eph. 2:2, 10; 4:1, 17; 5:2, 8, 15.
[36] Cf. 1 Thess. 4:9–12; 2 Thess. 3:6–13.

In summary, what was happening at Corinth was this: young, impressionable Christians were allowing themselves to become *slaves of human masters* (23). Young believers are easily swayed by what others, notably 'mature Christians', think and teach. They allow their discipleship to become a matter of following accepted practices, certain patterns of behaviour, cultural shibboleths. In Corinth there were still those who insisted on circumcision as the true mark of a bona fide believer. Equally, there were those who reacted violently against such legalism and insisted on the importance of another physical operation which removed the marks of circumcision.[37] The leaders of both groups were making slaves of immature believers, and Paul has to stress that circumcision and uncircumcision are both irrelevant (19). What matters is obedience to the Lord's commandments, and that has nothing to do with ritual religious acts.[38]

There were also influential people at Corinth making capital out of the slave–freeman issue. Paul brings that out into the open as well. His contention is simply that Christ overturns all human categories and all marks of distinction: *whoever was called in the Lord as a slave is a freed person belonging to the Lord, just as whoever was free when called is a slave of Christ* (22). Jesus himself is the one true reality for all men and women, whether bond or free, Jew or Gentile, male or female, married or single, black or white, rich or poor, young or old. Paul also appears to show which way the wind of the Spirit was beginning to blow in his own mind as far as the ethics of slavery were concerned: *if you can gain your freedom, make use of your present condition now more than ever* (21). Although that is a very tentative statement, it shows that he has no brief for slavery as such. In Christ we are united, we are one. From now on, therefore, Christians must never allow any human category to divide them, especially when others try to bring them into bondage by enforcing such divisions.

We all have one Master, one Teacher, one Saviour, one Lord: to him alone we owe our total allegiance. We have been *bought with a price* (23;

---

[37] In James Michener's book *The Source*, the story is told of a young Jew who wanted to become like the Greeks; so he went through a painful surgical operation to remove the marks of circumcision. This was common in the Greek games where athletes competed naked.

[38] We have a fascinating trio of parallel verses on the issue of circumcision in 1 Cor. 7:19; Gal. 5:6; and Gal. 6:15. The problem Paul faced with the circumcision party in the churches of Galatia, and not least in the whole saga of his confrontation with Peter on this issue, points to its being less pronounced a controversy at Corinth. In the churches of Galatia, the debate became so all-pervasive and determinative that the very heart of the gospel was perilously at stake. In both cases mentioned in Galatians there is explicit reference to certain individuals who were attempting to bring Christians into personal bondage.

the same phrase as in 6:20). With that allegiance we will each find a firm commitment to our present position, a growing flexibility about material things, and a liberating freedom from the countless distractions which confront us in our calling in the world.

5. Virgins (7:25–35)

Paul seems to have been asked for his thoughts about virginity. He writes first from the angle of overriding pressures in current circumstances (26–31), then from the pragmatic perspective of sanctified common sense (32–35), and finally in realistic terms about a young couple in love with each other (36–38).

Although two or three possibilities have been raised by scholars about the identity of these *parthenoi* (= virgins), it is most likely that Paul is here faced with another rigorist poser from the legalistic ascetics at Corinth.[39] Knowing his own preference for the single state (referred to again in 7:26, 32, 38, 40), they want from him a firm endorsement of his own preferences. Paul is scrupulously fair in this passage. He is not warning against marriage as such, but against the particular pressures (*thlipsin*, 28) and distractions (*merimnai*, 32ff.) which are the stock-in-trade of married people. He therefore gives advice to all those who are thinking, or planning, towards marriage.

One factor stands out in Paul's mind. It is the first time it has hit the surface of his thinking in the letter as a whole. In verse 26 he talks of *the impending crisis*; in verse 29 he says that *the appointed time has grown short*; in verse 31 he asserts that *the present form of this world is passing away*. What does Paul mean? Bruce comments, 'The whole discussion of marriage in this chapter is influenced by Paul's eschatological awareness in addition to his pastoral concern.'[40]

The first phrase, *the impending crisis*, could equally bear the meaning of 'the straitened circumstances which are bearing in on us at this very moment' (cf. NRSV margin). Jesus himself had spoken at length about such an *anankē*, such 'great distress', which would fall 'on the earth and wrath against this people' (i.e. the Jews – Luke 21:23). The immediate context of that 'distress' was the destruction of Jerusalem about fifteen years after

---

[39] For details cf. Bruce, pp. 73–74.
[40] Ibid., p. 74.

Paul wrote 1 Corinthians. One of the major pressures in such a crisis would be the shattering impact on family life. One has only to visit countries ravished by war to appreciate something of the inconceivable agony produced in such a war situation. Hardly a single family has not been personally and violently affected by the protracted wars in those countries over the years. Any sensitive Christian, especially one with the burning heart of a pastor like Paul, would have longed to spare those in his care any such suffering. The sheer facts of the matter mean that couples with families have to face the most ghastly experiences at such times: *those who marry will experience distress in this life, and I would spare you that* (28).

To appreciate Paul's thinking we need to take several factors into account. Persecution had been directed quite recently at Jews.[41] The Roman authorities, in the capital but even more in the provinces, found it very difficult to determine the real distinctives between the long-standing menace of Judaism and this emerging Christian sect. The degenerating sanity of the Emperor Nero was already beginning to make itself felt in debased and bestial treatment of a few Christians here and there around the empire. Paul himself had only recently been on the receiving end of particularly nasty persecution in Ephesus, the very city from which he was now writing this letter (cf. Acts 19).

In Paul's mind it is likely that the events surrounding the destruction of Jerusalem (foretold by Jesus) were seen as examples in microcosm (the Mediterranean world of the first century) of what would happen cosmically at the end of time. We should therefore expect Paul to counsel steadiness, flexibility and single-mindedness in the face of an imminent, if not actual, situation of great precariousness. In the context of a written request about the practical wisdom of entering upon the lifelong commitment of marriage, such counsel assumes added realism. Hodge comments: 'The apostle writes to the Corinthians as he would to an army about to enter on a most unequal conflict in an enemy's country, and for a protracted time.'[42]

It is, of course, not necessary to assume that Paul has any eschatological perspective in mind at all. It is possible that the church at Corinth was encountering unusually pressurized circumstances, about which we

---

[41] The presence of Aquila and Priscilla in Corinth as Paul's key colleagues had been due to an imperial edict expelling all Jews from Rome: cf. Acts 18:1–2.
[42] Quoted in Bruce, p. 74.

know nothing and he knew much. 'In view of the troubled times Paul felt it best for men to stay as they were. When high seas are raging it is no time for changing ships.'[43]

In Paul's second such phrase, *the appointed time has grown short* (29), he is (literally) saying, 'The crisis has been contracted.' The word for 'time' is *kairos* (cf. 7:5), designating a particularly important moment in the economy of God. This 'moment' has been shortened; by definition, it does not last very long anyway.[44] For whatever length of time is left, Paul is saying, be conditioned by non-worldly priorities:

> *let even those who have wives be as though they had none, and those*
> *who mourn as though they were not mourning, and those who rejoice as*
> *though they were not rejoicing, and those who buy as though they had no*
> *possessions, and those who deal with the world as though they had no*
> *dealings with it.*
> (29–31)

Marriage, bereavement, pleasures, possessions, commerce and business – let every Christian hold very loosely to all daily facts of human life.

We today also may not be able to think along these familiar tramlines for much longer. However accurate this assessment was in terms of Corinth in the first century, it might well turn out to be a word in season for Christians in the hitherto stable societies of the West in the twenty-first century. There are certainly many people today (unbelievers in particular) who are opting out of normal family responsibilities (e.g. many couples are choosing not to have children). Many are also opting out of the acquisitive existence expected of them in today's materialistic society.

Perhaps it is more than time for Christians to ask themselves questions which demand even more radical answers on the basis of Paul's teaching in this chapter. Michael Green sees the meaning of the phrase *the time has grown short* (29) as being literally 'furled like a sail'. Explaining this he expounds:

> God's time has been furled. The Lord has come in the mid-point of time, in the cross and the resurrection, and we live between that furled time

---

[43] Morris, p. 116.

[44] Cf. Eph. 5:16, where the bargains presented by such a *kairos* have to be snapped up with urgency.

and the second coming. We do not know how much wind is going to be opening that sail, but we do know that we are in furled-sail time.[45]

Paul's first two striking phrases in this paragraph provide a clear perspective on the third: *the present form* [Greek *schēma*] *of this world is passing away* (31). The best comment on this comes from John's pen:

> Do not love the world or the things in the world . . . for all that is in the world – the desire of the flesh, the desire of the eyes, the pride in riches – comes not from the Father but from the world. And the world and its desire are passing away, but those who do the will of God live for ever.
> (1 John 2:15–17)

It seems distinctively foolish to invest in a swiftly disintegrating 'scheme' of things.

This triple, yet single-minded, perspective on the contemporary scene at Corinth explains very adequately the advice Paul gives to virgins. In a sentence it is this: *it is well for you to remain as you are* (26; the principle of firmness in one's present situation). *Are you bound to a wife? Do not seek to be free. Are you free from a wife? Do not seek a wife* (27). Just in case his own known preference might cause an excessively guilty conscience, he adds: *But if you marry, you do not sin, and if a virgin marries, she does not sin* (28).

In verses 32–35 Paul introduces another, related issue in his concern to *promote good order and unhindered devotion to the Lord* (35). This gives a picture of quiet poise and uncluttered devotion to the Lord. The key word (which occurs six times in three verses) refers to 'distractions'. The basis of the Greek word is *meros*, or 'part'. When Paul writes, *I want you to be free from anxieties* (32), he is expressing his concern that Christians at Corinth should not have anything which divides their lives into parts and thus fragments them. The cares and chores of family life do precisely that. There is a conflict of concern for the married man: *the married man is anxious* ['fragmented'] *about the affairs of the world, how to please his wife, and his interests are divided* ['fragmented'] (33–34). The same is true for the married woman (34). Christians who are single can give more time

---

[45] An excerpt from a sermon preached at St Aldate's Church, Oxford, in December 1979.

to the spiritual disciplines which give a person distinctive depth and impact in ministry. Once a person accepts responsibility for a marriage partner, and even more for children, there is not as much time available for such things.

The apostle is not so naive as to assume that only unmarried Christians can serve the Lord in a thoroughly integrated way. He still talks of their undistracted concern as something which contains the seeds of non-integration, because being *anxious about the affairs of the Lord, how to please the Lord . . . [how to be] holy in body and spirit* (32 and 34) does not in itself actually produce holiness. That is the prerogative of God's Spirit. If unmarried men or women (and Paul probably has both in mind in this paragraph) have not come to terms emotionally and psychologically, as well as spiritually, with the call to singleness, they will find themselves being frequently distracted from pleasing the Lord, and drawn towards pleasing prospective marriage partners.

Furthermore, Paul is not passing any moral judgments in this paragraph, but purely stating the facts (cf. verse 35: *I say this for your own benefit*): the married man *ought* to be concerned to please his wife; he ought also to be concerned to please the Lord. In no sense does Paul intend, by his teaching here, to tie a halter (literal meaning of *brochos* in verse 35) around the necks of married Christians, and thereby bring them into heavy bondage.

So we return to Paul's original statement that both marriage and singleness are equally *charismata*, gifts of God's grace. The unmarried finds personal integration in the *charisma* of singleness: the married can secure undivided devotion to the Lord in the *charisma* of marriage.

6. Engaged couples (7:36–38)

Apparently, there were those at Corinth who imposed on engaged couples the discipline of abstaining from marriage for as long as possible – and longer. The people who advocated this were probably, like many who advocate lengthy engagements today, well established in the joys (and routine) of married life. To urge self-control was a simple matter for such folk. Paul, however, will not allow this kind of self-denial to be boosted into becoming the supreme virtue; nor is he prepared to countenance the free-and-easy approach to sexual relations advocated by some, more liberated, engaged couples. If a couple find their physical desires are so strong[46] that they can wait no longer, then let them get married and may God bless them: they do *well* (38); *it is no sin* (36). This is virtually the same as his advice in 7:9. If they can wait, they also *do well* (37). He urges them to be honest with each other: it must be a firm, thought-through decision, based on the assurance that sexual desires are so under control that they can genuinely do without satisfying them. The primary point is that engaged couples who wait for some time before marrying, and couples who find that 'it is better to marry than to be aflame with passion', *both* run no risk of missing God's best for their marriage.

7. Widows (7:39–40)

After stressing the lifelong permanence of marriage, Paul gives widows complete freedom to remarry. His only proviso is the one he adamantly lays down for all Christians contemplating marriage: *only in the Lord.*[47] This attitude is, at first glance, surprising in view of the overall emphasis of the whole chapter on remaining in one's present condition. He then acknowledges his own opinion that a Christian widow will be happier if she does not marry again, in spite of the need for sexual fulfilment.

From the early days mentioned in Acts, the church recognized a special responsibility for the widows in their fellowship (Acts 6:1ff.). It seems that a special 'order of widows' was instituted at an early stage, and that this care became a practical example of pure religion, 'undefiled before God, the Father' (Jas 1:27). After his experiences down the years in various local churches, Paul urged Timothy to establish clear guidelines for operating such orders (1 Tim. 5:3–16). In these instructions to his successor at Ephesus, from where he is writing this letter to the Corinthians, he actually tells Timothy to 'refuse to put younger widows on the list' (1 Tim. 5:11) for all kinds of negative – and a few positive – reasons. At that stage Paul's 'real widows' (1 Tim. 5:3) are 'not less than sixty years old' (1 Tim. 5:9). An older woman, facing the declining years of her life as a widow, misses the companionship, the fellowship, of her partner, and in the emptiness of her life she is tempted to plunge back into marriage just for companionship alone.

---

[46] 'If his passions are strong' is a paraphrase for the Greek word *hyperakmos* which could refer either to the man being oversexed, or to the woman being past her prime in terms of childbearing.

[47] This phrase could mean, more generally, 'only within the Lord's will'. In that case, attention would have to be paid to other matters besides whether the proposed partner is a Christian.

The fact that he once again (7:40) refers to his personal opinion (as in 7:25) might indicate the embryonic nature of his thinking at this stage. His final remark, *And I think that I too have the Spirit of God*, could well retain that faintly ironic nuance which often seems to colour his relationships with the church at Corinth.

1 Corinthians 8:1–13

8. Freedom and sensitivity to others

The next substantial section (8:1 – 11:1) covers Paul's answer to a very thorny issue in Corinth, as indeed throughout the early church: *Now concerning food sacrificed to idols* . . . (*tōn eidōlothutōn*). This is not immediately relevant today. Barclay explains:

> Sacrifice to the gods was an integral part of ancient life. It might be of two kinds, private or public. In *private* sacrifice the animal was divided into three parts. A token part was burned on the altar . . . ; the priests received their rightful portion . . . ; the worshipper himself received the rest of the meat. With the meat he gave a banquet. Sometimes these feasts were in the house of the hosts; sometimes they were even in the temple of the god to whom the sacrifice had been made . . . The problem which confronted the Christian was, 'Could he take part in such a feast at all? Could he possibly take upon his lips meat that had been offered to an idol, to a heathen god?' If he could not, then he was going to cut himself off almost entirely from all social occasions . . . In *public* sacrifice . . . after the requisite symbolic amount had been burned and after the priests had received their share, the rest of the meat fell to the magistrates and others. What they did not use they sold to the shops and to the markets; and therefore, even when the meat was bought in the shops, it might well have already been offered to some idol and to some heathen god . . .
>
> What complicated matters still further was this – that age believed strongly and fearfully in demons and evils . . . They were always lurking to gain an entry into a man's body and, if they did get in, they would injure his body and unhinge his mind . . . These spirits settled on the food

as a man ate and so got inside him. One of the ways to avoid that was to dedicate the meat to some good god . . . It therefore followed that a man could hardly eat meat at all which was not in some way connected with a heathen god. Could the Christian eat it? . . . To the Christian in Corinth, or any other great city, it was a problem which pervaded all life, and which has to be settled one way or the other.[1]

We see, then, that the question of *ta eidōlothuta* had two sides to it: taking part in idol feasts, yes or no? Eating meat bought in the shops but with dubious origins, yes or no? The situation was inevitably aggravated by the strict kosher laws of the Jews, as well as by the many articulate rigorists in the church at Corinth. Further complications would have been introduced by the famous Jerusalem decree (Acts 15:29), in which Gentile converts were urged to abstain from food sacrificed to idols.

Although Paul had never (as far as we can judge) used this decree at Corinth, it is likely that members of the Peter-party (cf. 1 Cor. 1:12) would have made very forceful capital from it to support their rigorism. Bruce makes the important observation that Paul is the only authoritative personality in the apostolic or sub-apostolic church who does not solve the 'food offered to idols' controversy by any absolute ban.[2] This serves to underline his determination not to let the legalists win the day on this absolutely central issue. This matter dealt with everyday habits of behaviour and it would have been fatal to yield one iota to the rigorists.

The Jewish rigorists in the Christian community at Corinth would have had three fundamental objections in prohibiting such food to fellow Jews: (1) It was tainted with idolatry; (2) the heathen would not have paid tithe on it; and (3) it probably would not have been killed in the right way. What, then, of Christians in general? There was the anti-rigorist group who would probably have regarded the whole debate as puerile and demeaning: what possible propriety could there be for those set free in Jesus Christ to develop pernickety scruples about food, especially when thereby they virtually cut themselves off from everybody else at Corinth? Not only would they become a laughing stock, but all effective evangelism would be virtually annihilated. So once again Paul would have found himself embroiled in a battle on two fronts: how can he keep both groups happy

---

[1] Barclay, pp. 79ff.
[2] Bruce, p. 79.

and still uphold the truth of the gospel? There were too many divisions between Christians at Corinth anyway, and he did not want to add fuel to those flames.

Taking Paul's arguments in 8:1 – 11:1 as a whole, it is plain that he is essentially for freedom: see especially 8:8; 9:1–12, 19a. He is advocating freedom of two kinds: absolute freedom in Christ (8:8; 9:19; and 10:29) *and* the freedom to restrict one's freedom for the sake of a fellow Christian ('one of them') whose conscience is less robust (8:13; 9:12, 15, 19). It is, perhaps, of some significance that Paul actually concludes the statement about his personal convictions (9:24–27) by admitting that he practises such voluntary restriction of his absolute freedom in Christ not least for his own personal benefit: 'so that . . . I myself should not be disqualified'.

After this general overview of the three chapters, we look more closely at chapter 8, where Paul has three major perspectives to bring on the whole problem. These concern the overriding principle at stake, the fundamental truth about God and the supreme consideration to be asserted in any such ethical debate.

1. The overriding principle: love builds up (8:1–3)

Let us remind ourselves of the two groups at Corinth: the legalists said, 'Do what the law says'; the libertines retorted, 'We know better – be free.' Paul's essential answer is this: love is what matters, not knowledge of the one (negative and legalistic) kind or of the other (permissive) kind. Paul is not here condemning 'knowledge' outright. He is concerned that true *agapē* love should control and characterize their *gnōsis* (knowledge). The spirit in which we say what is right is as much part of the truth as the knowledge we articulate. As Godet puts it, 'knowledge devoid of love and of power to edify, when we look at it more nearly, is not even true knowledge'.[3]

The word for *knowledge* (*gnōsis*) comes six times in these three verses, and we are clearly into what eventually became an explicit Gnostic debate. Some of the catchphrases of the libertines are quoted: *all of us possess knowledge* (1), with the emphasis no doubt on the personal pronoun. Two other slogans are discernible in verse 4. Paul is keen to reinstate knowledge in its rightful place, in its proper expression, and with its necessary

---

[3] Godet, 1, p. 408.

counterpart and context. Knowledge on its own, particularly of the kind paraded by these Corinthian experts, only *puffs up*, leaving its possessor like an inflated balloon. This is not the first time he has had to fire this warning shot across their bows.[4] Knowledge is important; we all possess some; but on its own it is inflated and empty. A Christian needs to be filled with love, because *love builds up* (1). Prick a balloon and it bursts; lean on a wall and it holds your weight.

Paul is concerned for the church at Corinth to be strong and firm enough to take heavy weights, and that requires a solid base of true Christlike love, which is not puffed up (cf. 13:4). When a Christian's character is controlled by love and is growing in true knowledge, he or she is no longer concerned so much with how well he or she knows God, as with being known by God. That actually is the proof of true love for God (Gal. 4:8–9). Any true knowledge does not lead to pride in what we know, but to humility about what we do not know.

That truth flew right in the face of the Gnostic approach to religion, which was essentially acquisitive and self-centred, asking such questions as 'How far can I go?' and 'What's in it for me?' That grasping approach is the exact opposite of *agapē* love, which wants to give, to help, to build up others. To love God, which can only be a response to his love for us revealed in his Son (supremely in his death for us – 1 John 4:10), is to begin the adventure of being known by God. All true knowledge is thus entering into that perfect knowledge which God has of us.

All our knowledge now is partial (13:8) and it is therefore extremely arrogant to put the greatest store by knowledge, especially the very esoteric and exclusive kind of knowledge paraded by the Gnostics.[5] Their version of spiritual 'one-upmanship' was the antithesis of true *agapē* love, as seen in the self-sacrifice of Christ. This love builds up the body of Christ.

We can now apply this overriding principle to the particular question of food offered to idols. Here is Paul's main point: specialist knowledge about the ritual and religious origins of a particular chunk of meat, either in the market or at your host's dinner table, will achieve nothing to build up the faith of fellow Christians. The important matter is the impact on my brother or sister of what I might do in this sensitive situation. My

---

[4] Cf. 1 Cor. 4:6, 18; 5:2.
[5] In referring to the Gnostics we must remind ourselves that, as a fully fledged heresy, Gnosticism was a second-century phenomenon. Paul addressed only an incipient Gnosticism.

knowledge of theological niceties, or even of Christian fundamentals, will achieve nothing except impressing others with my knowledge.

If, on the other hand, I carefully work out how my fellow Christians will react to my behaviour, and decide accordingly how I will behave, I will build up the body of Christ. We must, therefore, each strive to make our whole behaviour constructive by asking ourselves such questions as 'Are people brought closer to God? Are Christians strengthened in their faith? Are people glad to have met us?' When Christians' knowledge is radiated and released by love, they clearly demonstrate that they know God and that God knows them – that is, that there is a deepening personal relationship between the two.

2. The fundamental truth: there is one God (8:4–6)

Part of the 'knowledge' of the Corinthian 'in-group' was the obvious (to them) fact that there was nothing at all in this local idolatry: *no idol in the world really exists* (4). Paul readily agrees, and also endorses their other premise: *there is no God but one.* It is also perfectly true, says Paul, that *there may be so-called gods*, but 'all the gods of the heathen, they are but idols'.[6] This is fundamental and we must never allow ourselves to be shifted from this basis.

If, in fact, we simply took the catchphrase of the Corinthian Gnostics, *there is no God but one*, we could argue that everyone is indeed worshipping the same God, but by different names and in different ways. In the very common universalist–syncretist mood of today, the scandal of particularity in the message of Christianity is either rejected or gently sidestepped.

If we look more carefully at 8:6, however, we see Paul asserting: *for us there is one God, the Father, from whom are all things and for whom we exist, and one Lord, Jesus Christ, through whom are all things and through whom we exist.* There may be many *so-called gods in heaven or on earth – as in fact there are many gods and many lords* (5); but Paul categorically talks about *God the Father* (and we need to see in that phrase the richness of New Testament theology on the fatherhood of God) and *Jesus Christ* as equal in status and authority. They have differing functions, which are expressed in the Greek prepositions. The Father is the one *from* (Greek *ek*)

---

6 Cf. Ps. 96:5, Prayer Book version.

whom come all things: he is the source and origin; he is also the goal (Greek *eis*) and the purpose of our existence. Jesus Christ is the agent and mediator: the one *through* (Greek *dia*) whom everything and everyone comes into existence.

The most natural meaning of *us* and *we* in this passage is Christians: thus Jesus is the bridge to God, the go-between, the mediator, the way to God.[7] This is the fundamental truth from which Paul will not be shifted. There are fundamental and irreconcilable differences between the God who is Father of our Lord Jesus Christ and the deities worshipped in all other religions, however many peripheral similarities may be adduced.

What, then, of the many *so-called gods* and lords in heaven and on earth? The biblical perspective seems consistent and clear. They are *eidōla* = 'copies', that is, they do not have any reality. Thus the word 'idol' is used *both* for the image made of wood or of stone, *and* for the deity worshipped in such idolatry. In Isaiah we read, 'All who make idols are nothing, and the things they delight in do not profit' (Isaiah 44:9ff.). This is followed by a long list of craftsmen who join hands to make an idol: the ironsmith, the carpenter, the wood collector, the baker, the chef – all working with the same piece of wood from the forest, and then falling down to worship a dead log. It is all so manifestly unreal, devoid of spiritual truth: nothing.

And yet that is not the full story behind the Old Testament perspective on idolatry. There is an important passage in Deuteronomy, which reads:

> Jeshurun [i.e. Judah] grew fat, and kicked.
>   You grew fat, bloated, and gorged!
> He abandoned God who made him,
>   and scoffed at the Rock of his salvation.
> They made him jealous with strange gods,
>   with abhorrent things they provoked him.
> They sacrificed to demons, not God,
>   to deities they had never known,
> to new ones recently arrived,
>   whom your ancestors had not feared.
> (Deut. 32:15–17)

---

[7] Cf. John 14:6; Rom. 11:26; Col. 1:15ff.; 1 Tim. 2:5–6.

The gods of pagan worship are not gods in any full sense of that word; they are merely idols, that is, objects of worship made by human beings. But behind these 'copies' (*eidōla*) are spiritual forces, called 'demons' in the passage above.

That is by no means an exclusively Old Testament perspective. It is at least hinted at in 1 Thessalonians 1:9, and is expressly stated in Galatians 4:8–9, where Paul says to Christians,

> Formerly, when you did not know God, you were enslaved to beings that by nature are not gods. Now, however, that you have come to know God, or rather to be known by God, how can you turn back again to the weak and beggarly elemental spirits? How can you want to be enslaved by them again?

'Weak and beggarly' they may be, but they are still 'elemental spirits'.

It is clear that idol worship is both unreal and all too real. This is what Paul himself asserts in 10:19–20:

> What do I imply then? That food sacrificed to idols is anything, or that an idol is anything? No, I imply that what pagans sacrifice, they sacrifice to demons and not to God. I do not want you to be partners with demons.

These 'demons' are not identical with what heathen worshippers believe their 'gods' to be. To become involved in idolatry of any kind is to open the door to influence by demons, by agents of Satan who are lusting for our worship and are past masters of duping and destruction.[8]

This perspective has important pastoral application today. Those previously involved in non-Christian practices of worship are often in need of specific ministry in the area of the demonic. Paul himself is under no illusions at all that contact with demons is still very much a possibility for fully fledged members of the Christian community (10:19–22). This is not the same as suggesting that Christians can be demon-possessed, a possibility which theologically and pastorally seems lethal. Ministry for deliverance from such demonic forces needs, therefore, to be undertaken by wise, experienced and informed Christians. In addition, a whole mesh

---

[8] Is this not behind the uncompromising condemnation of certain elements in the churches at Pergamum and at Thyatira (Rev. 2:14, 20)?

of spiritual forces seems to be intricately at work wherever men and women are looking for satisfaction, fulfilment, identity and (especially) contact with 'the divine' – however loosely that last phrase may be defined. If there is a history of encounters with rival ideologies competing with the Lord Jesus Christ for a person's allegiance, we need to be ready for direct ministry to set people free from such bondage. The likely results of such involvement are confusion, aimlessness and the surrender of personal decision-making in a passive way to other forces. Such ministry is particularly important where there has been contact with cults linked with Eastern mysticism, or associated with brainwashing techniques, or directly involved with occult practices, or intermingled with drug-taking.

3. The supreme consideration: the fellow Christian for whom Christ died (8:7–13)

Again returning to the question of food offered to idols, Paul points out that there are Christians at Corinth who have not really grasped the fundamental truth just explained: *some have become so accustomed to idols until now, they still think of the food they eat as food offered to an idol* (7). Such people think that the idols *are* real and can therefore contaminate the eater. Because their contact with such idolatry has been long and comprehensive, Paul does not argue the point: he argues very strongly the need for the 'strong' (i.e. knowledgeable) person not to be self-pleasing, but to consider the weaker Christian. Having said that, he unambiguously states the spiritual principle: *Food will not bring us close to God. We are no worse off if we do not eat, and no better off if we do* (8).

The 'weak' person in this discussion is the person who is hypersensitive on such matters; he or she is the over-legalistic, rigorist Christian who tends to cut out anything and everything doubtful, just in case it might harm his or her relationship with God. Paul clearly wants such a 'weak' person to grow into a 'strong' position. Yet he does not here attempt to persuade that person into such a position of strength. His own stress falls on the 'strong' Christian who has been freed from human conventions and shibboleths: '*you* must voluntarily restrict *your* freedom'. Thus the strong must readjust to help the weak, not vice versa.

The arguments Paul accumulates in verses 9 to 13 are very powerful. First, a strong Christian's freedom can actually become a stumbling block to the weak Christian, causing that person's faith to weaken rather than to grow, and moving the weak Christian to act directly against what his or her conscience at that stage permits (10). In fact, a Christian is led to an action which is not based on faith, and such an action is seen by Paul as direct sin (Rom. 14:23).

Second, we must always pause to see our fellow Christian as someone *for whom Christ died* (11), not just as a good friend in the local church or even a committed member of our fellowship. When we discipline ourselves to this degree, we will do everything we can to avoid anything by which *this weak person is destroyed*.

Third, when we do sin against our brother or sister in this way and when we wound a weak conscience, we are in fact sinning *against Christ* himself (12; cf. Matt. 25:41ff.). The real presence of Jesus in our brother or sister is easy to ignore.

The inevitable conclusion of Paul's teaching in this chapter is that it is never a demonstration of true Christian liberty to do 'doubtful things' out of bravado. So Paul's assertion in verse 13 perfectly summarizes the thrust of this chapter: *Therefore, if food is a cause of their falling* [Greek literally = 'being scandalized' or 'made to stumble'; cf. Mark 9:42], *I will never eat meat, so that I may not cause one of them to fall. My brother or sister* – that is the emphasis which the hard-line men and women of knowledge needed to absorb.

Another major theme in this chapter is the place of conscience. It occurs three times (7, 10 and 12). On each occasion it is called *weak* (Greek *asthenēs*), and it refers obviously to the Christian whose life in Christ after rescue from paganism has been relatively brief. Such a person will have experienced a fairly dramatic change of lifestyle. His or her Corinthian way of life would have involved a good deal of socializing, both in giving and in receiving hospitality. Bruce gives an example from a contemporary papyrus: 'Chaeremon invites you to dine at the table of the lord Sarapis at the Sarapeion [*sc*. temple of Sarapis] tomorrow, the 15th, at the 9th hour.'[9]

There would have been a virtually total contrast between 'playing the Corinthian' and 'being a Christian'. Decisions about hospitality and general socializing would have taken up a considerable amount of their time. The less tender a Christian's conscience, the wider the field of Christian witness. The more sensitive the conscience, the greater the

---

[9] Bruce, p. 81.

temptation to withdraw into the Christian ghetto – or at least into its mentality.

There was, as a result, a crucial need for the consciences of Christians to be properly instructed over the things which really mattered in contemporary society. Paul picks up the same theme again in 10:23–30. If the Christian church at Corinth was going to cut ice in the rampant paganism of such a licentious seaport, the Christians needed to be less rather than more sensitive over 'doubtful things'. Paul wanted the life of faith to extend its frontiers into every dark alley and moral cesspit in Corinth. This required more robust consciences than many Christians, either at Corinth or at Rome, could muster. Therefore everyone had to be patient, non-judgmental, sensitive and absolutely committed to building up the life of the Christian community as a whole.

If a Christian is guided, by the example of someone seen to *possess knowledge* (10) or as a 'strong' brother or sister, into making a decision or taking a course of action over which he or she has not personally prayed and reached the Lord's will, then that is not a matter of faith. Paul's own judgment is that such a result is a sinful course of action: his or her conscience is wounded (12) or battered (Greek *typtontes*, used of beating somebody over the head); it then becomes even less equipped to reach mature, Christ-centred decisions.

For Paul, therefore, the 'strong' person is the Christian who allows the dictates of Christ's Lordship alone to determine daily behaviour; for such people the whole of life is their oyster. But there are many Christians for whom such strength is so distant as to be almost a chimera. What is the way forward? 'We who are strong ought to put up with [literally 'carry', *bastazein*] the failings [or weaknesses] of the weak [or inadequate], and not to please ourselves. Each of us must please our neighbour for the good purpose of building up the neighbour' (Rom. 15:1–2).

The key lies in that awkward little phrase 'not to please ourselves'. Such an attitude goes right against the grain, and particularly Corinthian grain, which was so nurtured on 'my rights'. The whole of Paul's argument in this chapter is a practical example of following the law of love: love will restrict itself for the sake of others. To cause any brother or sister, just one brother or sister, to stumble even once is such an appalling danger for Paul that he will not once touch meat to avoid such a disaster. That is true Christian love, and that, Paul would affirm with equal fervour, is true Christian freedom.

1 Corinthians 9:1–27

9. Freedom to restrict our freedom

Paul's great cry for Christian freedom is continued in this chapter. He is chiefly concerned with his own freedom to restrict his freedom for the sake of the gospel. He is expansive about his rights, thus echoing if not parodying the watchword of the Corinthians, but he concludes his whole argument with the self-discipline which this must promote (9:24–27). In fact, the real climax of Paul's argument in this section is the challenge of 11:1, 'Be imitators of me, as I am of Christ.'

1. Paul's freedom in Christ (9:1–6)

There were those at Corinth, as we know, who were constantly questioning the authority of Paul, especially his claim to be an apostle. They reckoned that they had far better credentials than he. They claimed to be apostles on far stronger grounds. Their idea of an apostle was a man with authority, who let everybody know that he was in authority. They lorded it over everyone; anyone who did not act in the same way could not possibly be intended to carry responsibility in the church. They saw Christian leadership in terms of being masters, not servants. They slated Paul because he was not like that; he was too 'weak', too 'soft', too willing to deny himself his freedom in Christ for the sake of others.[1]

So Paul explains precisely how he sees his freedom in Christ, especially how he has deliberately, and freely, chosen to restrict his freedom for the benefit of others. This, he maintains, is a sign of strength, not of weakness.

---

[1] If this seems to be a caricature, we only have to read 2 Cor. 10:7 – 11:15.

Throughout the passage Paul is talking of his rights as an apostle, rather than as any ordinary Christian. He has *seen Jesus our Lord* (cf. 15:8–9), and the sheer existence of the church at Corinth evidences the authenticity of his apostolic activity: these Corinthian Christians are, in fact, *the seal of my apostleship in the Lord* (2) – a seal being that which stamps something as specially belonging to someone.[2] Paul, if anyone, has a special right to claim the church at Corinth as his own responsibility and sphere of influence. He was the first to come all the way to them with the gospel, albeit with much fear and trembling; he had been through a great deal of personal pressure in order to see the church of Christ planted in such a city; he had given himself unstintingly for the total welfare of these people. But still he refused to claim his rights as an apostle.

What precisely were these rights? Paul lists three essential rights in the next three verses (4–6): the right to food and drink, to have one's wife present in a travelling ministry, and to have the freedom not to work for a living. *Do we not have the right to our food and drink?* he asks (4). Paul seems to be rather on the defensive. This is borne out in his use of the word *apologia* (3) to describe his procedure in this chapter; he is, indeed, answering charges about the legitimacy and the effectiveness of his apostleship. It is never easy to have one's whole ministry called into question, let alone written off. This is not the only time that Paul had to answer for his ministry to people who ought to have known better. The mere fact that he was prepared to spend time and thought giving a defence to those who would examine him on his basic credentials as an apostle of Jesus Christ stresses the essential meekness of the man.

The second apostolic right is of some interest: *Do we not have the right to be accompanied by a believing wife, as do the other apostles and the brothers of the Lord and Cephas?* (5). Are the Lord's brothers sons of Joseph by an earlier marriage or (more likely) later sons of Joseph and Mary? Did Peter make a habit of travelling around with his wife, and did that fact contribute to the emergence of a Peter-party? It is from such personal, rather than theological, distinctives that divisions in the church so frequently arise. Was Paul, in fact, the odd man out in travelling on his own without the practical support of a wife to look after him? Is the NRSV margin suggestively correct in talking of Paul having 'a sister as wife'? And

---

[2] Cf. 2 Cor. 12:12, 'The signs of a true apostle were performed among you with utmost patience, signs and wonders and mighty works' – probably Paul's own more detailed description of what he mentioned in 1 Cor. 1:6, 'the testimony of Christ has been strengthened among you'.

does that refer to Christian women who gave themselves to this supportive ministry, rather like Susanna, Joanna, Mary Magdalene and 'many others' who had provided for Jesus 'out of their resources' (Luke 8:2–3)? Or does it refer to Paul's actual sister who gave him this sacrificial support year in, year out? Whatever the answer to these questions, it seems obvious that a true apostle could legitimately claim proper care and maintenance for his wife as well as for himself – a practice which could well be followed with more sensitivity today when local churches benefit from travelling ministers.

In his third use of the word *exousia* (= right) in these three verses, Paul stresses the propriety of not having to work at an ordinary job in order to sustain his preaching ministry. In this way he avoided being any burden on the local church (6). We know, especially from the Acts of the Apostles, that Paul often worked long hours in a very enervating climate in order to get a local congregation off the ground. This was particularly true in Ephesus, a subtropical city where not much of any consequence normally happened during the hours of siesta (11 am to 4 pm) – as indeed happens regularly today in many similar places in Latin and Latin American countries. At these 'dead' hours (if the nrsv margin reflects accurately what took place) Paul daily argued in the Hall of Tyrannus, in the middle of a full day's manual labour as a leathermaker (Acts 19:9). Paul was able, at the end of those exhausting two to three years in Ephesus, to claim, 'I coveted no one's silver or gold or clothing. You know for yourselves that I worked with my own hands to support myself and my companions' (Acts 20:33–34). He made the same claim at Thessalonica,[3] and it was of paramount importance to the overall witness of the gospel at Thessalonica that he did thus model a pattern of sheer hard work and of dependence on nobody. There was a surfeit of 'eschatological parasites' in Macedonia, idlers who were waiting around for the return of Christ.

Rights, rights, rights – Paul had many, and claimed none. Incidentally, the mention of *Barnabas* in 9:6 is intriguing, not so much for any hint of reconciliation[4] between these two great men after their blazing row (*paroxysmos* = paroxysm) over John Mark (Acts 15:39), but because we know that Barnabas was a very wealthy landowner (Acts 4:36–37). It is

---

[3] 1 Thess. 2:9; 2 Thess. 3:7–9.
[4] Cf. 2 Tim. 4:11; Col. 4:10.

likely that Christians as touchy as the Corinthians thought it rather presumptuous for a man of considerable means to take advantage of their hospitality. If he was going to be a preacher of the gospel, they might have said, the least he could do was pay his own way.

2. Forgoing his rights (9:7–18)

The Corinthians needed some strong arguments to prise them free from their rights and their acquisitive attitude towards being Christians. So Paul adduces five solid reasons, as he argues initially that these rights lie entirely within his legitimate province: common practice, scriptural precept, intrinsic justice, Jewish custom and Christ's command.

a. Common practice (9:7)

The three metaphors here are all common biblical ones for the Christian ministry: soldier, farmer and shepherd. A fourth, equally common one (athlete), comes at the end of the chapter (9:24–25; cf. 2 Tim. 2:1–7). Whichever picture of a Christian minister he takes, Paul is arguing it is only right for the person to receive the appropriate 'perks': soldiers get their equipment and their uniform, without which they cannot fight; farmers, particularly fruit farmers, will not go to market to purchase some of their own apples; shepherds will have the bulk of their breakfast from the good things they have produced. What could be fairer, more normal, more proper? If it did not happen, the neighbours would reckon that someone needed his or her head examining!

b. Scriptural precept (9:8–10)

It is not only a matter of good rural common sense; the Lord of the harvest has laid down the law himself. Paul may appear to put it in a roundabout way, but the message is clear: *You shall not muzzle an ox while it is treading out the grain* (Deut. 25:4). Why not? Because hard workers deserve to be rewarded for their labours. God did not add that particular piece to the Deuteronomic law merely to make sure that oxen were properly looked after. He was explaining a principle: *It was indeed written for our sake* (10). Both ploughman and thresher should expect to receive a share of the profits, doubtless in kind. God had said so in his law; it was not just the milk of human kindness, but the method of divine sharing. After all, it is 'God who gives the growth' (3:7).

c. Intrinsic justice (9:11–12)

Paul's next argument in effect asks the Corinthians how much store they place by the gospel: what does it mean to you to have been brought from darkness to light? What do all these 'spiritual blessings' mean to you? Is there any gratitude in your heart for 'the grace of God that has been given you in Christ Jesus' (1:4)? One of the most instinctive habits in believers is the gift of hospitality and generosity: if we have been on the receiving end of spiritual blessing, we want to demonstrate our thankfulness to God in tangible ways.

In agricultural communities the area pastor (and in Africa the bishop in particular) will not return from his itinerant ministry without a few chickens, a sheep and a liberal supply of fruit and vegetables. Is such a 'harvest' so unreasonable? asks Paul. He knows in his heart that the Corinthians are completely accustomed to making this kind of 'love-offering' (as it is often called today): that much is evident from the not-so-veiled remark in verse 12, *If others share this rightful claim on you, do not we still more?* There were obviously others at Corinth who operated in this way with a fair degree of shamelessness, bringing this or that ministry and expecting to have a fairly substantial reward for their labours. These people had nothing like the same claims upon the Corinthians in terms of gospel blessings as Paul; but there was no hint of questioning their rights (*exousias*, 12).

Furthermore, Jesus himself had endorsed the same intrinsic right in his statement to the Seventy: 'Remain in the same house, eating and drinking whatever they provide, for the labourer deserves to be paid' (Luke 10:7).

d. Jewish custom (9:13)

The Corinthians needed to look no further than the Jewish temple to see the same principle in daily operation. In fact, it is likely that this was virtually commonplace, whichever temple you visited in the city. Paul, however, probably had the temple at Jerusalem chiefly in his mind. The Lord had told Aaron,

> I have given you charge of the offerings made to me . . . I have given them to you and your sons as a priestly portion due to you in perpetuity. This shall be yours from the most holy things, reserved from the fire: every offering of theirs that they render to me as a most holy thing, whether grain-offering, sin-offering, or guilt-offering, shall belong to you and

> your sons . . . All the best of the oil . . . of the wine and of the grain, the
> choice produce that they give to the LORD, I have given to you. The first
> fruits of all that is in their land . . . shall be yours.
> (Num. 18:8ff.)

The list is long and thorough, and is followed by a similar injunction to the
Levites: 'To the Levites I have given every tithe in Israel for a possession in
return for the service that they perform, the service in the tent of meeting'
(Num. 18:21).

e. Christ's command (9:14)

Paul's clinching argument is, even to the Corinthians, incontrovertible: the Lord Jesus himself has laid it down *that those who proclaim the
gospel should get their living by the gospel.* 'You received without payment;
give without payment. Take no gold, or silver, or copper in your belts, no
bag for your journey, or two tunics, or sandals, or a staff; for labourers
deserve their food' (Matt. 10:8–10). To make the preaching of the gospel
completely free is altogether different from accepting any gifts which
meet your necessary expenses. The NEB version of Paul's instructions to
Timothy takes this command of the Lord one interesting step further:

> Let the elders who rule well be considered worthy of double honour,
> especially those who labour in preaching and teaching; for the scripture
> says, 'You shall not muzzle an ox while it is treading out the grain', and,
> 'The labourer deserves to be paid.'
> (1 Tim. 5:17–18)

f. A timeless challenge

With these five arguments Paul spells out an extremely powerful case for
claiming all his personal rights, not merely as a Christian, but as an
apostle. The Corinthians expected an impressive apostle to be very firm
on his rights. Paul makes a completely contradictory case, and in so doing
builds up an approach to the ministry of the gospel which is a timeless
challenge to everyone called to share in the gospel. We will take each
statement in sequence.

9:12, 15. *Nevertheless, we have not made use of this right . . . But I have
made no use of any of these rights, nor am I writing this so that they may
be applied in my case.* We might almost call this Paul's password. He simply

is not concerned about rights: he has deliberately chosen to forgo each and every one of them. He had the inner freedom to do so, which few Christians actually achieve. By thus freely ignoring his rights, he was actually celebrating his freedom. And if, by any chance, the Corinthians were beginning to think he was surreptitiously slipping in a request for some material provision of his daily needs, they could forget that as well (15). Paul's emotional involvement in his ministry might well be a matter for evaluation; his integrity was completely above board.

9:12. *We endure anything rather than put an obstacle in the way of the gospel of Christ.* Paul's whole autobiography would endorse that statement. He was passionately gripped by Jesus Christ. He would do literally anything to ensure that Christ 'might come to have first place in everything' (Col. 1:18). His whole attitude to Christian ministry was to 'endure' rather than to 'enjoy' his daily calling.

The overwhelming impression is of a man so utterly dedicated to the gospel that he was constantly worrying about this drawback and that hindrance. Barrett puts it powerfully:

> The gospel, which turned upon the love and self-sacrifice of Jesus, could not fitly be presented by preachers who insisted on their rights, delighted in the exercise of authority, and made what profit they could out of the work of evangelism.[5]

The word translated *obstacle* (*enkopēn*) is

> a graphic and somewhat unusual word (only here in the New Testament). It means literally 'a cutting into', and was used of breaking up a road to prevent the enemy's advance. Paul had avoided doing anything which might prevent a clear road for the gospel advance.[6]

The fact that Paul writes of enduring anything to prevent such irresponsibility also speaks of his great love for those outside Christ (cf. 9:19–23). The word for *endure* is one of the eloquent verbs he uses of true *agapē* love (13:7). This kind of love 'endures all things', and it is salutary to hear the heart of an evangelist expressing itself in this way. We have only

---

[5] Barrett, p. 207.
[6] Morris, pp. 135f.

to read the lists of Paul's sufferings in the Corinthian correspondence to appreciate something of what it cost him personally to ensure that the gospel road was free of obstacles. A man who is ready to endure anything for the gospel is not interested in his rights.

9:15–18. *I would rather die than that – no one will deprive me of my ground for boasting! . . . What then is my reward? Just this: that in my proclamation I may make the gospel free of charge, so as not to make full use of my rights in the gospel.* If Paul had any rights left in his apostolic heart, it was the right to make the gospel free of charge – and that was so close to his heart that he regarded it as his chief cause of pride. We know, from other parts of the Corinthian correspondence, that Paul's boasting was a major source of inner conflict (cf. 2 Cor. 10 – 12). He was driven to it by the unique pressures of the Corinthian situation. Barrett seems to be right in noting here (9:15) the beginning of the Pauline paradox of 'glorying in weakness . . . Not only will Paul glory in circumstances that must have meant hunger and weariness; he will glory in a situation which can have brought him little but mockery and insult.'[7]

Paul's stance on boasting was that its only proper target is the Lord himself (1:31). He was certainly not proud of preaching the gospel: how could he be proud of doing something which he was inwardly and irresistibly compelled to do? If he had been compelled, for whatever reason, to stop preaching the gospel, he would simply have been consumed with intolerable frustration. Paul had been arrested by Jesus and therefore he had no option: *an obligation is laid on me, and woe betide me if I do not proclaim the gospel!* (16).

Because the Corinthians had become so obsessed with their rights, they found it almost impossible to believe that Paul could be inwardly driven purely by his love for Jesus Christ and his passion for the gospel. They would have reckoned it the ultimate disaster if they had had all their supposed rights stripped from them. For Paul, on the other hand, it would have been the ultimate catastrophe if he had been compelled to stop preaching the gospel. The penultimate catastrophe would have been if he had been prevented from doing so 'free of charge'.

Paul posits the theoretical situation where he is spending his time preaching the gospel, but with his heart and soul actually elsewhere: *if not*

---

[7] Barrett, p. 209.

of my own will, I am entrusted with a commission (17) or NEB, 'I am simply discharging a trust.' That is the lowest approach Paul could envisage towards preaching the gospel. He was so thrilled with the amazing privilege of proclaiming such a gospel that he could not really empathize with those who saw it simply as a job to be done. At the same time he recognized that, at its most humdrum and prosaic, he was simply a man entrusted with a commission, a steward in trust with the resources of the Lord (17, *oikonomian*; cf. 4:1). A steward (an *oikonomos*) has no rights and no rewards, only responsibilities: and that is precisely the major thrust of Paul's *apologia* (3) in this chapter. He did have rights, apostolic rights, rights as founder of the church at Corinth, which were unique and overriding. But he was utterly overwhelmed with the privilege of being an evangelist, and he repudiated as abhorrent the very idea that a person can do God any service, favour or kindness.

Paul's whole attitude is paralleled closely by the instructions of Jesus himself:

> Who among you would say to your slave who has just come in from ploughing or tending sheep in the field, 'Come here at once and take your place at the table'? Would you not rather say to him, 'Prepare supper for me, put on your apron and serve me while I eat and drink; later you may eat and drink'? Do you thank the slave for doing what was commanded? So you also, when you have done all that you were ordered to do, say, 'We are worthless slaves; we have done only what we ought to have done.'
> (Luke 17:7–10)

3. Choosing slavery to all (9:19–23)

The rest of chapter 9 spells out Paul's position, both in terms of his personal relationship to all sorts and conditions of people (19–23) and in terms of his own personal self-discipline (24–27). In both he provides a stimulating incentive to single-minded discipleship as a free man in Christ. He was completely free (*free with respect to all*, 19), but he did not intend to allow that freedom to provide him with an excuse for the indulgence even of an odd personal whim or two. Why? *I do it all for the sake of the gospel, so that I may share in its blessings* (23). As Barrett comments: 'The gospel has been entrusted to him, but it has not been put

145

under his control.'[8] Every encounter, every personal habit, was now overtly under the control of Jesus Christ as Lord, because the gospel dominated his whole life. He was living his daily life *sub specie aeternitatis* (i.e. in the light of eternity), and that meant evangelism with integrity, relationships with adaptability, and personal holiness with single-mindedness.

Paul wanted, like his master, to lay down his life. He had learnt that 'happiness lies more in giving than in receiving' (cf. Acts 20:35). In verses 19–23 he gives a few examples of what it meant for him, a wealthy, educated, religious Jew, to make himself *a slave to all*. He had sacrificed matters of racial identity, religious sensitivity and conscience. He had done that with one goal: *that I might win more* (19).

The word for *win* (*kerdainō*) comes five times in this paragraph. Then the nuance is changed by moving from 'winning' people to 'saving' them (22). The word *sōzō* (= save) states what *kerdainō* (= win) can only imply: that what is at stake is not simply the failure or success of human persuasion, but a person's eternal destiny. This is subtly implicit in the contrast between *that I might win more* (19) and *that I might by any means save some* (22). Paul did not thereby exclude any legitimate 'means' from efforts to win people, but he was at least tacitly acknowledging that the most enlightened, far-reaching, imaginative and 'mass-production' methods will not save anyone.

His fundamental philosophy was to discover the methods which combined the greatest integrity with the greatest impact – some might say 'success': *I have made myself a slave to all, so that I might win more of them* (19). There is a gold mine of evangelistic methodology in that single sentence, particularly when we remember the way that Jesus himself modelled the servant–slave way of life: 'whoever wishes to become great among you must be your servant, and whoever wishes to be first among you must be slave of all' (Mark 10:43–44). Martin Luther summed up this truth as follows: 'A Christian man is a most free lord of all, subject to none. A Christian man is a most dutiful servant of all, subject to all.'

Taking a closer look at Paul's slave-likeness, we see that (for example) he was ready to forgo the determinative power of his Judaism (20), if that would open a door for the gospel. He was concerned for the desires, the inclinations, the sensitivities of his hearers. 'His Judaism was no longer of

---

[8] Ibid., p. 216.

his very being, but a guise he could adopt or discard at will.'[9] There were occasions, notably in the circumcision of Timothy (Acts 16:3) and in discharging a Nazirite vow in the temple of Jerusalem (Acts 21:23ff.), when he was quite ready to go through with actions which in Christ were unnecessary – and, by contrast, he refused to bow to pressure from Judaizers who wanted Titus to be circumcised (Gal. 2:3). Bruce comments,

> If Paul felt no longer any necessity to comply with Jewish regulations and ceremonies as matters of divine obligation, he did not go to the other extreme and regard these things as forbidden to a Christian; henceforth they ranked as morally and religiously indifferent things, to be observed or not as occasion might indicate.[10]

A matter of minor importance may, nevertheless, have had some more direct bearing on Paul's remarks here. We read that, on the eve of his departure from the Corinthian hinterland at the port of Cenchreae, 'he had his hair cut, for he was under a vow' (Acts 18:18). Corinthians being Corinthians, that particular action could have had some kind of long-lasting impact on the libertine–legalist controversy.

The most radical implication of Paul's words, however, was in the area of racism: *To the Jews I became as a Jew.* It may be difficult to appreciate the profound freedom Christ brings to individuals and families who have, for years, generations or even centuries, been gripped by racial prejudice. It is an indescribable liberty to learn to relate to people as human beings. Paul had discovered freedom from racial pride and prejudice in Christ. He is, nevertheless, prepared to forgo the fruits even of that freedom *in order to win Jews.* In similar, but different, racial contexts today many Christians are walking that costly path in order to win racists to Christ.

Because the next two examples (i.e. being under the law and being outside the law) of becoming *all things to all people* are so riddled with exegetical complexity, it is better to refer to competent scholarship, rather than work through the whole range of possibilities. Barrett and Bruce[11] are reliable guides. The nub of the matter seems to be this: Paul had been a slave to religious ceremony and ritual in the Jewish law. This consisted of 613 written precepts in the Pentateuch, together (probably) with their

---

[9] Ibid., p. 211.
[10] Bruce, pp. 86f.
[11] Barrett, pp. 211–215; Bruce, pp. 87f.

oral amplification (called by Jesus 'the tradition of the elders'). These were accepted as the divinely appointed way to life, but had been discovered by Paul to be an instrument of spiritual death (Rom. 7:7–13). But in certain – unusual and infrequent – circumstances Paul was actually prepared to come again under the law, in order to avoid starting off a relationship on the wrong foot, and thus to win such people to Christ. Equally, he was prepared to ignore all religious obligations, in order to win those totally beyond the pale of religious establishment and orthodoxy.[12]

In both approaches Paul would have run the risk of – and actually succeeded in – offending Christians. Such people, notably at Corinth but certainly not confined to Corinth, would have been concerned less with winning unbelievers to Christ as Lord than with keeping spotless the purity of the fellowship. Once again, the cliques at Corinth needed to stop worrying about this right and that right, or this reward and that reward, and to take with full seriousness their own responsibility for obeying the commission of the risen Lord to preach the gospel and make disciples.

Of course, there were dangers in Paul's own methods of evangelism. Even in this short paragraph he has to make two key disclaimers, in order to pre-empt any accusation of his being a heretic. For example, the libertine element at Corinth would have been appalled to hear the apostle of freedom say that he was prepared to become *as one under the law* (20), even for evangelistic purposes. He therefore has to stress that he is himself *not under the law*. Likewise, the legalists would almost have had apoplexy to hear Paul talk of being *one outside the law* (21): and so he had to cover his tracks with the claim, *not free from God's law but am under Christ's law* (21). It all seems a rather sad commentary on the truth of 8:1, 'Knowledge puffs up, but love builds up.' One would have thought that Paul's own integrity and whole-heartedness, quite apart from his godly wisdom, would have made him above suspicion, even in Corinth.

Racial identity and religious sensitivity have been two major issues in Paul's statement of true freedom in Christ; the third is the whole matter of conscience, which brings us back to the overall discussion on food offered to idols. The 'strong' and the 'weak' were the two groups which mattered in chapter 8; here Paul says, *To the weak I became weak, so that I might win the weak* (22). This would seem to be a wider application, especially in the context of evangelistic opportunities, of his foundation

---

[12] Cf. his most striking sermons at Lystra (Acts 14:15ff.) and at Athens (Acts 17:22ff.).

principle in 8:9, 'But take care that this liberty of yours does not somehow become a stumbling-block to the weak.' He was a 'strong' person with an informed and robust conscience, quite prepared to exercise his freedom in appropriate circumstances, and equally prepared to curtail that freedom if required. It is worth recalling that, before he came to know freedom in Christ, Paul had been completely harassed by a guilty conscience, especially in the matter of covetousness (cf. Rom. 7:7–8). Now, he was clean and free to respond to the Holy Spirit.

Paul clearly exercised the most imaginative and sensitive adaptability in his relationships with unbelievers. He did it all *for the sake of the gospel*, so that he might share its power and reality as far and wide as possible. Paul was the most versatile of men, never locked into any single way of operating and always listening to God's ideas in each new situation: *I have become all things to all people, so that I might by any means save some* (22) – a veritable spiritual chameleon. Paul's versatility in seeking to win men and women of all backgrounds to Christ challenges us to cross the culture gap between the Christian subculture of cosy meetings and holy talk and the pagan culture of our local community. The task of identification with and incarnation into our contemporary paganism, of all kinds, is one of the biggest tasks confronting the church.

4. Running to win (9:24–27)

Paul sensed that the Corinthians had become spiritually flabby. They had been wanting the rewards without the hard work. They had been more concerned for pleasant surroundings than for proper training conditions. He had a ready metaphor at hand. Corinth was the centre of the Isthmian Games, which took place every two years. The streets of the city and the hillsides of the Acrocorinth would have been full of athletes in training for these prestigious events. It was self-evident that *Athletes exercise self-control in all things*, and 'self-control' is part of the fruit of the Spirit (Gal. 5:23). If such self-discipline was crucial to gain a 'crown' made of pinewood, then let us all run this Christian race with total dedication: 'run to win' (24) is Paul's watchword.

He was not suggesting that we can miss out on the prize, because 'the crown of righteousness' awaits 'all who have longed for [Christ's] appearing' (2 Tim. 4:8) – that is, all whose goal in life is to know Christ and who are pressing forward for the prize of the upward call of God in Christ

(Phil. 3:14). In the contests in the athletic stadium at Corinth, only one person received the actual prize. In the Christian race, rewards are not additional to the gospel, but integral to it: but running does not automatically assure winning. Both perseverance and self-discipline are needed.

It is important to avoid the danger of drawing a wrong conclusion from Paul's words here – that you can put all your energies into running the Christian race and end up *disqualified* (*adokimos*, 27). If this is what Paul thought might happen to him, what hope would there be for anyone? The whole teaching of the New Testament makes it plain that such a verdict is impossible. At this point Barrett is dangerously wrong: he says,

> Paul clearly envisages the possibility that, notwithstanding his work as a preacher, he may himself fall from grace and be rejected . . . His conversion, his baptism, his call to apostleship, his service in the gospel, do not guarantee his eternal salvation.[13]

Indeed, they do not guarantee anything: only the finished work of Jesus Christ on the cross can provide such a guarantee, and that is why Paul began his main theological exposition in this letter on that theme (1:17 – 2:5). Morris is more accurate when he writes: 'Paul's fear was not that he might lose his salvation, but that he might lose his crown through failing to satisfy his Lord (cf. 3:15).'[14]

There is a particularly close word-link between 9:27 and 3:13 which makes the meaning of Paul's teaching unambiguous. The context in 3:11–15 is the way any Christian, but particularly those involved in church-building, will have to face extremely thorough examination about the quality of his or her work for the Lord. This will be 'tested' by fire (*dokimasei*), to a degree which will expose the materials used in building on the foundation, the only foundation which can be laid, Jesus Christ himself. The root word from which both *dokimazei* (3:13) and *adokimos* (9:27) are taken appears in 2 Corinthians 13:5–7, where it occurs five times in a context where the validity of Paul's own apostleship is being queried. Those who are in Christ cannot lose their salvation, but can find that their service for Christ has been followed through with their own resources and for their own glory. That is supremely what Paul feared.

---

[13] Barrett, p. 218.
[14] Morris, p. 140.

In verses 26 and 27 Paul is warning the Corinthians (and himself) of the need not to *run aimlessly*. He then switches from running to boxing and emphasizes the need to pummel his body and to subdue it. He did not see his body as evil,[15] but he recognized that our bodies can be 'presented' either to sin 'as instruments of wickedness', or to God 'as instruments of righteousness' (Rom. 6:13).

Paul writes that he subdues his body, literally 'I lead my body around as a slave' (*doulagōgō*). He had spent his life preaching the good news of Jesus to others, using every bodily faculty at his disposal and getting not a few bruises and pains in the process. He, for one, was not going to miss out on all the rewards inherent in the gospel and only just be saved by the skin of his teeth.[16] Paul had no intention of failing the test on that day, a day not of judgment on sin but of scrutiny of service. Just as competitors at the Isthmian Games could take no short cuts to physical fitness, so there are no easy options or routes of self-indulgence when we are serious about spiritual freedom. 'Just as you once presented your members as slaves to impurity and to greater and greater iniquity, so now present your members as slaves to righteousness for sanctification' (Rom. 6:19). Forget your rights, Corinthians. Follow hard after that imperishable reward. Fulfil daily your responsibilities to yourselves, to one another and to the Lord himself.

---

[15] Cf. the teaching in 1 Cor. 6:9–20.
[16] 'Only as through fire' (1 Cor. 3:15).

1 Corinthians 10:1 – 11:1

10. Freedom and its dangers

In dealing with the problem of food offered to idols, Paul has so far been spending much of his time addressing those with over-scrupulous consciences or simply defending his own voluntary self-limitation in the area of Christian freedom. In 10:1–22 he tackles the Corinthian libertines, who obviously reckoned that their approach to the whole subject, and to Paul himself, was the only really mature way of thinking. There was in their attitude not only yet more evidence of their presumptuous arrogance, but also a very serious risk indeed of mixing true worship of the Lord with the worship of demons.

These first two sections (10:1–13 and 14–22) contain some of the most salutary teaching in the whole letter, not so much for the content (which is straightforward), but because Paul does not pull his punches in addressing remarks to Christians at Corinth who, in all likelihood, reckoned these insights were more for 'them' than for 'us'.

Paul's thinking appears to run like this. Among the Christians at Corinth were a group of people who were confident in their own spirituality and maturity; they did not have much time for Paul as an apostle, or as a teacher. They had just noted his mention of the real (to him) possibility of failing to meet the test of God's close scrutiny of his life. We have no means of telling what reaction such teaching would have produced in this self-confident group in the church at Corinth. They may have thought that Paul was trying to give them something of a fright with all this talk of being 'disqualified'.

There is at no stage any assertion that Christians lose their salvation or are disinherited from the family of God. There *are* very strong warnings against falling away from God and against presuming on his goodness. The fact that, in calling the Corinthians (both Jewish and Gentile believers) yet again 'brothers and sisters', he refers to 'our fathers' indicates the solidarity between the people of God under both old and new covenants.

All the way through the chapter Paul is underlining the truth of Christian freedom. In so doing, he warns about the dangers of presumptuousness, compromise and legalism.

1. The danger of presumptuousness (10:1–13)

Paul takes his lessons from the way God dealt with his people under the old covenant, during the time of the wanderings in the wilderness under Moses. In that generation, God's people knew many blessings, but they also were guilty of many sins, for which they were severely punished.

a. Their blessings (10:1–4)

The people of Israel enjoyed many repeated blessings from the Lord: protection, guidance, sustenance, forgiveness. All these took place in a series of remarkable incidents in which God intervened to demonstrate his sovereign control of their lives (cf. Exod. 13ff.).

Paul chooses to concentrate on two particular facets of these experiences in the life of the people of God in the time of Moses. They *were all under the cloud, and all passed through the sea, and all were baptized into Moses in the cloud and in the sea, and all ate the same spiritual food, and all drank the same spiritual drink.*

It is misleading to translate *pneumatikos* by the word 'spiritual', because Paul is not denying that the manna and the water were anything but very physical. He seems to be indicating that, as well as being necessary for physical sustenance, they were also of spiritual value, nourishing their whole relationship with God. This is borne out by the way Paul equates the rock (which provided the water – Exod. 17:6) with Christ himself (4). In other words, Paul is stressing the divine origin of the people's provision. A later incident in these forty years (Num. 20:1–13) indicates that water came forth from a rock towards the end of the wilderness wanderings, as well as towards the beginning. In fact, the two events (though in detail very similar) are in spiritual significance totally contrasted: in the original story Moses acted in obedience to God's clear command, whereas in the later incident the operative mood was one of presumption. The Lord looked upon Moses' presumption with such seriousness that it was for this particular sin that he was refused admission to the Promised Land.

Before the people of Israel received this physical and spiritual sustenance ('supernatural food' and 'supernatural drink'), *all were baptized into Moses in the cloud and in the sea* (2). The use of the word *baptized* is, of course, highly significant. To be *baptized into Moses* meant that they were voluntarily and unconditionally placing themselves under the leadership of Moses. Paul's very striking, but unusual, language in this passage emphasizes the parallels between the privileges of God's people under Moses and the privileges of God's people under Jesus. In both historical epochs there were two events which were pregnant with meaning: being baptized to denote loyalty to God's appointed leader; and being provided with 'supernatural' food and drink on a regular basis.

Paul is clearly comparing the presumptuous attitude of God's people under Moses to the arrogance of certain Corinthian Christians in his own day. They too had been through the waters of baptism, with all the deep significance this carried for allegiance to Jesus as Lord (6:11). They too were involved regularly in common meals,[1] during which they were both physically and spiritually nourished. These Christians, like God's people under Moses, were on the receiving end of great blessings; but to receive blessing is by no means the same as to enter into the privilege and responsibilities of blessing. They had become so absorbed with rights that they were now presuming on the efficacy of their relationship with the Lord.

We note that the *spiritual* importance of baptism is stressed by the fact that the children of Israel were never actually *in* the cloud or *in* the sea. In the same way the pre-eminent significance of the baptized life is what Paul underlines in Romans 6:1ff., not the actual experience of baptism. The Israelites were baptized *into Moses*; the Christians of Corinth were baptized into Christ. Both actions denoted allegiance, but the Christians were not working out the practical implications of that allegiance. What led Paul to make such an accusation?

b. Their sins (10:5–10)

Before we enumerate these, we need to note the cryptic statement of verse 5: *Nevertheless, God was not pleased with most of them, and they were*

---

[1] Considered later in 10:14–22 and 11:17–34.

struck down in the wilderness.[2] Indeed, of the generation which left Egypt under Moses, it is recorded that only two reached Canaan: Joshua, the son of Nun, and Caleb, the son of Jephunneh (Num. 14:30, 38). That is the solemnity of God's displeasure with a presumptuous generation. We need to stress, in passing, that this is all the text says: *they were struck down in the wilderness.* Nothing is said in terms of their eternal destiny, because that is not the point of these stories. That point is made plain in 10:6: *Now these things occurred as examples for us.*

The sins of the people of God under Moses have an ominous ring in terms of the known and the likely sins of the Christian community at Corinth: covetousness, idolatry, immorality, straining the patience of the Lord and grumbling against the Lord. Specific events in the wilderness wanderings were doubtless in Paul's mind, and he especially recalled the golden calf (Exod. 32), the hankering after the fleshpots of Egypt (Exod. 16), the mass immorality with the daughters of the Moabites and the story of the brazen serpent.[3] The narrative of events during that period does not make very pleasant reading.

Paul effectively told the Corinthians in their presumed spirituality not to boast about their spiritual condition. We are all in a perilous position, says the apostle, if once we allow ourselves the indulgence of thinking that sin does not matter. They thought that the combination of the sacraments and their spiritual experiences was sufficient to protect them from falling away. They were relying (in an almost quasi-miraculous way) on God-given means of grace and God-given experiences, rather than on God himself in Christ. Paul has just mentioned his own need to be self-disciplined, lest he should fail to receive all God has for him. He wants the Corinthians to develop the same determination and discipline.

c. Their punishment (10:5–10)

This can be summarized in three dramatic and tragic phrases: *they were struck down* (5); they *fell* (8); they *were destroyed by the destroyer* (9–10). The last example is a similar situation to that described in 5:5 (cf. Num. 16:41–49). Destruction of the flesh, in this case of thousands, did not necessarily involve eternal destruction as well. These people did not see the Promised Land, but nothing is said of their eternal destiny. Paul wants

---

[2] A quotation from Num. 14:16.
[3] Num. 25 and 21.

these beloved, but boastful, brethren to be the very best that they can be for the Lord. The same things which spoilt the lives of God's people in those distant days under Moses wreck Christian communities today. They have been written down 'to instruct us' (11). They happened to them to act as a warning on the slippery slope into rejecting God. They are in the Bible for our benefit, to drill sense into us (that is the basic meaning of the *nouthesian* [11], literally = to put '*nous*' into us).

d. Their warning (10:11–13)

But there is more to the timelessness of the Passover–exodus saga than to teach us a little more wisdom. Paul's own contemporaries were living in a uniquely privileged generation, one *on whom the ends of the ages have come* (11). These *ages* could be a combination of 'this present age or world order' and 'the age to come' (heralded by the first coming and to be consummated by the second coming of Christ). On this explanation, every person in Christ is living in crucial days 'between the ages' (what theologians often call 'living in the overlap'), with each extra day a bonus. Bruce summarizes: 'The pattern of divine revelation, human disobedience and divine judgment manifested in the Israelites' experience from Egypt to Canaan is reproduced in the New Testament era.'[4]

On the other hand, this striking phrase in verse 11 could be saying this: the story of the exodus and the wilderness wanderings was recorded for our benefit (i.e. for the edification of Christians); we are the people whom God, the Lord of history, had in mind when these events took place and were recorded.[5] Obviously certain incidents in the 'salvation history' of the people of God under the old covenant had more central and pivotal meaning than others. The exodus is arguably the cardinal event of all.

To claim that God's activity on the stage of world history is all focused on the Christian church may sound relatively harmless to most Western Christians. What we need to realize is that a Latin American or a black African theologian, committed to liberation or *uhuru*, will find such exegesis of Old and New Testament history (with the exodus as pivotal, both in its Old Testament occurrence and in its New Testament interpretation) absolutely foundational. Indeed, the health of the worldwide church

---

[4] Bruce, p. 93.
[5] Cf. 1 Pet. 1:10ff.; also Luke 24:25–27; Acts 2:16; 1 Pet. 1:20.

and the integrity of her witness to the kingdom of God may well depend on the exodus being accurately expounded and properly applied. The very least we can – and must – say is that the exodus was *sui generis* (because the Jews were the covenant people) and therefore cannot be applied to any and every liberation from oppression. We are, in any case, dealing in these verses with one of the most volatile theological time bombs in the world today.

The injunction of 10:12, *if you think you are standing, watch out that you do not fall*, is not merely a warning shot across the bows of Corinthian super-spirituality. No doubt it includes that, but there would be little need for Paul to talk in the evocative language of verse 11 if all he wants to convey is the spiritual danger of thinking that we have moved beyond the reach of certain temptations. The root meaning of *peirasmos* is not so much 'temptation' as *testing* (13). Paul is warning the Corinthians, 'You are facing many powerful testings because of the weakness of your spiritual resources; but the major point about temptation/testing is not the force of sin's attractiveness, but the make-or-break nature of your trial. Are you going to come through them with a tougher resilience and acuter faith in the living God? Or will your determination to endure to the end have been subtly sapped?' (cf. 1 Pet. 1:5ff.).

Equally, let people today who feel like devaluing the significance of the exodus as determinative for the kingdom of God be careful lest they find themselves overtaken by violent and irresistible events; and let those who think they *do* understand the tempestuous forces at work in today's world reconsider their theological appraisal in relation to such particular events as the North–South struggle and the nuclear menace. Christians who think they are impervious to these forces have begun to appreciate that, in the turbulence of today's global village, nobody can claim to have found a position of permanent stability (that is the force of the perfect tense *hestanai* = 'stand'). There is only one place for that security:

The LORD is exalted, he dwells on high;
   he filled Zion with justice and righteousness;
he will be the stability of your times,
   abundance of salvation, wisdom, and knowledge;
   the fear of the LORD is Zion's treasure.
(Isa. 33:5–6)

Therefore, 1 Corinthians 10:12 is not so much a personal summons to take the vulnerability of being a Christian disciple more seriously, as an eternal perspective on the activity of God in history, and particularly in salvation history; if people blessed with all the 'supernatural' blessings lavished on the children of Israel in the time of Moses fell, and went on falling in different ways, then the Christians at Corinth certainly had no immunity. And if, furthermore, we happen to be those *on whom the ends of the ages have come*, then we are facing all that Paul meant by the phrase 'the impending crisis' (cf. 7:26) and much more.

If we think this is all too much for us, Paul characteristically comes to us with a classic word of encouragement: *God is faithful* (13). We can rely implicitly on him. We may feel that our own personal trials are too great and beyond the ability of anyone to grasp, let alone to alleviate. But *no testing* [= trial] *has overtaken you that is not common to everyone*. God has himself been along this path in Jesus. He knows how much we can endure. He also knows the way he is taking, the way through the valley, the way of escape, the day of release and the joy of endurance because victory is secure: all these he has himself experienced.

The way out (*ekbasis*) is almost exactly the same word as 'exodus', and Luke (Luke 9:31) describes the redemptive death of Jesus as the 'exodus' he will achieve at Jerusalem. God himself provides the oppressed and sorely tried with his exodus. He is not vindictive. He is not waiting to hit the presumptuous with punishment. Nor are we on our own; we are in this situation along with countless others, for whom the time of testing is equally, if not more, nerve-racking. It is the certain consummation of an exodus already achieved that enables us to endure: we see the light at the end of the tunnel and we press on.

2. The danger of compromise (10:14–22)

After his weighty warning to complacent Christians in danger of basing their eternal security on doing all the right 'religious' things, Paul urges them: *flee from the worship of idols* (14). The command is the same as in 6:18, 'Shun fornication!' The Christian who revels in his or her God-given freedom in Christ, like many at Corinth, can so easily compromise the truth. Having asserted the priority of the Christian's freedom, Paul now warns against a flippant, careless attitude towards the worship of idols – the particular problem facing the Corinthians, which he has investigated in some detail in chapter 8.

He has just noted (7) the way the children of Israel allowed their lives to be contaminated by idolatry. The narrative of the golden calf in Exodus 32 is full of the most illuminating and penetrating insights into the degeneration which idolatry always produces. Paul is not prepared to put any ifs and buts into his rejection of idolatry. He recognizes that he is not speaking to those who cannot reason, but to *sensible people* (15).[6] He therefore appeals to them to *judge* for themselves what he is saying (15: *krinate* may contain an oblique reference to the Corinthians' love of passing judgment on this or that).

Paul bases his argument on the sacrament of the Lord's Supper, and it runs like this. The central ceremony of Christian, Jewish and pagan worship is more than mere words and actions. Those who take part in these ceremonies become actual 'partners'. The root word (*koinōnos*) comes four times in this paragraph, and there are two occurrences of the word *partake* (17, 21). The partnership acts in two ways: with one another as fellow worshippers and with the god/gods/God whom they worship. The worshippers share together in the spiritual reality behind all that happens. Barrett renders *koinōnia* 'common participation': in other words, the stress falls both on that in which we share and on the shared experience of all who take part. We may compare the well-known phrase 'the fellowship [or 'communion'] of the Holy Spirit' (2 Cor. 13:13 [NRSV]; 13:14 [other English versions]). We all share in him as Christians, and it is that common participation which unites us all as Christians.

Let us note the four ways Paul uses *koinōnia/koinōnos* in this section. First (16), all who share in the *cup of blessing* in the celebration of the Eucharist at the love-feast of God's people share *in the blood of Christ*, that is, in the results of Christ's atoning death – in *all* those results.[7] Whether in relation to Christian communion, Jewish sacrifices or pagan ritual, those who partake are doing far more than simply performing a 'memorial' of some past event in history. Calvin wrote: 'The soul has as truly communion in the blood, as we drink wine with the mouth.'

The phrase *the cup of blessing* is usually taken to refer to the third cup at the Passover meal, over which the following prayer of thanksgiving was

---

6 He does not actually use the emotive word *sophoi*, but *phronimoi* = 'having sense'.

7 Cf. the prayer towards the end of the 1662 Prayer Book service of Holy Communion: 'that we and all thy whole church may obtain remission of our sins, and all other benefits of his passion'.

pronounced: 'Blessed are You, O Lord our God, who gives us the fruit of the vine.' In saying that the cup was blessed, Paul is using shorthand for saying that God was blessed over the cup. There are those who believe that the use of the first person plural, 'the cup of blessing that *we* bless', indicates that any Christian was able to celebrate this eucharistic meal in the sense of presiding over what took place; Barrett says: 'it will be noted that Paul does not appear to confine the saying of the thanksgiving to a limited group of Christians'.[8] The same reasoning applies to *a sharing in the body of Christ* (16). More perspectives on the significance of taking part in the body and blood of Christ will become apparent when we examine 11:17–34.

The second couplet of verses in which partnership is central comes in 18 and 20, and in both cases the reference is not to abstract participation, but to people who are active partners. *Consider the people of Israel*, says Paul; *are not those who eat the sacrifices partners in the altar?* The priests had special parts of the meat reserved for them, while the ordinary worshippers had other portions set apart for them. The worshippers had no responsibilities whatever in the ceremonies around the altar; they simply received some of the benefits of the ritual meal.[9]

By analogy, it is plain where Paul's argument is moving. Christians are partners with the Lord and with one another in their central act of communion, a partnership that is so intimate and complete that he says (17): *Because there is one bread, we who are many are one body, for we all partake of the one bread.* Any *sensible* person could conclude that the same truths apply in idolatrous worship. Morris writes:

> The *devils* [*demons*] make use of men's readiness to worship idols. Thus, when men sacrifice to idols, it cannot be said that they are engaging in some neutral activity that has no meaning. They are in fact sacrificing to evil spirits . . . To share food is to establish fellowship. Thus they are entering into *fellowship* with *devils* [*demons*]. Paul does not wish this to happen to his Corinthian friends.[10]

In asserting that *You cannot drink the cup of the Lord and the cup of demons*, Paul is saying that the two experiences are mutually exclusive.

---

[8] Barrett, p. 232.
[9] Cf. Lev. 10:12–15 for the priestly menu; 1 Sam. 9:10–24 for the ordinary Jew's meal.
[10] Morris, p. 147.

The two simply cannot mix: we must not put ourselves in any situation where such a choice might have to be made.

Paul is not reversing his original denial that 'food offered to idols is anything' or that 'an idol is anything' (cf. 8:4). He still affirms the nonentity, the unreality, of idols as such; but he equally affirms that behind all idolatry is demonic activity: *what pagans sacrifice, they sacrifice to demons and not to God* (20). There is only one true God, anyway, and idolaters have no time, desire or ability to worship him. But they are creatures with the capacity and the inner drive to worship when they focus this worship on 'beings that by nature are not gods' (Gal. 4:8). Paul's own conviction is that the spiritual truth of such a situation is that such people offer their sacrifices to demons (20), are partners with demons (20), drink the cup of demons (21) and partake of the table of demons (21) – and as a result share in the 'benefits' of such fellowship.[11] Christians, there-fore, who become involved in idolatrous feasts are exposing themselves and the Christian community to demons: *You cannot drink the cup of the Lord and the cup of demons. You cannot partake of the table of the Lord and the table of demons* (21).

Such contact with demonic forces provokes the Lord to jealousy (22) and unleashes devastating forces of disintegration. Paul clearly believes in the reality of an unseen spirit world, that idolatry is not just meaningless but positively evil. It is evil because it robs the true God of the glory due to him, and because such actions bring people not simply into contact with lower spiritual powers but actually into subjection to them. Paul consistently sees these powers as subordinate to Jesus as Lord, but as having been stripped once and for all of their impact through his triumph over them on the cross (cf. Col. 2:15).

Having made that unmistakably plain, Paul is adamant (especially to the 'strong' people of knowledge at Corinth) that Christians can never dare to play around with these demonic forces. Whatever his temporary feelings of impatience and intolerance towards these puffed-up hyper-spiritual experts, Paul's sense of deep concern for them as his *dear* brothers and sisters in Christ (14) compels him to speak as plainly as he

---

[11] Bruce (pp. 96f.): 'Paul is thinking of feasts which are explicitly under the patronage of a pagan deity, involving in some degree the acknowledgement and even worship of that deity. Those who shared such a feast . . . were considered to have "perfect sacrificial communion" with him . . . In the cool light of next morning, a Christian guest might well realize that he had joined in words or in practices totally at variance with his Christian profession . . . he had been the victim of a demonic force associated with the worship of the "idol".'

knows how: *flee from the worship of idols.* The Lord is a jealous God who brooks no rivals, no comparisons, no alternatives.[12] There are dangers in presumptuousness and complacency, especially the danger of finding ourselves victims of the humiliating fall which inevitably follows all pride. But there is, if anything, even greater danger in compromise, because we smudge the issues and let in all kinds of spiritual counterfeits which confuse the truth as it is in Jesus, as well as being in obvious conflict with it.

3. The danger of legalism (10:23–30)

This paragraph draws together the threads of the last three chapters, stressing the fact of Christian freedom. Paul quotes again the great watchword of the Corinthian libertines, *All things are lawful.* He agrees, but urges them always to take into account both the overall good of the Christian community and the best interests of each individual fellow Christian. He requires such liberated Corinthian Christians to ask themselves this simple question: 'Am I building up the body of Christ?' Paul then re-stresses the freedom of the individual (25–27) in the whole area of food touched by idolatrous practices: 'when you go to the meat market (25), stop asking all kinds of leading questions about its origins; when an unbeliever invites you round for a good dinner (27), enjoy it without having a quiet session in the corner with your conscience. And, in any case, remember that "the earth is the LORD's and the fullness thereof".[13] If you can say a (?silent) prayer of thanks over the meal, then all is well and good.'

Even so, in verse 28 Paul indicates another possible ground for abstaining: having reinforced the primacy of Christian freedom, he also re-stresses the individual's freedom to curb his or her freedom for the sake of a fellow Christian, a weaker Christian (28–29), 'however tiresome he might be',[14] however pernickety or even narrow-minded. Paul's own foundational principle seems to be stated in verse 29: *why should my liberty be subject to the judgement of someone else's conscience?* In other words, says the apostle, 'I do not make up my mind on things on the basis of what others think; but I am prepared to do what others believe to be right if that will ensure that their edification is not impeded.'

---

[12] Cf. Deut. 32:21; Isa. 42:8; Jas 4:4–5.
[13] Cf. Ps. 24:1; 1 Tim. 4:1–5; 6:17.
[14] Barrett.

4. Conclusion (10:31 – 11:1)

Paul ends this whole section with four verses full of entirely positive guidelines for the life of the Christian community, which is neither Jewish nor Greek but 'a third race': *the church of God* (32). Paul is not concerned at this stage with barriers or stumbling blocks, with rights or responsibilities. We find Christian freedom in its true creativity when we follow Paul's five ground rules for life together in Christ. They really need no more than stating, contemplating and obeying.

   i. *Do everything for the glory of God* (31) – not to establish my freedom.
  ii. *Try to please everyone in everything* (33) – not claiming my rights.
 iii. *Not seeking my own advantage* (33) – not my benefit or fulfilment.
  iv. *Seeking . . . that* [*many*] *may be saved* (33) – not being preoccupied with my personal salvation.
   v. *Be imitators . . . of Christ* (11:1) – not boosting my reputation. That is Christian freedom: being free from ourselves to glorify God by being like Christ.

1 Corinthians 11:2–34

11. The Christian community at worship

We now move into the next major area of controversy between different groups at Corinth, namely, the Christian community at worship. There are two major themes in chapter 11: the behaviour of women and attitudes to the Lord's Supper.

1. Introduction (11:2)

It is a pleasant surprise to discover that Paul is able to commend the Christians at Corinth, *because you remember me in everything and maintain the traditions just as I handed them on to you.* He refers to these *traditions* explicitly both in 11:23, in recalling the institution of the Lord's Supper, and in 15:1 and 3, in passing on the fundamentals of the gospel. The word denotes the twin process of hearing and of passing on, and is normally used to refer to those essential Christian truths which are at the heart of the gospel.

These *traditions* (the English word actually enshrines the same process from a Latin, not a Greek, root) were passed on orally from evangelists and teachers to new believers. This body of tradition became authoritative reproduction of apostolic truth. Considerable mention is made of them and great store is laid by them in the Pastoral Epistles, where Paul underlines the need to follow the pattern of sound teaching passed on from older men to able successors.[1]

---

[1] Cf. 1 Tim. 4:6; 2 Tim. 1:13–14; 2:2; 3:14; 4:3–4; Titus 1:9; 2:1.

In a culture that was basically non-literary, the fundamental importance of reliable oral tradition took on added emphasis. In fact, oral tradition is very reliable, as the elementary example of nursery rhymes indicates. Once something is embedded in the culture of a community, it remains a firm part of it. In thinking of the Corinthian church at worship, we need to remember that Paul had spent eighteen months teaching the church, and this teaching had a strong inner consistency. He was thus able to write of a similar, if not identical, pattern 'in all the churches' (cf. 14:33). It is today suggested with some conviction that there was in the early church a body of Christian catechesis, which dealt with ordinary discipleship and basic doctrine: the scholars call this body of teaching 'house-tables' – what we might call Christian ground rules.[2]

In terms of such traditions affecting the worship of the Corinthian church, Paul had little to bother him. Yet it is clear from 11:3–16 that there was a 'contentious' element at Corinth who were spoiling for a fight and made the particular issue of head-coverings for women a major bone of such contention.

2. The behaviour of the women (11:3–16)

In first-century Greece, dress for men and women was apparently very similar, except for the women's 'head-covering' (here called *kalymma*, or 'veil'). This, incidentally, was not the equivalent of the Arab veil, but a covering for her hair alone. The normal, everyday dress of all Greek women included this *kalymma*. The only women who did not wear them were the *hetairai*, who were the 'high-class' mistresses of influential Corinthians. Also, slaves had their heads shaved, and the same practice was enacted as punishment for convicted adulteresses. It has further been suggested that the sacred prostitutes from the local temple of Aphrodite did not wear veils.

Now there was no special 'dressing-up' for attending the fellowship meetings of the church at worship: the men came without any head-coverings; the women came with them, as in normal everyday life. Apparently, in the 'excitement' of the worship, certain women were tempted to throw back their head-dresses and allow their hair (which they always wore long) to fall loose. Bruce thinks that Paul knew that pagan

---

[2] Cf. Michael Green's *Evangelism: Now and Then* (IVP, 1979), pp. 88f.

prophetesses in the Graeco-Roman world prophesied with uncovered and dishevelled heads.[3] This naturally caused severe distraction to the men at worship and was, in addition, a denial of the submission in the Lord of married women to their husbands. In Jewish temple worship, the women were kept on their own, out of sight behind a screen; the men always prayed with their heads covered. Paul was thus bringing Jewish Christians, both men and women, one significant step further; he tells the men to pray with their heads uncovered (4), and he expects the women to take an active part both in prayer and in prophecy (but under submission, 5).

One factor undergirds Paul's arguments in this paragraph: he starts from the doctrine of creation, not from the doctrine of redemption. This simple rhetorical technique immediately undercuts the objections of those who claim that Paul was in inner conflict with his own teaching in, for example, Galatians 3:28: 'There is no longer male and female; for all of you are one in Christ Jesus.' In fact, verse 11 of this chapter enshrines precisely the same truth, 'Nevertheless, in the Lord woman is not independent of man or man independent of woman.' Whatever he may have just said about subordination (a matter we shall examine later), the phrase 'in the Lord' (which carries all the special emphasis in the Greek) clearly indicates that the man and the woman are completely interdependent in Christ – and *only* in Christ. Paul's four themes in this paragraph are submission, glory, interdependence and nature.

a. Submission (11:3–6)

Paul stresses first of all the pattern of relationships which God has written into the Christian community: *Christ is the head of every man, and the husband is the head of his wife, and God is the head of Christ* (3). In other words, the divine order is: God … Christ … husband … wife. The husband is no more superior to his wife than God is superior to Christ. But as Christ chose to submit himself to his Father, so the wife should choose to submit herself to her husband. The word for *head* is *kephalē*, which on rare occasions means the ruler of a community, but normally carries the sense of source or origin. It is used of the source of a river. So God is the source of Christ, Christ (as creator) is the source of man, and man ('out of his side' – Gen. 2:21ff.) is the source of woman (so 11:8). A third sense of *kephalē* (apart from its literal meaning) is the determinative and

---

[3] Bruce, p. 105.

directive sense, which is far closer to what we mean now by headship or leadership.

Now this fundamental order of relationships, writes Paul, is to be clearly reflected in Christian worship. It is important what people look like in public worship. There must be no distractions. In Christian worship we are demonstrating openly the essence of what God has done in Christ: he has set us free to serve him and to worship him. This freedom must be visibly demonstrated; compare 2 Corinthians 3:13–18, where we read that Moses (by contrast) had to cover his head in the presence of God. Christian men do not have to cover their heads; they have been set free and the glory of Christ is to be made plain through the ministry of prayer and prophecy led by the men with bare heads:

> And all of us, with unveiled faces, seeing the glory of the Lord as though reflected in a mirror, are being transformed into the same image from one degree of glory to another; for this comes from the Lord, the Spirit. (2 Cor. 3:18)

Christian women at Corinth (and theirs was equally a ministry in prayer and prophecy) were to keep their heads covered, because otherwise there was not freedom to worship, but instead a substantial degree of distraction. It was a sign, therefore, of the woman's submission for her to cover her head. The man's submission was to Christ alone; the woman's *veil* indicated her submission to others present. That was true in the secular community in the city outside; there was no reason, affirms Paul, to drop that convention inside the church. If she did, the woman was behaving as though either a slave or an adulteress (5).

Bruce has some words worth weighing on the whole subject of the dictates of convention. 'There is nothing frivolous about such an appeal to public conventions of seemliness. To be followers of the crucified Jesus was in itself unconventional enough, but needless breaches of convention were to be discouraged.'[4]

If a Christian woman became so uninhibited in public worship that she dispensed with the outward symbol of her submissiveness, then she ought (following the logic of her lack of submission) to have cut off her hair and thus removed at a stroke the distracting impact of her 'crowning glory'.

---

[4] Ibid., p. 107.

But that was obviously not the Christian way to behave (and certainly would have flouted the norms of Corinthian society); therefore she ought to accept the discipline of keeping a veil on her head, especially when so moved by the Spirit in prayer or in prophecy that she was tempted to fling all her inhibitions to the wind. The force of Paul's argument from creation in verse 3 is that God did not make one principle of divine action at one point in time, only to turn it upside down later. He is a God of order, of consistency, of non-contradictoriness: he cannot deny himself (cf. 2 Tim. 2:13).

b. Glory (11:7–10)

Just as Christian worship should visibly reflect the divinely ordained pattern of relationships, so it should also reflect the fact that we have been created to bring glory to God (cf. 10:31). Our worship together is intended to give God the glory due to his name. Man (used generically, 'Adam') was created directly by God alone, for his pleasure, his joy and his glory. In the same sense the woman was created to be the glory of man, deriving her being from man and finding her fulfilment in being his helper. In this sense the woman is the man's 'better half', being in fact his 'glory' (7, NRSV margin). In Genesis we read of God saying, 'Let us make humankind in our image . . . So God created humankind in his image, in the image of God he created them; male and female he created them' (Gen. 1:26–27). The image of God is, therefore, to be seen only in the full complementarity of male and female.

It is the theme of the glory of God which exercises Paul in this passage: *man is the image and reflection* [or 'glory'] *of God; but woman is the reflection* [or 'glory'] *of man.* If God alone is to be glorified in the worship of the church, then it is the joint responsibility of both the man and the woman to do all within their ability to make this happen. So long as the woman remained properly covered on her head, she was free to bring a prophecy or to lead in prayer. In herself, in her created being, she is the glory of man; in covering her hair (her supreme glory, 15: *doxa*, the same Greek word as in the rest of the discussion), she was acknowledging that God alone must be glorified in Christian worship – not her husband. Thus, the veil (or *kalymma*) represents her *authority* (10: *exousia*) to pray or to prophesy during a time of worship – the authority given to her within the ordered life of the worshipping congregation, given in recognition of the fact she has been clearly gifted by the Lord to bring such a ministry.

Bruce stresses that, 'in a letter in which *exousia* (= authority) is a key-word', its presence here is a sign of the Christian woman's authority. 'In Christ she received equality of status with man: she might pray or prophesy at meetings of the church, and her veil was a sign of this new authority.'[5] Barrett agrees: 'Her veil represents the new authority given to the woman under the new dispensation to do things which formerly had not been permitted her.'[6] It is very possible, on the other hand, that Paul's reference to a woman wearing *a symbol of authority on her head* (10) applies to her submission in Christ to the authority of her husband. Only in such a submissive spirit would she have been free to minister in the worshipping life of the church. It is not unlikely that Paul was thinking of *both* aspects of authority. Morris suggests as much: 'By covering her head the woman secures her own place of dignity and authority. At the same time she recognizes her subordination.'[7]

Throughout this exegetical maze the golden thread seems to be the desire in Paul's heart to ensure that the worship of the church at Corinth is 'done decently and in order' (cf. 14:40). There were all kinds of disorder, and perhaps even of indecency, although some commentators represent these malpractices in the most bizarre ways; for example, that the real problem in the worship services at Corinth was presiding bishops (i.e. 'angels') with roving eyes and impure hearts. It is impossible to know what Paul means by asserting that a woman ought to have a symbol of authority on her head *because of the angels* (10). Was it in deference to the acknow-ledged presence of angels at the worship of the church? But if we are as concerned as Paul for the glory of God to dominate our worship as his people, we shall not go far wrong.

c. Interdependence (11:11–12)

This parenthesis is a necessary corrective to Paul's strong teaching on the distinctiveness of the man and the woman as created in God's image. *In the Lord*, that is, in Christ, the man and the woman (husband and wife) are completely interdependent. He has been arguing strongly for the wife to be submissive to her husband, and for that attitude to be publicly spelt out whenever God's people gather for worship. Here he argues with equal strength that the two are one in Christ, totally bound up with each other,

---

[5] Ibid., p. 106.
[6] Barrett, p. 255.
[7] Morris, p. 154.

inseparable and interdependent. It is true physically (12), but it is even more true in the Lord. Both the man and the woman owe their existence to God: *all things come from God*. Christian worship is expressed best when together such married couples visibly give the Lord the glory of their interdependent lives.

d. Nature (11:13–15)

Paul brings this somewhat complex and at times (to us) remote discussion to an end by an argument drawn neither from the distinctiveness of men and women, nor from their mutuality; neither from their independence of each other, nor from their interdependence upon each other. He simply goes back to nature: *Does not nature itself teach you that if a man wears long hair, it is degrading to him, but if a woman has long hair, it is her glory? For her hair is given to her for a covering* (14–15). Precisely how culturally universal this actually is may be difficult to answer, but Paul's major point is undeniable: God has made men and women different, so *vive la différence!*

No doubt there are many cultural conventions when it comes to masculine and feminine roles, jobs and rights which need to be revised or rejected. As Creator, however, God intends that men and women should have different, but complementary, functions.

Each human being is to give glory to God by being what God intends him or her to be. The man is to be truly masculine and the woman truly feminine, without allowing stereotypes of either to dictate our perceptions, but rather basing our understanding of what it is to be fully human on the perfect model of Jesus. This principle will make us chary of going overboard on the modern theme of 'unisex'. The fullness of Christian worship can be experienced only as each man and each woman, created for God and redeemed by God, allows his or her humanness to be expressed according to God's pattern.

e. Conclusion (11:16)

What does all this add up to? Paul wants the women to dress normally and naturally in Christian worship. He wants such worship to give glory to God and to make it obvious that Christians have been set free to worship and to glorify God. So he urges the Corinthians: 'Do not ignore the obvious pointers of creation or of nature. God made us like this. Do not flout all the dictates of common sense and decency in your worship. Let it be

Christ-centred and God-glorifying.' There will always be Christians who love an argument, and there seem to have been plenty such at Corinth (16). Paul concludes the matter by saying that every other Christian congregation accepted these guidelines: why should the Corinthians be different?

3. Attitudes to the Lord's Supper (11:17–34)

The next aspect of corporate worship to absorb Paul's attention clearly touched him on the raw. The Corinthians were making a mockery of the Eucharist and of the *Agapē*. So incensed was he by reports of what was going on that he wrote bluntly: 'When you come together, it is not really to eat the Lord's supper' (20). We need to investigate the reasons behind such a direct statement, in order to appreciate the situation at Corinth, the significance of the fellowship meal and the seriousness of any abuse.

a. The situation at Corinth (11:17–22)

Although he had been free to 'commend' them for their observation of certain traditions he had passed on to them about public worship (2), he cannot commend them now (17, 22). The divisions (*schismata*) in the church at Corinth had reached schismatic proportions: there were now not merely personality cults around certain figureheads (1:12), nor differences of emphasis over food offered to idols; there were hints of a rather obnoxious kind of snobbishness (11:21) between the rich and the not-so-rich. The church was badly splintered, and these schisms made their times of worship and fellowship so negative that Christians went away in a worse state spiritually than when they arrived (17).

Now Paul was not naive; he expected any church to be full of different emphases on this or that matter. To that extent he was not surprised by the situation at Corinth: *there have to be factions [haireseis] among you, for only so will it become clear who among you are genuine* (19). Such selectivity[8] in Christian convictions among those submitted to the Lordship of Jesus is inevitable. But there is absolutely no need, let alone any propriety, for Christians to sunder fellowship on the basis of such distinctives. When such schism actually penetrates the public worship of the congregation, the situation is scandalous.

---

[8] See commentary on 1:10ff.

Paul expected schism because he was a realist, but he deplored it and sought to remove it. One of the incidental results of heresy (selectivity) in a local Christian community is that it provides an acid test of genuine commitment to Christ and to the body of Christ, as distinct from religious bigotry or simply love of theological debate. Paul had constantly to warn young church leaders like Timothy and Titus about such professing Christians.[9] When those who claim to be Christians love nothing better than empty and profitless arguments about theological niceties, that indicates their real spiritual condition. Such folk are not *genuine* (*dokimoi*), they have not passed the test,[10] and their loud claims about theological 'soundness' will not impress the Lord on that crucial day when our Christian service is scrutinized.[11]

It is no wonder that Paul could not call the gatherings of the church at Corinth 'the Lord's Supper': they were not under the Lord's authority; there was hardly any awareness of the Lord's presence; the purpose behind them seemed to be scarcely directed towards remembering the Lord's death. How could such an occasion be 'the Lord's Supper'? Each person was far more concerned with satisfying his or her own hunger and thirst (21). If the purpose of coming together was to satisfy physical appetites, why not stay at home? *Do you not have homes to eat and drink in?* (22).

There seems to have been a peculiarly callous insensitivity to the physical needs of those with very little, almost to the point of humiliating them. When they came together, there was no sense of being one family in the Lord. Each group kept to itself. The food brought was not shared in a common pool, but each enjoyed his or her own provisions. Some managed even to get drunk. The arrangements, in brief, emphasized the divisions in the church at Corinth, not their fellowship.

b. The significance of the meal (11:23–26)

Paul then reminded the Corinthians what the Eucharist-plus-*Agapē* was originally meant to be. He recalled the actual institution by the Lord Jesus himself *on the night when he was betrayed*. Paul's anonymous reference to Judas may have been an incidental challenge to the Corinthians in their own behaviour.

---

[9] E.g. 1 Tim. 1:3–4; 6:3–5, 20–21; 2 Tim. 2:14–18, 23–26; Titus 1:10–14; 3:9–11.
[10] Contrast Apelles (Rom. 16:10).
[11] Cf. 1 Cor. 3:11–15; 9:27.

He passed on to the Corinthians what he personally had *received from the Lord* himself. We cannot be sure precisely how Paul received this revelation. He did not receive the gospel itself 'from a human source, nor was I taught it, but I received it through a revelation of Jesus Christ' (Gal. 1:12). He could have been claiming the same direct revelation concerning these words of instituting the Lord's Supper. However, the word translated *received* (*parelabon*) is the technical word for oral transmission down the generations and across different groups. Perhaps the facts came from oral transmission, but their interpretation and application came directly from the Lord. Whatever the nature of their source, these words are to determine the whole meaning, atmosphere and behaviour in any celebration of the Lord's Supper. It is pre-eminently the death of the Lord which must dominate the proceedings, and this was clearly not the case at Corinth.

The head of any Jewish home would have performed such actions with bread and wine at any meal, and with special solemnity at the Passover meal. It is, thus, the *words* which give the *actions* their unique significance, as well as the identity of the Person who uttered the words. He *took . . . bread . . .* he gave *thanks, he broke it and said, 'This is my body that is for you'* (23–24). And then he added the world-shaking statement/ command: *Do this in remembrance of me.*[12] He followed these actions with similar ones with the cup, after supper, saying, *This cup is the new covenant in my blood. Do this, as often as you drink it, in remembrance of me* (25).

The words over the cup would have evoked memories of key Old Testament passages (e.g. Jer. 31:31), but Paul's own stress is on the way every such celebration is a public proclamation of the Lord's death, *until he comes* (26). There is an anticipatory element in every celebration of the Lord's Supper.[13] It looks back to his death; it looks forward to his return.

The main word Paul uses to describe what has happened is *covenant*. Through the shedding of the blood of Jesus, the paschal lamb (5:7), it is now possible for Jews and Greeks, rich and poor, libertine and rigorist, men and women, to know the glorious freedom of forgiveness and to have personal knowledge of God. Those who enter into this personal

---

[12] Bruce writes: 'In the biblical sense "remembrance" is more than a mental exercise: it involves a realization of what is remembered. At the Passover feast the participants are one with their ancestors of the Exodus; at the Eucharist Christians experience the real presence of their Lord. As the Passover meal was "a memorial of the departure from Egypt", so this breaking of bread was to be a memorial of Jesus after "his departure (*exodos*) which he was to accomplish at Jerusalem"' (p. 111).

[13] Cf. the Lord's own teaching in Luke 22:16, 18.

relationship, this covenant relationship, with the Lord naturally enter at the same time into a covenant relationship with one another. Thus, the covenant community is established – and that is precisely what the Corinthians were undermining by their behaviour. For them the death of Christ was not central; the return of Christ was not dominant; the love of Christ was not in control. It was, in a word, not 'the Lord's Supper'.

c. The seriousness of abuse (11:27–32)

The whole of this paragraph has a specially solemn ring about it. Paul is insistent that the Corinthians must stamp out of their worship around the Lord's Table anything which is *unworthy*. The privilege and the high calling involved in sharing in the Lord's Supper demand the strictest form of self-examination. To take part in the sacrament 'unworthily' is to become *answerable for the body and blood of the Lord* (27).

The Greek word for *answerable* (*enochos*, 'guilty') has a forensic application, and this atmosphere is maintained throughout the paragraph with the root word for *judgement* (*krinō*) coming five times in verses 29–32. We may be involved in another of Paul's personal word games with the Corinthians over their love of litigation and spirit of judgmentalism. Here, he may well be saying explicitly, is an area where they truly ought to be exercising a strict discipline of judgment. When Paul talks of anyone who eats the bread and drinks the cup unworthily as *answerable for the body and blood of Christ*, essentially he means you become guilty of *shedding* the blood of Christ: that is, you place yourself, not in the company of those who are sharing in the benefits of his passion, but in the company of those who are responsible for his crucifixion.

How, then, should we approach the inestimable privilege of taking part in the Lord's Supper? This is, in fact, one of the most frequent pastoral dilemmas in a local church. There are many who hold back from partaking because they do not feel worthy. There are also those (probably fewer in number) who presume to take part without beginning to exercise even the slightest self-examination. So Paul's instructions here are topical and essential: *Examine yourselves, and only then eat of the bread and drink of the cup* (28). Bruce interprets as follows: 'The context implies that his self-examination will be specially directed to ascertaining whether or not he is living and acting "in love and charity" with his neighbours.'[14]

---

[14] Bruce, p. 115.

The process of self-examination is, etymologically, again linked with the root word *dokimos*.[15] Each Christian is obliged, not to reach some moral or spiritual standard of perfection (imaginary or otherwise), but to pursue rigorous and honest self-scrutiny.

The danger comes from eating and drinking *without discerning the body* (29): such people *eat and drink judgement against themselves*. What, then, does it mean not to discern the body? There are two possibilities. First, not giving due weight to the church as being the body of Christ (cf. 10:17): this was clearly where the Corinthians, with all their divisions, were actually placing themselves in considerable peril. Second, we fail to 'discern the body' when we do not recognize the special presence of the risen Lord in his worshipping community and, more particularly, in this sacrament of his body and blood. For the Corinthians there was the added danger of sharing in this particular meal as though it was no different from any other common meal. This is a frequent occurrence for us today, when we catch ourselves proceeding through the liturgy of the Lord's Supper by rote, without properly feeding 'on Christ by faith with thanksgiving'.

Paul was clear enough about the seriousness of such abuse to attribute sickness, weakness and even death in the Christian fellowship at Corinth to such unworthy reception of the bread and the wine in their public worship. Such events, he asserts, would not have been at all necessary if they had judged themselves truly (31). For the children of God there is no judgment on sin, because that has already been paid once and for all by Jesus himself (cf. John 5:24). Any way in which God does thus preserve the purity of his Table is part of the Father's disciplining of his children (cf. Heb. 12:5–11).

All Christians should ask themselves a leading question along the lines suggested by Paul's teaching in verses 30–31: how much weakness and illness is, in fact, part of the wise, loving, painful but productive, discipline of a perfect Father? It is, according to Paul, of that order rather than divine punishment: *when we are judged by the Lord, we are disciplined so that we may not be condemned along with the world* (32).

d. Conclusion (11:33–34)

So Paul concludes his heartfelt plea to the Corinthians about two aspects of their life as a worshipping community. He is so perturbed about the way

---

[15] Cf. 1 Cor. 3:13; 9:27; 11:19; Rom. 16:10.

they are exposing themselves to the judgment of God in their approach to the Lord's Supper that he underlines its nature as a love-feast: *wait for one another. If you are hungry, eat at home* (33–34). It is conceivable, according to Schlatter, that this marks the beginning of a separation between the love-feast and the Eucharist. This may not be correct, but it is a timely reminder that Christian worship in Corinth was of a more informal nature, took place (in all probability) in private homes, incorporated both liturgical and spontaneous elements, and was not confined to one hour's devotions in a specially constructed building which remained virtually unused for the rest of the week. Some further implications of this kind of worship Paul proceeds to tackle in chapters 12–14.

1 Corinthians 12:1–31

12. Concerning spiritual gifts

1. Proclaiming Jesus as Lord (12:1–3)

As we examine the next subject brought to Paul by the Corinthians, *Now concerning spiritual gifts*, we need to remind ourselves of the pagan background from which most of the Christians in Corinth had been delivered. This was essentially based in the Greek mystery-religions, in which spiritual experiences were the norm. They had grown accustomed to being *enticed* (2) by some kind of supernatural or demonic force, either into a state of trance, or into ecstasy, or into some strange course of action. Such 'inspiration' was regarded not merely as normal and to be expected, but as a clear authentication of the reality of the divine force involved. If there was no such clear manifestation of inspiration, the power of the relevant divinity was suspect.

In line with his two-edged argument earlier about meat offered to idols (8:4–5), Paul asserts both the impotence (*idols that could not speak*) and the potency of the forces present in these mystery-cults (*you were led astray* – pointing to a definite power at work and leading people). These forces were not in any sense what their exponents taught them to be; indeed in comparison with the truth as it is in Jesus, these *idols* were 'dumb' (rsv).[1] But Paul would have had great difficulty persuading the Corinthians that there was nothing in them at all. They knew all too well that there was.

---

[1] The word 'dumb' or 'speechless' (*aphōna*) does not mean that such heathen practices were carried on in silence; the very opposite was the case. As Conzelmann points out, it 'merely points to the fact that the pagan cult is vain . . . surrenders its devotees to the power of the demons' (p. 206). Cf. Ps. 115:4–8; Hab. 2:18. We have an example from Lucian (*Dialogi Mortuorum* 19.1): 'A sort of god (*daemon*) carries us away wherever he wills, and it is impossible to resist him.'

In the Western world of the twenty-first century, as increasing disillusionment with technology and materialism eats into most people, and certainly in virtually every non-Western culture, there is a plethora of religions and a multitude of spiritual experiences which are real but which, because of their very diversity and popularity, we need to evaluate properly with adequate criteria. What comes from God? What is the result of a disturbed personality or psychological trauma? What happens in certain drug-induced states, whether under medical supervision or in certain unrestricted subcultures? What is the direct inspiration of satanic forces?

In the light of the frequent and normal experiences of this kind to which the Corinthians had been subject, it is not surprising that Paul does not want them to remain 'ignorant' about 'spiritual things'. The word *gifts* in the NRSV is gratuitous and Paul probably is referring to what today is, in a broad sense, called 'spirituality' – that is, all the many diverse ways in which we experience spiritual reality. Although the discussion later narrows down to particular *charismata* and later still (chapter 14) to two particular gifts, the general reference seems more likely. The Corinthians were thoroughly absorbed with things supernatural and needed some firm, wise, corrective but encouraging advice from Paul. Incidentally, although it is most unlikely that the *tōn pneumatikōn* (1) is masculine (i.e. referring to 'spiritual people', as in 3:1ff.), Paul's own description of the Corinthian Christians as 'unspiritual' could not have been far from his mind. This is the probable force of his saying *I do not want you to be uninformed* about these matters: they thought they already knew all there was to know. He has told them that they have not begun in that area; so here is lesson number one for ignoramuses.

Paul is thus still pricking Corinthian pride, this time about their supposed super-spirituality. And the first lesson is indeed elementary, but crucial: *I want you to understand that no one speaking by the Spirit of God ever says 'Let Jesus be cursed!' and no one can say 'Jesus is Lord' except by the Holy Spirit* (3). Whatever other spirits, divinities or demons they have previously encountered, the Spirit of God, the *Holy* Spirit, is committed to proclaiming that Jesus is Lord. There is thorough discussion in the commentaries on the apparent impossibility of any Christian, even in the church at Corinth, descending to the allegedly inspired cry *Let Jesus be cursed!* (*anathema*). Is Paul perhaps posing the opposite of the true Christian confession, *Jesus is Lord*, in order to remind the Corinthians of the kind of utterance which they might well have heard in their pagan days while attending a local cult ('A curse on Jesus')? He would then be saying that by contrast the Spirit (*pneuma*) of the one true God lifts up Jesus as Lord.[2] This was almost certainly the earliest Christian creed, and there is evidence that, in Christian meetings, outsiders and even baptismal candidates were asked to leave the room before this statement of faith was affirmed.

This burning desire of the Holy Spirit to glorify Jesus (cf. John 16:14) is Paul's overall criterion of genuineness in this matter of spirituality. Indirectly but cardinally, it pervades all these three chapters. Thus chapter 12 concentrates on the church as the body of Jesus Christ; chapter 13 unfolds the essential character of Jesus Christ; chapter 14 takes two particular gifts (speaking in tongues and prophecy) and shows how any spiritual gift exercised with true Christlikeness serves to build up his body, the church – at Corinth or anywhere. As the church is thus consolidated and begins to function effectively, so Jesus of Nazareth is seen to be Lord of the universe.

This growth into maturity on the part of the local church also fulfils the inbuilt potential of each individual Christian, but it is important to see that this perspective on individuality is part of the growth of the whole body; it is not seen by Paul in any detached way. The supreme Lordship of Jesus is to be demonstrated by the church as his body. No appeal is made to the desire of any individual for personal fulfilment, which has always been the attraction of non-Christian and sub-Christian groups, from the Greek mystery-cults onwards. By concentrating on the church at Corinth as the body of Christ, Paul is again contrasting the false spirituality of contemporary religions with the genuine work of the Holy Spirit.

The phrase *Jesus is Lord* (3) is so familiar and fundamental that today we need to unpack its particular uniqueness. In 8:5 Paul mentioned the multitude of gods and lords in the world at that time. Each different culture had its own deities, and they demanded the loyalty and allegiance of their devotees. Christians stand outside, over and against these 'lords' and proclaim boldly together: 'Jesus is Lord', identical with Yahweh in the Old Testament, supreme over the Roman Emperor, the risen conqueror of every conceivable cosmic or demonic principality and power (cf. Col. 2:15). To enter the waters of baptism and to declare 'Jesus is Lord', to mean it and

---

[2] For other possible interpretations see Bittlenger, *Gifts and Graces*, pp. 16–18.

to adhere to it through everything until death – that requires the inspiration of the Spirit of God himself.

Obviously Paul does not mean that someone cannot even utter the words 'Jesus is Lord' without the Spirit; he is talking of a public confession of a personal faith in a living Saviour in front of a hostile world. No-one could maintain such a creed in any century or culture *except by the Holy Spirit*.

To be truly 'spiritual' drives a person neither to ecstasy nor to individualism nor to other-worldliness, but into the life of the local church as an expression of his or her personal commitment to Jesus as Lord and to his body here on earth. It is there that the implications of what it is to be 'spiritual', men and women of the Spirit, will be worked out. In times of persecution and martyrdom, such as many of Paul's contemporaries were to face in the days of Nero and Domitian, the meaning and the inspiration of being members of the body of Christ begin to make themselves felt. To distance ourselves from other Christians is to waver in our allegiance to Jesus as Lord: this is the unmistakable thrust of what Paul now proceeds to unfold in the ensuing three chapters.

2. For the common good (12:4–7)

How, then, does the Spirit of God underwrite and spell out the fundamental fact that Jesus is Lord? By enabling the church to embody his presence in the world in a variety of ways, through each individual member, but always pointing to Jesus as Lord.

Paul expects the church, even the divided and arrogant church of Corinth, gradually to provide a model of Christian community. The church is the means by which Jesus Christ is uniquely present and distinctively expresses himself in the world. In the church there is a rich diversity both of people (13, 28) and of gifts (4–11). There are many members in this body, and each member is different. No person, no gift, is a replica of another. God never imitates; that is Satan's nature, when he attempts to mimic all the good gifts of God with his own counterfeits. In fact, the nine gifts specifically mentioned in verses 8–10 are exactly paralleled in spiritualist practices.[3] Any desire, let alone any effort, to extinguish or diminish this rich diversity is not inspired by the Holy Spirit. Just as the very grace of

---

[3] Cf. Raphael Gasson, *The Challenging Counterfeit*.

God is 'many-coloured' (cf. 1 Pet. 4:10), so is the way he distributes his gifts and creates us as individuals.

Paul now spells out this diversity. The actual word translated *varieties*, *diaireseis*, can mean either diversity or assignment. The verb from the noun is used obviously with the latter meaning in verse 11: 'the . . . Spirit . . . allots to each one individually just as the Spirit chooses'. It might well be that Paul intends a double nuance, both to stress the diversity in God's church and to maintain the focus of the whole chapter on God's sovereign action in his church. There are four key verbs in the text which illustrate this sovereignty: verse 11, God 'apportioned/assigned/allotted'; verse 18, 'God arranged'; verse 24, 'God arranged'; verse 28, 'God appointed'. From beginning to end, from the smallest detail to the broad scope of church life, God is in control. That ensures variety, because he is infinitely rich in mercy and grace, always working out creatively new ways of demonstrating his love and truth.

There are, first of all, *varieties of gifts*, of *charismata*, that is, grace (*charis*) made concrete or actual. Timothy is urged by Paul to 'rekindle the *charisma* of God that is within you' (2 Tim. 1:6). Peter urges his readers: 'serve one another with whatever *charisma* each of you has received' (1 Pet. 4:10). The modern Greek word means 'a birthday present', which maintains the important emphasis of a love-gift, even if it also suggests the personal possession, for private enjoyment, of the receiver. Paul wants his readers to understand that all the variety of God's grace is not a matter of earning his favour or attention: out of his love God gives to everyone in his church.

Second, *there are varieties of service*, of *diakoniai*, that is, of ways in which we can be deacons, servants of one another, of our neighbours, of God (cf. 4:1). Paul is here emphasizing the attitude of mind towards the things of the Spirit which he wants the Christians at Corinth to develop. They probably tended to see the church as an arena for demonstrating their own talents and prowess, almost a stage on which to perform. The temptation remains with us today, but Paul is reminding us of our essential calling to be servants one of another. That attitude of mind supremely points to Jesus as Lord (cf. Phil. 2:4ff.). There are infinitely diverse ways in which the Spirit will inspire willing servants to this kind of diaconate. As Bittlenger says, 'It is not a matter of waiting till something comes over me and forces me, but a readiness to give out what God has placed in me.'[4]

---

4 Bittlenger, p. 21.

Third, *there are varieties of activities,* of *energēnata,* that is, God's energy going to work within Christians and spilling out into the life of the community. Here Paul is stressing the sheer power and inherent energy in each Christian. The operation of God's Holy Spirit is not a theory, and we must not reduce it to a matter for theoretical debate. The Spirit produces results, varied results which can be noticed: changed lives, transformed relationships, increasing congregations, effective testimony, released talents. As each of these is energized by the Spirit, the Lordship of Jesus is demonstrated in as many diverse ways as there are people who possess this energy. Samuel Chadwick wrote of his own discovery of this divine energy in the following evocative way:

> Every part of my being wakened up. I did not get a new set of brains, but I got a new mentality. I did not get a new faculty of speech, but I got a new effectiveness of speech. I did not get a new dictionary, but a new Bible. Immediately I was a new creature, with the same basis of natural qualities, energized, quickened, reinforced into a bigger vitality and effectiveness that nobody would ever have dreamed possible. That is what happens to those upon whom the Spirit comes.[5]

A fourth phrase is used in verse 7 which also illumines this facet of variety, and the whole verse stresses the overall theme of community: *To each is given the manifestation of the Spirit for the common good.* Again and again Paul is bringing the Corinthians back to the good of the community, not the personal whims of the individual. But the most important truth here stressed is that individual Christians are intended to *demonstrate* that they have the Spirit of God within them. Tom Smail has written: 'The Spirit must not be "spiritualised". He operates in the body and his business there is to produce visible glory, which all who have eyes for reality can see.'[6] He intends to make himself felt and known through his gifts, as well as by his fruit (cf. Gal. 5:22–23). Often the reason for the church's lack of credibility as the community of the Holy Spirit lies precisely here. Many Christians do not, or cannot, manifest their distinctive gifts in the life of their local church. The rich variety of the Christian community is thus hidden, and its corporate life appears to the outsider as dull and conformist, instead of diverse and colourful.

---

[5] Samuel Chadwick, *The Way to Pentecost* (Hodder, 1966), p. 32.
[6] T. A. Smail, *Reflected Glory* (Hodder, 1975), p. 29.

It is important to appreciate that the rich variety of such operation by the Holy Spirit in the body of Christ is completely unrelated either to Christian maturity or to personal deserts. Paul is adamant that 'to *each* is given the manifestation of the Spirit'. That refrain runs through the chapter like a theme in a symphony. The Christian community is the community of the Holy Spirit, of the living God. He is a richly diverse God, and every single member contributes to this living diversity.

3. God's grace in action (12:8–11)

Paul now gives nine examples of this rich variety. In Romans 12:6–8, Ephesians 4:7–11 and 1 Peter 4:7–11 we have three other lists, which overlap but also delineate over twenty clear gifts of the Spirit. Classic Pentecostalism used to teach firmly that these nine gifts in verses 8–10 are the special, 'supernatural' (*sic*) gifts of God to his church. This distinction between natural gifts and supernatural gifts clearly needs our fuller attention.[7]

It would seem wrong either, on the one hand, to *confine* the gifts of the Spirit to natural abilities harnessed and released by God, or, on the other hand, to assert that the *real* gifts of the Spirit are only those which are manifestly supra-natural.

It is also important to stress that, in certain cases, a person's natural talent

> will not be translated into a spiritual gift, because the person feels that he has misused it so seriously in the past that it has only bad associations in his mind. A further explanation is that the Lord does not motivate the person to use the talent in his service because of the immaturity of the individual. The Lord knows the gift would prove more of a stumbling block than a piece of service. It would lead to pride and self-sufficiency through reliance on the gifts, rather than on the Holy Spirit's enabling.[8]

For example, a highly trained and eminent ballerina in the USA did not feel able or free to use her dancing talents in the life of her local church for

---

[7] See additional note on spiritual gifts at end of chapter 14 (pp. 237–239).
[8] Eddie Gibbs, *Body-Building Exercises* (Falcon, 1979), p. 60.

several years, until she had found release from her driving ambition for personal recognition and public acclaim.

As both Creator of our natural abilities and Redeemer of our whole being so that we receive new abilities, God works in a variety of ways to produce many diverse examples of his grace in action in the Christian community. This will become clearer when we look later at the different gifts mentioned. It is also implicit in the tense of the verb 'is given' in verse 7, which indicates firmly that such endowment is not necessarily, or even normally, a once-for-all gift, but a constantly new provision of whatever may be needed in the variety of circumstances faced by the Christian community.

We now look at the list of particular gifts in verses 8–10. Although the list has been broken down in a number of ways (e.g. into 'doing gifts, speaking gifts and knowing gifts'[9]), this seems an arbitrary way to proceed. We will take each as it comes here in the biblical text.

a. The utterance of wisdom (12:8)

The literal Greek is *logos sophias* (= *the utterance of wisdom*) and it is necessary both to root this in the general Corinthian approach to wisdom and to note the specific nature of the *logos*. Such a gift could well be revealed by a thoroughly wise Christian (a pastor or teacher, for example) who has learnt consistently to fear the Lord (cf. Prov. 3:5–6), and does not lean towards or upon his or her own understanding, so that he or she clearly is a wise person, both in counsel and in behaviour. Such a person will sometimes manifest a specific gift on a specific occasion, as the wisdom of God is communicated with succinct and precise clarity, so that this particular 'utterance' manifestly reflects the wisdom of God. Such a 'word of wisdom' will shed light on one confused situation, bring perspective on another, provide an irrefutable frame of reference in a third.

Solomon was given such a *charisma* when confronted with two women laying claim to a baby (1 Kgs 3:16–28), and the particular words which enshrined the wisdom of God were these: 'Divide the living boy in two: then give half to one, and half to the other.'

Jesus himself was constantly revealing such enabling grace in his ministry. Examples can be seen in the way he conducted himself when his adversaries were trying to lure him into speaking falsehood, contradicting

---

[9] Michael Green, *I Believe in the Holy Spirit* (Hodder, 1975), pp. 161ff.

himself or speaking contrary to the manifest meaning of God's law. His use of the counter-question is a fascinating ploy and often led to or itself encapsulated 'the utterance of wisdom'.[10]

Having underlined the specific nature of such a gift for a particular occasion, we need also to stress that any Christian who has been growing steadily in Christ, who is the wisdom of God (Col. 2:3) and whom God has made our wisdom (1 Cor. 1:30), could for that reason be regularly used to utter wise words. The tense of the verb *is given* (*didotai*) indicates that this is not necessarily a gift which is given for permanent possession and for regular manifestation by one particular Christian. It *could* mean that, but its far more likely meaning is to focus on God meeting the need of a particular situation by equipping one member of the body with this gift. The next time he might well use somebody else in a similar way. This is of pastoral importance, because there is often a strong tendency to speak, in a rather possessive and clinging way, of '*my* gift'; whereas Scripture teaches us here as elsewhere that they are *God's* gifts to the *body* for the purpose of establishing Jesus as Lord.

It is also important to remember that these are gifts of God's *grace* – that is, they are not rewards for or indicators of spiritual maturity. For that reason the youngest Christian can be used in any of these ways, including the utterance of wisdom.

God does, however, give to his church both gifts and people.[11] It would seem likely that, in certain areas of ministry (to which we shall come later), a person is gifted frequently and consistently in such an obvious way that the church then recognizes in that person thus regularly gifted a gift of God to his body, perhaps as an evangelist or a teacher or a pastor. It is, however, unhelpful to see these gifts as necessarily or even normally located in the same individual: that is part of God's wisdom in ensuring that every member retains a steady expectation of being able to be used by God to build up his church. It also minimizes the 'guru mentality', which prevents many Christians from receiving much from God except through certain gifted individuals, whom they have come to regard as expert in some particular ministry.

If a Christian falls into the trap of appropriating any gift or ministry to herself or himself, then the Lord may well steer that person away from a

---

10 Cf. Luke 2:40–52; 13:17; 14:6; 20:19–26.
11 Cf. 1 Cor. 12:28; Eph. 4:7–11.

situation where she or he assumes (or it is assumed by others around) that *that* gift and ministry are crucial for the body of Christ in that place. Such a sense of importance, even indispensability, subtly takes the focus off Jesus as Lord, and the sensitivity of the Holy Spirit in this very area ('He will glorify me' – John 16:14) leads him to move the person on from the situation or into another area of ministry. This is a painful experience, and we do well to remember that God is very sensitive about the sovereignty of his Spirit in his church (cf. Jas 4:5). The Spirit himself is also very sensitive about the prominence of Jesus as 'head over all things for the church, which is his body' (Eph. 1:22–23). This is the thrust of 12:11: 'All these are activated by one and the same Spirit, who allots to each one individually just as the Spirit chooses.' Any tendency nowadays to talk of 'my church . . . my gifts . . . my ministry' can have Corinthian overtones.

b. The utterance of knowledge (12:8)

The Greek, *logos gnōseōs*, literally means 'a word of knowledge'. Another Corinthian preoccupation comes into view again: *gnōsis*, or 'knowledge'. The Holy Spirit is concerned to equip the body of Christ with knowledge of the 'truth . . . in Jesus' (cf. Eph. 4:21), both in the wide arena of truth and with specific knowledge of specific facts. In these ways the Spirit enables the kind of ministry which makes Jesus Lord of people's lives and of different situations. Jesus himself clearly demonstrated such knowledge in his overall teaching. There were also specific occasions when he spoke directly into a situation; for example, in establishing his identity and his salvation to the Samaritan woman (John 4:18), or in authenticating his ministry to the paralysed man (Mark 2:8–12), or in firing an apparently callous but crucial question at a congenital invalid (John 5:6).

Peter seems to have been similarly equipped in dealing with incipient hypocrisy in the early days of the church (Acts 5:1–11). The story of Ananias and Sapphira illustrates how the Holy Spirit apparently equipped a particular Christian (Peter) with a specific gift (a word of knowledge) to deal with a clear situation which might never have been known, let alone dealt with, except by such a manifestation of the Spirit.[12] Without this particular equipment from the Spirit, the church would have gradually lost its distinctive hallmark of integrity and transparency. Hypocrisy

---

[12] This is the interpretation of, for example, E. H. Plumptre (*Acts* [Cassell, 1893], p. 81), E. Haenchen (*The Acts of the Apostles* [Blackwell, 1971], p. 241) and I. H. Marshall (Tyndale Commentary, *Acts* [IVP, 1980], pp. 110–112).

would have become normal in the community of the Spirit. It is proper to ask how much the Christian community today has lost its distinctiveness because of the absence of such a manifestation of the Spirit. The result of this particular gift being firmly exercised in an extraordinarily difficult situation was that

> great fear seized the whole church and all who heard of these things . . . many signs and wonders were done among the people through the apostles . . . more than ever believers were added to the Lord . . . And every day in the temple and at home they did not cease to teach and proclaim Jesus as the Messiah.
> (Acts 5:11ff., 42)

In other words, the Lordship of Jesus was asserted.

There are obvious applications and equally obvious dangers in any such specific exercise of this gift today. It is so manifestly relevant and powerful that it could be very dangerous either in the wrong hands (indeed, repeatedly in the same hands) or in the wrong spirit, that is, without the love on which Paul concentrates in chapter 13.

Not all commentators accept an interpretation of these first two gifts which emphasizes such specific and precise manifestation of wisdom and knowledge. In general it seems true to say that less emphasis is placed by commentators on the specific 'utterance' than on wisdom and knowledge in general. For example, Godet, Bruce, Hodge and Morris debate the possible distinction between *sophia* and *gnōsis*, but come to no definite conclusion, beyond feeling that Paul is talking in general terms about putting both into words in one way or another. It would seem reasonable *both* to envisage the widest possible scope for wisdom and knowledge, as embodied in Jesus himself,[13] *and* at the same time to expect very specific articulation in precise words of whatever God wants the local church to know at a given stage in its life together.

c. Faith (12:9)

It is probably best to say what this particular gift is *not*, before we describe what it is. It is clearly neither the 'saving faith' by which every Christian is enabled to receive the salvation of God (e.g. Rom. 10:8–10), nor the

---

[13] Col. 2:3, 'in whom are hidden all the treasures of wisdom and knowledge'.

faithfulness which comes as fruit of the Holy Spirit's work in a Christian's character (Gal. 5:22). Equally, it is not the tendency of the optimist to be positive about everything, summed up in the words of J. B. Cabell: 'The optimist proclaims that we live in the best of all possible worlds; and the pessimist fears this is true.' Faith as a gift of the Spirit in this sense is also not to be equated with a dogmatic, almost defiant, assertion that 'the pain will go' or 'she will not die', which can degenerate into stating that the pain has actually gone when it very clearly and painfully has *not* gone.

Faith is neither credulity, nor gullibility, nor optimism, nor 'easy believism'; faith looks at God's character and stands firmly on God's promises. Like all true faith of whatever kind, this gift of faith in certain members of the body looks through the immediacy of the situation to 'him who is invisible' (Heb. 11:27) and brings the confidence that God will move in apparently impossible situations. In practice, this gift often seems linked with miracles and gifts of healing. We see this in the life of Jesus on numerous occasions, but most notably at the death of Lazarus.[14]

The gallery of the heroes of faith in Hebrews 11 certainly lends reality to this gift, as seen consistently in the lives of men and women of God who, through faith, were assured of things they could neither see nor prove, and consequently pressed on with God through the most testing circumstances conceivable. There have always been examples of this kind – for example, George Müller, Hudson Taylor, William Wilberforce, the Reformation martyrs, as well as many in our own day who are not such household names but who manifest equal faith and are a constant encouragement. For this reason a regular diet of Christian biography greatly strengthens personal growth in the Lord.

These individuals all demonstrate the gift of faith. But it would be a pity if we allowed such pinnacles of faith in action to take this gift beyond the experience of any local church and any Christian. The stage may be Coventry rather than China; the drama may be to do with a church's budget rather than the abolition of slavery; the plot may revolve around discouragement in the youth club rather than establishing a network of orphanages in Bristol. But every scenario in each local church requires the gift of faith, distributed by the Spirit as he chooses to boost the flagging morale of his people. The steady perseverance of the local church in

---

[14] See especially John 11:41–42, in his prayer of faith, and cf. Jas 5:13–15, with the ministry of the elders to any sick person.

pursuing the upward call of God, either in its general life or over a particular issue, truly underwrites our obedience to Jesus as Lord. The most insignificant member may well be used to impart such faith to the whole body at a crucial moment of decision-making. There is an Eastern saying (attributed to Rabindranath Tagore): 'Faith is the bird that knows the dawn and sings while it is still dark.'

d. Gifts of healing (12:9)

The literal translation of the Greek seems to be of unusual significance here: *gifts of healing*, *charismata iamaiōn* – both are in the plural. Paul is not talking about 'the gift of healing' or 'the healing ministry'. He is encouraging the Corinthians to expect many different ways in which God in his sheer grace gives healing of all kinds to different people, relationships, even situations. Writing about sickness which is not simply physical, Hans Burki comments:

> Sickness is always related to conflict. We become sick if a conflict becomes unbearable – the conflict between body and mind . . . ; between the conscious and the unconscious . . . ; between individual need and social integration; and between our temporal struggles and our eternal destiny. When tensions in one or all of these areas grow beyond our bearing, we get sick and we need healing, healing in all these areas.[15]

These *charismata* are referred to in the same words at the end of the chapter (28 and 30), although the RSV wrongly turns the phrase into 'healers' in verse 28. For many reasons, since this removes the only New Testament reference to 'healers' with such a connotation, this is a most important linguistic fact. At once the focus comes off individuals who might exercise such a ministry, and the stress is allowed to fall where it is consistently placed in the teaching of this chapter, that is, on the gifts distributed to the body to demonstrate that Jesus is Lord. We are, then, more free to respond to God who says, 'I am the LORD who heals you' (Exod. 15:26), whenever sickness of any kind comes.

James urges any member of the church who is sick in any way to call for the elders, so that they may pray with faith (Jas 5:14). It is the Lord who heals. The means, the method, the moment, the mystery all belong to him.

---

15 Hans Burki, speaking at the Pan African Christian Leadership Assembly, Nairobi, in 1976.

In both Old and New Testaments it is plain that the Lord brings healing through his chosen instruments to all kinds of people in all kinds of need. Often this healing bypasses human agency. Such healing continues into the early days of the church. There were always those who were not healed. Sometimes these are mentioned and occasionally the reason for lack of healing is given. It is legitimate to infer that there were many who did not receive healing – as, for example, there were many who were not healed when Jesus was carrying out his ministry in those three short years.

It seems proper to say, also, that similar healings have continued (even though spasmodically in terms of written records) throughout the history of the church. It is certainly true, in terms of sheer statistics, that there are more frequent manifestations of these gifts of healing in parts of the world where people do not have ready access to sophisticated medical treatment. This fact should not be used either to make modern Western Christians feel guilty because they resort to doctors, or, on the other hand, to confirm in anyone the feeling that such gifts of healing have been outdated by medical progress. There is still a vast amount of sickness in modern society; indeed, there are illnesses that seem to be peculiar to our century and civilization. Many of these are clearly beyond the ability of the medical profession. If the Lord is our healer, there are surely gifts of healing for all kinds of sickness, both through the training and skill of medically qualified people and through the faith and availability of ordinary Christians.

This is not to say that the Lord always brings physical healing. He clearly does not. Physical healing is not ultimate wholeness. That comes through death for the Christian (or through the return of Jesus in glory). The Lord is the healer; and he distributes gifts of healing through members of the body of Christ to those who are sick. The gifts are for the sick, not for those chosen to receive the gifts. The variety of these gifts and the variety of healings to which they are directed both encourage us not to exclude any form of sickness from such ministry. There is a gift of healing suitable for every area of disease, disintegration, trauma or pain.

In brief, both Paul's teaching here and James's instructions to call for the elders encourage us to rethink our actions and reactions whenever there is any sickness in the body of Christ. When we become sick, do we turn first (however momentarily or briefly) to the Lord? Such prayer need take only a few seconds and frees us to see medical means and the ministry of the elders or of the body as a whole as his healing provision in this situation. In any particular sickness medical resources will perhaps be the only means, or perhaps only one means, or perhaps a means to be bypassed.

Of course this begs all kinds of questions about the basic structures of our local churches. If such ministry is to be available in any realistic way, we need to have basic units of pastoral care which are small enough for every member to have access to gifts of healing, through the elders or in the body as a whole. This ministry does not necessarily have to be brought to the sick person at home or in hospital. Much sickness is of the kind which we carry round with us in our daily routine, our work and our worship. We bring it with us when we gather with others for worship. Why not call for 'the elders' then and there? Why should not 'the elders' make available such a ministry in every gathering of the church, whether in a home or more formally? Gifts of healings then become as normal as any other aspect of Christian ministry. Occasionally there will be healing of a more unusual and remarkable nature, but a continuous ministry of healing will be maintained across the whole spectrum of human sickness. Such a Christian community will inevitably become a healing community in every sense of the word. And so gifts of healing will glorify Jesus as Lord.

e. The working of miracles (12:10)

Literally, 'inworkings of powers', *energēmata dynameōn*. Moffatt's translation is 'miraculous powers'. The first word is the same as in verse 6, referring to God's energy manifested in powerful ways. Godet writes:

> Paul has in view the power of working all sorts of miracles other than simple cures, corresponding to the wants of the different situations in which the servant of Christ may be placed: resurrections from the dead, the driving out of demons, judgments inflicted on unfaithful Christians, deliverances like that of Paul at Malta.[16]

It is here that we undeniably encounter a gift which is impressive and beyond the ordinary. The ministry of Jesus himself impressed people with its amazing power of an extraordinary kind. A similar ministry was

---

[16] Godet, 2, p. 197.

carried through by the apostles (cf. Acts 19:11). Paul reminds the Corinthians later that 'The signs of a true apostle were performed among you with utmost patience, signs and wonders and mighty works' (2 Cor. 12:12). Paul also appeals to such miracles as evidence of God's supplying the Spirit to the Galatians, when they had lapsed into formalism and legalism (Gal. 3:5). The fact that Paul describes such miracles as indicators of his own apostleship is taken by many commentators[17] to indicate that their major (though not exclusive) function was to authenticate a fresh stage of revelation (e.g. the law, the prophets, the incarnation, the apostolic preaching of the gospel). A person's attitude to such miraculous gifts will depend upon the way she or he perceives the biblical doctrine of miracles and their purpose.

Some scholars think that Paul is here speaking specifically of exorcism, or setting people free from the grip of demonic forces.[18] As we have seen,[19] such spiritual forces were commonplace in the pagan lives of Corinthians, most of whom would have encountered or even been controlled by evil spirits.

It seems reasonable at least to include such ministry under the title of *the working of miracles*. Whenever occult practices increase in a society, the need for this manifestation of the Spirit becomes very great. In that sense we can call it common and usual, not least in the way contemporary Western society has moved in recent decades. The problems caused by occult involvement are a major factor in any Christian ministry today. Again, the issues are complex; but the nature of the conflict is very plain, not least because the worldview of the Bible fully endorses the reality of such events. Those who have found themselves involved in such ministry agree in asserting the way it truly establishes the Lordship of Jesus over the darkest forces of evil. Particular gifts to enable the church to operate effectively in this area are available to the body of Christ, says the apostle: 'the working of miracles', or the power within to express the sovereign victory of Christ, is such a gift.

It must be stressed with special care in this area of ministry that this gift, like all the gifts in this paragraph, is to be exercised in the worshipping life of the Christian community. When so-called healers and exorcists embark on itinerant ministries of a specialist nature, operating usually

---

[17] E.g. Hodge.
[18] See, e.g., Conzelmann, p. 209 footnote.
[19] 1 Cor. 10:20; 12:2.

on their own apart from any local church, it is a sure sign that something is badly wrong with both individual and, probably, the local church. By placing this gift firmly within the body of Christ, Paul had an inbuilt safeguard both against overvaluing this gift and against specialists in such a ministry. Without doubt no Christian should ever be drawn into such ministry individually; Paul certainly would not have envisaged such a situation without the guiding presence of 'elders'. On the other hand, we must be careful not to overreact; any Christian in the body can be used in this gift as in any other.

f. The ability to distinguish between spirits (12:10)[20]

The Greek phrase is more cryptic: *diakriseis pneumatōn* = 'discernings of spirits'. In the context of the above discussion, this could refer very specifically to the ability to discern the presence and the nature of evil spirits in a person, place or situation. More widely, it probably means an ability to recognize from what source any purported spiritual manifestation comes. Of such sources the Bible seems to identify three: the Holy Spirit, the human spirit and evil spirits. In the general area of spirituality, therefore, and in the specific area of spiritual gifts of varying kinds, the Spirit provides the gift of discernment as to which of these three spiritual sources is in operation in a particular case.

The highly complex nature of the human personality, especially when in a disturbed state, reminds us of the extremes (for good and evil) to which the human spirit can be taken. It is often crucial to distinguish to what extent particular phenomena are produced from the human spirit, and how much influence is also being exercised either by the Holy Spirit on the one hand or by evil spirits on the other. This discernment also shows how important it is for psychiatrists and Christian ministers to seek more ways for expressing real partnership in dealing with such cases.

It is difficult to decide whether this gift is simply supernatural intuition or whether it is linked in some way to the process of testing spiritual manifestations.[21] There is a clear example of the former in Paul's approach to the slave girl at Philippi who was pestering him with the cry: 'These men are slaves of the Most High God, who proclaim to you a way of salvation.'

---

[20] The three other gifts in this passage – prophecy, speaking in tongues and interpretation of tongues – will be examined in detail in our study of chapter 14. Any superficial treatment at this stage would be unhelpful and misleading.
[21] Cf. Matt. 7:15–20; 1 Thess. 5:20–21; 1 John 4:1ff.

Even in such sound and true words Paul saw clearly the operation of an evil spirit (Acts 16:16–18).

Once again, we can see the importance of these gifts being exercised within the worshipping life of the body of Christ. It is very easy for someone who has been used in this discerning ministry to slip into the habit of seeing evil spirits in any unusual situation or behaviour. This tendency can again be minimized by stressing that all these gifts are available to any member of the body and are distributed by the Spirit in the worshipping community to meet a particular need. This passage does not necessarily refer to any regular practice of any one gift by any one person.

The most crucial – although obvious – point to stress in this whole area of ministry is the need to conform not just our thinking but our practice to the teaching of Scripture. Jesus' ministry in the field of the demonic provides a model of incisive, authoritative, quiet assurance. He saw the reality of demonic forces where we might not and his own contemporaries often did not. But he also discerned between sickness due to demons and sickness due to purely physiological factors. A study of Mark's Gospel, with special attention to the way he operated, yields great rewards. Those who allow the Spirit of Jesus to reproduce such quality in their own ministry will truly demonstrate the Lordship of Jesus today.

This is the rich variety of spiritual gifts of a particular kind which the Spirit of God makes freely available to every local church. Along with this variety, harmonizing and arranging it for maximum effectiveness, is the unity of God himself. There is an implicit and spontaneous trinitarian ring to verses 4–6, 'the same Spirit . . . the same Lord . . . the same God', with an apparently natural emphasis on gracious giving on the part of the Spirit, sacrificial service on the part of the Son and purposeful power on the part of the Father. However diverse the gifts, however different the people both in background (13) and in abilities (8–10), it is all the work of the one God, Father, Son and Holy Spirit. In particular, the Spirit delights in this variety and Paul endorses this by the phrase *the same Spirit*, which he repeats in verses 4, 8, 9 and 11. Thus it is true equally that the Spirit never imitates himself and that the Spirit never contradicts himself. Only God can sustain such variety in unity. Only God knows the best way for the body of Christ to be built up and to grow up into maturity: he inspires this variety and he *allots to each one individually just as the Spirit chooses* (11).

The three verbs in verse 11 are all crucial for a proper approach to these gifts – he wills, he inspires, he apportions. There is a plan, a divine purpose, into which we are to fit sensitively without any attempted manipulation either of God or of others in the body. The desire to make these gifts available to God for the service of others comes from God alone; it cannot be produced by purely human exhortation or pressure. There may be a place for both the whip and the carrot, but many local churches have suffered from those who force the pace or paint too rosy a picture of involvement in the life of the body. As far as distribution of gifts is concerned, that also is firmly in the hands of the Spirit: he excludes no single member from his largesse, but the decision about which gift for which person at what time lies entirely within his discretion. There is nothing either haphazard or discriminatory about this distribution of gifts.

4. Unity in diversity (12:12–13)

The phrase *the body*, introduced in verse 12, perfectly illustrates these two themes of variety and unity. *Many members . . . one body* is Paul's summary of the matter. The way he ends verse 12 is highly significant. We would expect him to say: 'Just as the body is one and has many members . . . , so it is with the church.' In fact, he says, *so it is with Christ*. It is important not so to identify Christ with his church that we lose sight of his pre-eminence and transcendence. Nevertheless, Paul is clearly referring here to the way Christ today manifests himself by the Spirit to the world through his church. Bittlenger comments: 'In order to accomplish his work on earth, Jesus had a body made of flesh and blood. In order to accomplish his work today, Jesus has a body that consists of living human beings.'[22] Paul is affirming both the rich variety and the deep unity in Christ himself. In this all Christians share as members of this *one body* (13) through this *one Spirit*.

This particular verse (13) has been the focus of much diverse and contradictory interpretation. Its context makes it clear that there can be no legitimate exegesis which divides Christians into two (or more) groups, let alone into first-class and second-class Christians. This by itself precludes the classical Pentecostal interpretation, which asserts that Paul here describes a two-stage initiation into Christ: regeneration (the first

---

22 Bittlenger, p. 55.

part of the verse) followed by 'the baptism of the Spirit' (the second part). John Stott has argued cogently against this position, stressing that the experience described in this verse is one shared by all Christians.[23] The Greek preposition *en*, sometimes translated '*by* the Spirit' at the beginning of the verse, ought to be rendered either 'in' or 'with' the Spirit. This then brings this verse into line with the six other passages in the Gospels and Acts where being baptized with/in the Spirit is clearly said to be the distinctive work of Jesus. Jesus is the baptizer; the Holy Spirit is the 'element' in which all Christians are baptized.

There is another side to the discussion aroused by verse 13. John Stott, for example, says that the two parts of the verse refer to the same event and experience. 'The being baptized and the drinking are clearly equivalent expressions.'[24] If it is true that Paul is here talking of being baptized by Jesus with/in the Holy Spirit, we need to note the meaning of the word *baptized* in such a context. It is likely that the word carries the double connotation of 'being initiated into' and 'being overwhelmed by'. For example, contemporary secular Greek sources spoke of a submerged ship being 'baptized'. That ship was not merely 'initiated into' water; it was thoroughly 'overwhelmed by' water. Indeed, we can go on to say that it was 'made to drink of' the water: in other words, the water was inside the ship as well as the ship being underneath the water. Paul seems, then, to be saying both that Christians are in the Holy Spirit, and that the Holy Spirit is in Christians, parallel to our being in Christ and Christ being in us. By reverting to another metaphor used to describe the Holy Spirit, wind or air or breath, we can see the same truth: a new body is surrounded by air, but must also breathe in the air, if it is to carry on living and growing.

If all Christians have been initiated into and overwhelmed by the Spirit through the work of Jesus the baptizer, if Jesus has made all Christians drink of the Spirit, it is legitimate to ask today whether the church as a whole or a particular local church or an individual member is genuinely experiencing what Paul is describing. It is certainly not pastorally sensitive to assume this to be happening, let alone

> to tell believers who know themselves to be spiritually inadequate that
> rivers of living water are pouring from them, to tell those who feel futile

---

[23] See John Stott, *Baptism and Fullness* (IVP, 1975), pp. 38–43.

[24] Ibid., p. 43.

and fruitless in their Christian service that the outpoured energy of the Holy Spirit is freely at work in them.[25]

'This is to run into complete unreality,' says Smail, and he goes on to show that the Corinthians had *both* received the preaching of the cross in faith (2:1ff.) *and* experienced the powerful results of that preaching in lives totally transformed: 'you were washed, you were sanctified, you were justified in the name of the Lord Jesus Christ and in the Spirit of our God' (6:9–11).

In verse 13 Paul can appeal, not just to an event, but to an experience in the life of every Corinthian believer. This event, this experience, transformed them from pagans to Christians, introduced them into the community of Christian believers, and began 'an experiential participation in the Spirit's presence and power'.[26] We need today to point one another with expectancy to Jesus the baptizer as the person who longs to take us all deeper and deeper into the reality of the Spirit's power and presence. It is not a question of one special experience to be imposed upon all; but it is a reality to be experienced, and that experience can be continuous and daily. This expectant openness to experience the Spirit more and more on the part of every Christian will unite the body in eager dependence upon Jesus. We must not allow fear of wrong or superficial experiences to keep us from the birthright of the church from Pentecost onwards: 'they were all filled with the Holy Spirit'.

It is worth pointing out that people in cultures less dominated by the analytical and cerebral emphasis of Western education seem far more free to enter expectantly into such experience of the Spirit. Africans and Latin Americans, in particular, are far less prone to extricate their minds from the rest of their persons: they respond as persons. The Corinthians tended to set great store by the non-cerebral (see chapter 14), and they needed to be taught the importance of a proper use of the mind (*nous*): a timely reminder that their experience of being baptized in the Spirit by Jesus did not guarantee either their wholeness or their spiritual maturity.

It is probable that the African–Latin American understanding (however instinctive) is far closer to that of the Judaeo–Christian perspective of the Bible.[27]

---

[25] Smail, *Reflected Glory*, p. 33.

[26] Ibid., p. 142.

[27] See Lausanne Occasional Paper No. 2, on Gospel and Culture, p. 14: 'Some Third World cultures have a natural affinity to biblical culture.'

The reference in verse 13 to *Jews* and *Greeks*, *slaves* and *free*, reminds us of the many-coloured diversity of the body of Christ. Corinth was a cosmopolitan seaport full of people from many different cultures. That presented difficulties, but it offered immense potential for a full-blooded testimony to Christ. The more we today draw on the richness of the worldwide community of believers, the more pungent and attractive will be our testimony.

5. We are Christ's and each other's (12:14–27)

Paul now uses the human body to illustrate truths about life in the body of Christ. It is not an exact parallel and Paul's language strays beyond straight comparison: for example, limbs of the body do not actually suffer or rejoice (26). In this section particularly we see the two themes of community and individuality, notably in verse 27: 'Now you are the body of Christ and individually members of it.' The similar passage in Romans has this perspective: 'we, who are many, are one body in Christ, and individually we are members one of another' (Rom. 12:5). On this basis at least three facts are spelt out: we need one another, we differ from one another and we are to care for one another.

a. We need one another (12:15–16, 21)

There are two sides to this particular coin. The stress in verses 15–16 is on a wrong kind of independence which could be based either on feeling not needed and unimportant, or on resenting not having been made or gifted differently. The other aspect (verse 21) is an attitude of superiority on the part of some members towards others. Both an independent spirit and a superior attitude bring atrophy and paralysis to the body as a whole, because it is deprived of certain contributions without which it must degenerate. If we are together the body of Christ, we need one another, not only for the health of the body as a whole, but also to enable each individual to operate at full potential. Any Christian who operates independently from others is reducing his or her own effectiveness and that of the body as a whole. The practical application of this truth in a local situation is surely obvious: at the very least it means a genuine effort by those in pastoral oversight to recognize, train and release the gifts of every individual for effective service. That means recognizing hidden talent, crossing denominational and other boundaries, moving away from clerical monopoly, and developing partnership in ministry outside the immediate locality and indeed with a global perspective. We need one another and we live in a world where communications of all kinds make it possible for this to be practically realized.

b. We differ from one another (12:17–20)

Many members, yet one body is Paul's conclusion. A body which is all eyes and ears is not a body. Each member is unique, distinctive, irreplaceable, unrepeatable. As we have already seen earlier in the chapter, this is the glory of the church as the body of Christ. Instead of allowing ourselves to be cast in any one mould, we ought to relish the differences and learn to capitalize on them. It is true of most churches that there are many round pegs in square holes: they become jammed. Equally, there are many square pegs in round holes: they are either too big to belong or too small to fill the need. There are also many pegs trying to fill several holes at once. That leads to many others lying around unused. Another variation on the same theme happens when new pegs are forced to fit into existing holes, instead of being allowed to find their own niche of a totally new kind. We differ from one another, because God wants those differences to be moulded into a special unity which is demonstrably his own doing.

Rather than build up community out of diversity, we often tend to let each sub-group form its own unit and grow in isolation from other natural groupings. The community which is alive to the Spirit is committed, by Scripture, to the costly struggle of living out the reconciliation of all people to one another and to God, by uniting black and white, intellectual and action-oriented business person, new believer and mature disciple, Jew and Gentile, young and old, male and female, single and married.

There are many other, more subtle, distinctives which we can easily and unconsciously stifle, to the point where the body has effectively lost several limbs by social, cultural or intellectual amputation. For example, a local church needs both the traditional and the avant-garde; those on the political right, left and centre; those who lean different ways over 'charismatic renewal'. More particularly, the distinctive insights and priorities of evangelist, prophet, pastor and teacher all need to be held together and not reduced to the lowest common denominator. We differ from one another and only God, who made us different, can hold us together.

c. We are to care for one another (12:22–26)

This mutual care, says Paul, is also intrinsic to the body: this is the way *God has so arranged* [= 'adjusted'] *the body* (24). The Greek word, *synekerasen*, has the basic meaning of mixing different parts together with a specific purpose in mind, namely, to produce mutual support and interdependence. 'The word may be used of mixing colours.'[28] God wants the members of a local church to recognize how much they depend on one another, because that is an incentive to remove *dissension* (25, *schisma*)[29] and to deepen true concern.

Paul underlines this in two ways. First, we pay particular attention to the less presentable parts of our physical bodies; we should be similarly ready to give special care to 'weaker' brothers and sisters, those who might feel readily dispensable but are in fact vital to the health of the body. Second, this care is to be expressed both by 'rejoicing with those who rejoice' and by 'weeping with those who weep' (cf. Rom. 12:15). Some Christians find more difficulty with the former than with the latter: it requires the grace of true humility to be genuinely glad when another is being blessed, used and praised. When one member suffers in any way, it is essential for the body to feel the pain together.

> If pain causes us to go inward, there is no more communication with the world outside; if it causes us to go outward in retaliation, then we lose the message we bear . . . If pain causes us to go forward, then we are not bearing the pain, we are using the pain.[30]

Throughout the world today, the way the Christian community faces and uses suffering is crucial to the integrity of its testimony. In the West we have become so accustomed to finding escape routes from pain of all kinds that we can learn deep lessons from our brothers and sisters in other parts of the world for whom suffering is normal and inevitable. We learn this in the relatively manageable fellowship of a local church, especially in a smaller microcosm of the church meeting regularly in a home. Care is shown by entering into the joys and sorrows of other members of the body. That is automatic with our physical bodies, as a toothache or a septic

---

[28] Morris, p. 177.
[29] Cf. 1 Cor. 1:10; 11:18.
[30] Dr Samuel Kamaleson, speaking at the Pan African Christian Leadership Assembly in Nairobi in December 1976.

toe will soon indicate. When there are no such sensations, there is something seriously wrong. Do we know one another well enough in our local churches to be able to rejoice or to suffer at appropriate occasions?

d. Our individuality (12:27)

As the body of Christ operates in this way, so the individual members will find their real needs met. The need for security is met in the assurance that 'I belong to the body.' The need for identity is met in recognizing and working at the fact that 'I have a distinctive contribution to bring to the body.' The need for a proper sense of responsibility is met by assuming concern for others in the body: 'I need you; I feel with you; I rejoice with you.' So each individual grows as a person and as a Christian in direct relation to finding his or her place as a member of the body. The Scriptures speak of individuality, not of individualism. The latter phenomenon is a perversion of our calling in Christ. It plagues the church of God, spoiling its witness and shrivelling individuals.

This discovery of our individuality within the life of the Christian community remains as revolutionary a message in today's world as it was in that of Paul and his Corinthian readers. It is a radical alternative both to the tyranny of totalitarianism and to the empty dreams of personal fulfilment through individualism.

There is a further perspective in this chapter, one which prevents such a community turning in on itself and becoming a pious ghetto of religious fanatics. The body of Christ is placed in the world to serve. Ministry is its daily vocation. As the community is mobilized under the Holy Spirit within the real world, its throbbing vitality will be sustained. Gifts are to be used in practical, costly and often very ordinary service (cf. 12:5). The ministry of Jesus through his physical body on earth is continued in the ministry of his body, the church. It is the same ministry: he came 'not to be ministered unto, but to minister, and to give his life a ransom for many' (Mark 10:45, AV). That is the purpose of the body of Christ now: 'As the Father has sent me, so I send you' (John 20:21).

6. God has appointed . . . (12:28–30)

To be effective in such ministry, the church must work with God's own appointed methods, motives and people. This seems to be the force both of this paragraph and of chapters 13 and 14. The list in verse 28 repeats some from verses 8–10, omits others and adds four new ones. In this way Paul is summarizing all that he has said in chapter 12. He is repeating the fact of variety, the need for unity and the call to ministry. There are slight, but important, differences in presentation. Instead of concentrating on what the Spirit gives to each individual for the common good, Paul writes of God appointing people in the church as *apostles . . . prophets . . . teachers.* The phrases *first . . . second . . . third . . .* may refer to priority of *time* rather than of *importance.*[31] Certainly the apostles founded local churches; the prophets proclaimed God's word into each situation; the teachers built securely on this foundation (cf. Eph. 2:19–20). On the other hand, Paul is firm that the church has been 'built on the foundation of the apostles and prophets', and in this sense their ministry was first both in time and in importance.[32] Again leaving *prophets* and *various kinds of tongues* until our examination of chapter 14, let us look at the four additions: *apostles, teachers, forms of assistance* and *forms of leadership.*

a. Apostles

Christ appointed his apostles (lit. = 'those sent out') to plant churches and to give them authoritative teaching. In the original founding of the church at and after Pentecost, that ministry was in the hands of the Eleven, plus Matthias (cf. Acts 1:15ff.). To these twelve were added James, Paul and perhaps Barnabas.[33] Clearly these men had a special commission and an unrepeated authority. They were, uniquely, witnesses to the resurrection of Jesus and had been specially chosen by Jesus 'to be with him, and to be sent out' (Mark 3:14) to teach and preach with his authority. Bittlenger divides these into the apostles in Jerusalem (the twelve plus James) and the apostles from Antioch (he adds Silvanus or Silas to Paul and Barnabas).[34] Many other people, especially at Corinth, laid claim to be apostles;[35] many since have claimed to be on a par with Paul (e.g. in today's Old and New Apostolic Church). In both cases the claims have been specious.

---

[31] Morris says of 'first . . . second . . . third' that they 'rank these various gifts to the church in order of honour' (p. 178). The Ephesians 4 list, however, is different and any sense of superior gifts does not fit Paul's context in these chapters very easily.

[32] See John Stott, *God's New Society* (IVP, 1979), p. 107.

[33] The inclusion of Barnabas is based on the reference in Acts 14:4, 14 to Paul and Barnabas as 'apostles'. There is actually no explicit evidence that Barnabas was given a resurrection appearance or that he was on a par with Paul when he was included in the original group. It could be that, in Acts 13 and 14, both Paul and Barnabas are seen as apostles of the church at Antioch (in line with the 'apostles of the churches' in 2 Cor. 8:23 and Phil. 2:25), whereas overall only Paul was seen as an apostle of Christ.

[34] Bittlenger, p. 67.

[35] See 2 Cor. 11 and 12.

Although it is true that nobody since the first apostles has been invested with their authority, it seems right to say that one essential ingredient of their ministry, namely, planting churches in virgin territory, is of prime importance in every age. A church is planted when individuals in an existing congregation are commissioned and sent out (at least in pairs) into an area to found there a church which is grounded in the teaching of the first apostles. This 'apostolic ministry', as distinct from the unique work of those first apostles, is essential if vast areas of the world today are not going to remain unevangelized. It is this foundational ministry which Paul seems to have in mind here (cf. Eph. 4:11). Such apostles appear to have a wide spread of gifts – in evangelism, prophecy, teaching and pastoring. They use these gifts to establish a church and then move on, after the pattern of Paul's own ministry;[36] in this way he left behind a team of 'elders' in each town to carry on and increase the work he had begun. In Ephesians Paul indicates that these elders will include between them four ministries: prophets, evangelists, pastors, teachers (Eph. 4:7–14). They will have the responsibility of equipping the body of Christ 'for the work of ministry'. In this more general sense, therefore, God appoints 'church apostles' (as we might call them) in order to establish new congregations.[37] Perhaps that is why Paul writes *'first* apostles'.

Another strand of this apostolic ministry today, in the view of many, is its itinerant nature.[38] For such people are always on the move and in this way share in the very nature of God himself, who sent his Son into the world with such an apostolic commission (cf. Heb. 3:1). The Holy Spirit constantly keeps some on the move in this way. They are pioneers and, by virtue of their mobility, they can encourage the wider church with their wisdom and experience. In today's world such itinerant ministry is common, and one of God's intriguing developments in recent years has been in setting aside certain people for such far-flung itinerant work, as distinct both from ministry confined to one local situation and the necessarily more restricted travelling ministry of missionaries and evangelists before the age of aviation. The example of Paul and Barnabas reporting back to, being supported by and thoroughly involved in the life of their sending church, the body of Christ at Antioch (Acts 13 – 15), underlines

---

[36] E.g. at Derbe, Lystra and Iconium, Acts 14:20–23.
[37] There is, in fact, mention of such 'apostles of the churches' in 2 Cor. 8:23 and Rom. 16:7, and also in Phil. 2:25.
[38] Cf. Michael Harper, *Let My People Grow* (Hodder, 1977), pp. 49ff., 61ff., 186ff.

the importance of rooting such itinerant ministers in the life of a local congregation. This helps the local congregation to have a truly missionary[39] outlook, and it prevents those on the move from becoming isolated, lonely or out of touch with the realities of local church life. It also gives flesh and blood to the international character of the church.

b. Teachers

The church at Antioch (Acts 13:1) had both prophets and teachers, of whom Barnabas and Paul were two. It is not clear whether the five mentioned were all both prophets and teachers, or whether some were prophets and some teachers. Howard Marshall thinks it probable that at that stage 'the dividing-line was not very clear, both groups being involved in exposition of the significance of the prophetic Scriptures and in exhortation'.[40] He contrasts the teaching activity of Barnabas and Paul at Antioch[41] with the inspired messages of prophets like Agabus (Acts 11:27ff.).

It is clear that the teaching ministry soon became highly valued and respected in the church. James has such a high view of it that he actually discourages his readers from becoming teachers, for 'we who teach will be judged with greater strictness' (Jas 3:1). Apollos was clearly a teacher (Acts 18:24ff.), and Paul describes Apollos's ministry at Corinth as being a necessary follow-up to evangelism and church-planting: 'I planted, Apollos watered' (1 Cor. 3:6). Teachers thus enable Christians to grow up towards maturity. Without such teaching ministry new life simply dries up. Those called and gifted in this area need to concentrate fully on it, because it requires single-minded application.[42] The list in Ephesians 4:11 could place pastors and teachers together as a combined ministry, but that is by no means the only possible interpretation. To feed the sheep, pastors need to provide teaching from God's Word; but pastoring requires more than teaching. Many teachers actually are not good pastors; many pastors do not have the gift of teaching. Sheer observation would lead us to expect the two to be separate. The main point is that *all* such ministries are needed in the local church.

---

[39] The English word 'missionary' has exactly the same etymological root (through the Latin) as 'apostle'.
[40] I. H. Marshall, *Acts* (IVP, 1980), p. 215.
[41] Acts 11:26, 'for an entire year they associated with the church and taught a great many people'.
[42] Cf. Acts 6:4; Rom. 12:7.

It is worth remembering that there were no books available to members of the early church, that Jewish Christians had a working knowledge of the Old Testament (but heavily overladen with rabbinic additions and interpretations), and that writing and education in general were confined to a privileged minority. All this enhanced the value of the teacher. The ready availability of all these things today does not diminish the importance of teachers in each local church, but inevitably must affect the methods used. Much teaching today would be made far more effective by imaginative use of audio-visual aids and by the kind of dialogue situation Paul used at Ephesus in the Hall of Tyrannus (Acts 19:9). It is also very necessary, in the cerebral atmosphere of much Western Christianity, to ensure that any teaching which is given is genuinely worked out into people's daily lives. That is where the pastoral instinct will not be satisfied with teaching which reaches only the mind, but will discover structures of pastoral care which enable the congregation to encourage one another in practical obedience.

c. Forms of assistance

If the essence of Christian ministry is to 'support the weak' (according to Paul's quotation of the words of Jesus in his farewell speech to the elders of the Ephesian church – Acts 20:35), there will be numerous people to offer *assistance* in the local church. This is probably the most common gift of the Spirit, exercised by the greatest number of Christians. The Greek word, *antilēmpseis*, refers to the gift rather than the person, again suggesting that any Christian should expect to render such assistance in the Christian community. Certainly no Christians ought to consider themselves above such ordinary, even humdrum and often unrecognized, service. Bittlenger believes that this word has a more limited and specialized meaning, being closely related to the handling of money: 'according to recently discovered papyri the Greek word for administration was a technical term in the field of banking and referred to the chief accountant'.[43] This possibility would no doubt be strongly favoured by many clergy who, like the present writer, find that their minds virtually go into reverse when money matters are being discussed. The facilitating ministry of people gifted in all areas of finance in a church is crucial and is indeed a gift of God's Spirit.

---

[43] Bittlenger, p. 70.

The most common interpretation of this word, however, applies it to the general ministry of practical assistance of all kinds. It would refer to such service as cooking and catering, washing-up and cleaning the church, moving chairs and providing transport, flower-arranging and secretarial help, answering the telephone and running errands, gardening and painting, repairing and redecorating. Such vital ministry is needed in visiting the sick and housebound, welcoming people to church services, fetching and carrying, putting out books and clearing them up afterwards – indeed, a thousand and one little chores which any Christian can fulfil 'as to the Lord and not to men and women' (Eph. 6:7). The root meaning of the word is 'to take a burden on oneself instead of another', and that nuance indicates the attitude of mind which releases such ministry in the congregation: as we look at the jobs which need to be done, we shall be motivated to divert such burdens away from others, especially those who are heavy-laden, on to our own shoulders. In most churches the load falls on too few willing helpers, who end up carrying virtually everything.

d. Forms of leadership

The literal translation of the Greek, *kybernēseis*, is 'pilotings'. The reference is to the helmsman of a ship, the person with the responsibility of steering the vessel, keeping it on course, avoiding dangers, recognizing changes in weather and adjusting accordingly. The helmsman knew well the capabilities of both the craft and the crew. He knew which expertise to call on at which moment. The most effective helmsman had a quiet confidence and an immediate rapport with the crew. He neither panicked nor relaxed his vigilance. He had his eye on the destination and was above all concerned that his ship and his crew reached journey's end safe and sound.

It is intriguing to discover that modern Greek uses the same word of an airline pilot. Travelling across the Atlantic one time, my wife and I were invited into the cockpit of a DC-10 as the plane was reaching the American coastline. Those flying the plane were receiving constant messages from two or three airports and were regularly readjusting the flight path accordingly. Yet at the same time the captain was responding to our very simple request for some memento of our presence in the cockpit to give to our two boys back in England. He called the chief steward and, about an hour later, one of the cabin crew gave us what we wanted. The pilot or helmsman, knowing every one of his crew, knew whom to ask for our needs to be met.

Such ministry is indispensable in the local church: those who have the ability to steer a service, a meeting, a conference, or indeed the whole church; to hold it on course and keep it moving towards its destination; to call on the right person with the right gift at the right time; to cope with trivial requests, which are important to the individual making them, without becoming impatient or taking their eyes off the main issues and the ultimate goal. Such helmsmen will be people both of vision and of sensitivity.

Increasingly in today's church the reality of team ministry is being pursued. Old habits unfortunately die very hard and most teams are in fact influenced significantly by one strong personality. There is much talk about non-status and the vital importance of each person on the team. Genuine concern is expressed about preserving the headship of Christ over his body. But still secular or traditional styles of leadership predominate. Then come the rationalizations, encapsulated in aphorisms like 'the buck must stop somewhere'. If the gift of helmsmanship along the lines just explained is fundamental to the body of Christ, then it really comes into its own as a church genuinely pursues what it means to have shared responsibility carried out by a team. The helmsman is the one who holds the team together and keeps it on course; he or she will be in such touch with each member of the team that the right person is called on to bring the right gifts at the right time. It is unlikely that a person with one of the more 'up-front' ministries (e.g. evangelist, teacher, prophet) will have this gift of steering; it is probable that it will reside in someone else. Most churches would benefit substantially from identifying and releasing such helmsmanship at the heart of their worship, decision-making and organizational life.

The dictionary definition of the modern business science of cybernetics (the word comes from the same Greek root) affords a fascinating insight into this matter: 'study of system of control and communications in animals and electrically operated devices such as calculating machines'. We can reduce this to simple language: making people tick and making things work. In other words, this is the essential enabling ministry of the body of Christ. It is both very demanding and absolutely irreplaceable. It may be right to call it 'administration' (cf. RSV); if so, it must be free from any narrow interpretation and be brought right into the heart of every local church.

7. The more excellent way (12:31)

Variety ... unity ... ministry. These are Paul's three themes in this chapter. Each theme undermines Corinthian pride and complacency. The rhetorical questions in verses 29–30 also nail their self-sufficiency. The last verse of the chapter (31) may well pin them down even further, as a prelude to the devastating message of chapter 13. Most English translations assume that the Greek verb, *zēloute*, is imperative: *strive for the greater gifts*. It could well be indicative, that is, stating as a fact that the Corinthians covet the higher gifts. Paul has already chastised them for their covetous spirit (3:3). The rest of chapter 12 has been a thorough attempt to stress the equal value of each person and every gift in the body of Christ. The Corinthians always tended to have a league table of gifts, prizing the more dramatic above the more ordinary. For these reasons it seems best to accept Bittlenger's interpretation of this verse,[44] when he concludes, 'There are, in other words, two ways of receiving and manifesting gifts: by *striving* after them or by attaining them through *love*.'

The competitiveness of the Christians at Corinth is often repeated today. Gifts of the Spirit are thus discovered and used, but such churches often become hard and full of criticism. Those who have certain gifts develop a proud attitude to those who do not; those who want these gifts become depressed because they do not seem able to receive them. If, on the other hand, it is love which controls and prevails in a church, then every member will be freed to bring his or her particular gift and to ask God for more gifts, not for his or her own sake, but for the benefit of all. Such is the desire of those controlled by the love of God. The way of love is, therefore, not an alternative option to the way of spiritual gifts. Spiritual gifts are absolutely essential for every church; but there is a more excellent way of discovering them: through love. The less excellent way, through an unhealthy desire to be a lively or successful church (*more* lively and *more* successful than the one across town), leads to pride, hardness, human-centredness and rivalry.

---

[44] Cf. Bittlenger, pp. 73–75.

1 Corinthians 13:1–13

13. If I do not have love . . .

This magnificent song of Christian love[1] reveals its fullest and most challenging meaning only when carefully applied into the community life of a local church, such as the one at Corinth. The chapter is frequently read at weddings or memorial services. It is often used on occasions which require lofty sentiments, literature of a high quality, but no overt Christian statement.

Thomas Merton provides a pungent example of such misapplication of the true message of the chapter. He describes the chaplain at his boarding school in the following way:

> He was a tall, powerful, handsome man, with hair greying at the temples, and a big English chin, and a broad, uncreased brow, with sentences like 'I stand for fair-play and good sportsmanship' written all over it.
>
> His greatest sermon was on the thirteenth chapter of First Corinthians – and a wonderful chapter indeed. But his exegesis was a bit strange . . . 'Buggy's' interpretation of the word 'charity' in this passage (and in the whole Bible) was that it simply stood for 'all that we mean when we call a chap a "gentleman"'. In other words, charity meant good sportsmanship, cricket, the decent thing, wearing the right kind of clothes, using the proper spoon, not being a cad or a bounder.
>
> There he stood, in the plain pulpit, and raised his chin above the heads of all the rows of boys in black coats, and said: 'One might go through this

---

[1] Some commentators assume that this chapter was written on some previous occasion and incorporated into the text of 1 Corinthians at this point.

chapter of St. Paul and simply substitute the word "gentleman" for "charity" wherever it occurs. "If I talk with the tongues of men and of angels, and be not a gentleman, I am become as sounding brass, or a tinkling cymbal . . . A gentleman is patient, is kind; a gentleman envieth not, dealeth not perversely; is not puffed up . . . A gentleman never falleth away."' . . .

The Apostles would have been rather surprised at the concept that Christ had been scourged and beaten by soldiers, cursed and crowned with thorns and subjected to unutterable contempt and finally nailed to the Cross and left to bleed to death in order that we might all become gentlemen.[2]

It is clear, then, that chapter 13 must be studied in the context of the rest of Paul's letter to the church of Corinth. Otherwise it remains mere words – noble, even ennobling, but only words. When applied to a local church, it becomes dynamite. It uncovers all the weaknesses, gaps, failures and sins in any Christian community. It is a particular challenge to any church which has seen outward success in its ministry. These words cut us down to size; they humble us, because we begin to see what really matters to God. They redirect us as the body of Christ to our true calling. It is probably good for any congregation to assess its life together from time to time in the mirror of this chapter.

Because of the grandeur of its language, because it is acknowledged to be 'great literature', this chapter needs to be linked immediately with Paul's discussion of spiritual gifts in chapter 12. In a word, Paul is saying that all the most dramatic and wonderful gifts we can imagine are useless without love. As Bruce says, 'the most lavish exercise of spiritual gifts cannot compensate for lack of love'.[3] Before we look at what Paul has to say about love, a few preliminary comments are necessary.

It is well known that the Greek word for love in the New Testament, *agapē*, was not previously in common use. It was taken into the Greek of the New Testament specifically because the love of God, seen in Jesus of Nazareth, required a new word. God's love completely transcends all human ideas or expressions of love.

---

[2] Thomas Merton, *The Seven Storey Mountain* (Sheldon Press, 1978), pp. 73–74.
[3] Bruce, p. 124.

It is a love for the utterly unworthy, a love which proceeds from a God who is love. It is a love lavished on others without a thought of whether they are worthy to receive it or not. It proceeds rather from the nature of the lover, than from any merit in the beloved.[4]

This is the love which, according to Jesus, has to characterize and control the Christian community, if it is in any sense to be recognized as Christian (cf. John 13:35) and if he is to be recognized as God's Son and the world's Saviour.

For these basic reasons Paul spells out why Christian community life without love is nothing, worse than nothing (1–3). He then describes what love is, what love is not and what love does (4–7). Finally, he paints vividly the lasting and eternal quality of love (8–13), outliving both knowledge and spiritual gifts – the two great priorities for the Christians at Corinth.

1. The absence of love (13:1–3)

Paul makes three strong statements about the loveless Christian.

a. Without love I offend others (13:1)

In 8:1 he has already established the key principle that 'love builds up'. When spiritual gifts are exercised in love, not in a competitive spirit, the body of believers is edified. That is Paul's constant plea throughout his discussion of prophecy and tongues in chapter 14. The inevitable result of not using spiritual gifts in love is that others are offended.

The way Paul puts this is by an oblique reference to the devotees of Greek mystery-cults at Corinth, who worshipped Dionysus (god of nature) and Cybele (goddess of wild animals). Dionysus, the Thracian and Phrygian god of the reproductive energies of nature, was worshipped with orgiastic rites, including the tearing in pieces and devouring of animal, possibly also human, sacrifices. Worshippers, especially women, losing their own personality, were identified with him. He tended to specialize as the god of wine. Cybele, the mistress of wild nature, was often shown with lions and other beasts. Phrygia appears to have been the centre of her cult, which was introduced into Rome and had great popularity during

---

[4] Morris, p. 181.

the early Roman Empire (i.e. the first century AD), especially among women.

No doubt the streets of Corinth resounded with the noisy gongs and clashing cymbals which were a feature of such worshippers. A *chalkos* (*gong*) was a piece of copper; a *kymbalon* (*cymbal*) was a single-toned instrument incapable of producing a melody. Both were used in the mystery-religions, either to invoke the god, to drive away demons or to rouse the worshippers. They were neither melodious nor capable of producing harmony. Both beat out a heavy monotone and caused as much offence as constantly barking dogs.

Equally offensive, maintains Paul, are those who use the gift of speaking in tongues without the controlling motive of love. It does not matter whether the tongues are human languages (as they sometimes seem to be) or even 'the language of heaven' (which some people rather tendentiously assume): if there is no love they come across as unattractive and boorish.[5] Some Christians with this particular gift insensitively impose it on others in the congregation; with considerable self-indulgence rather than a deep desire to build up the church, such people override the feelings of those who are either unaccustomed or unsympathetic to this gift.

b. Without love I am nothing (13:2)

If lovelessness actively repels people from the church and the gospel, thus being the biggest single obstacle to effective witness in a community or a nation, it also evacuates Christians of their significance before God. They become nonentities, ciphers. God cannot use loveless Christians for his glory, even if they are gifted with prophetic speaking; even if they are able to understand and explain the deep things of God, man and Satan;[6] even if they are knowledgeable about a vast field of truth and experience; and even if they have the most incisive and bold measure of faith envisaged by Jesus himself – the faith which moves mountains (cf. Matt. 17:20).

It would be tempting to assume that Paul is using rhetorical hyperbole in this passage – that is, that the full impact and value of these important gifts (prophecy, revelation, knowledge) is diminished when love does not

---

[5] It is a moot point whether the gift of tongues can actually be, in any sense, 'the language of heaven'. In Rev. 14:2ff., John gives a description of 'a voice . . . like the sound of harpists playing on their harps' as one of the features of worship on 'Mount Zion'. It seems far-fetched to take such a passage (from such a book) to explain Paul's reference in 13:1 to 'tongues . . . of angels'.

[6] Cf. 1 Cor. 2:7–11; Rev. 2:24.

flow. That is not what Paul writes. If there is no love, he maintains, there is nothing of any real value in my ministry. I may be successful; I may get results; I may be admired, appreciated and applauded – but, as far as God and eternity are concerned, I am nothing. 'The Corinthians clearly thought that the possessors of certain gifts were extremely important persons . . . Not only are they unimportant, they are actually *nothing*.'[7]

c. Without love I gain nothing (13:3)

Paul now mentions two acts of self-sacrifice which most closely approximate to practical love of the purest and most unselfish kind. What if he were 'in one grand sweeping gesture' (Morris) to *give away* everything? What if he were to hand over his *body to be burned* (RSV)?[8] Are not such actions inherently valuable in the sight of God? Do they not achieve something for the kingdom of God? Are they not meritorious? No, he replies, not at all, because such actions can be motivated by self-interest, not by the interests of others. So nothing is gained: the effort, the sacrifice, is wasted.

2. The nature of love (13:4–7)[9]

If love is so fundamental, irreplaceable and determinative for our life together as Christians, we need to know more clearly what it is. The next four verses give a crisp cameo.

It is important that Paul uses *verbs* in describing such love: loving people will behave in a certain way; they will do, and not do, certain things because of the kind of people they are becoming, through the love of God shed abroad in their hearts by the Holy Spirit. These qualities, these actions, are top priorities for every Christian in a local church. If these are absent, the church will languish and fail, if not disintegrate, however active, successful and large it may be.

The verbs Paul uses are all in the present continuous tense, denoting actions and attitudes which have become habitual, ingrained gradually by constant repetition. They sound ordinary, obvious, almost banal;

---

[7] Morris, p. 183.
[8] 'To be burned' is the most likely reading. An alternative would make the sentence read: 'if I hand over my body so that I may boast [i.e. about it]' (see NRSV here). But, as Barrett points out, such an action is obviously lacking in love if it is done to promote one's own glory, and this makes the key phrase 'but do not have love' tautologous. Paul is certainly not tautologous, especially in this chapter.
[9] On the whole of this section, see Bittlenger, *Gifts and Graces*, pp. 82–89.

but they are probably the most difficult habits to cultivate. It is not coincidental that these four verses perfectly describe the character of Jesus himself, and of nobody else. This becomes clear when we substitute 'Jesus' for 'love' in this passage, and then by contrast insert our own name instead.

Several writers[10] have used Karl Barth's headings for this passage; and, because it is very difficult to improve on them, we will also use them.[11] The first two phrases, however, seem to introduce the theme: 'Love has a big heart and practises sheer goodness' renders the Greek accurately. Such love, which is therefore *patient* and *kind*, can face up to the darkness within and around us, in three directions.

a. Love and the darkness in ourselves (13:4b–5a)

By using five negatives, one in front of each verb, Paul emphasizes that an essential part of true Christlike love is to recognize such alien realities for what they are, and to renounce them positively and decisively. Love simply does not do these things: it does not give in to jealousy, showing-off or arrogance; it resists the temptation to react rudely or selfishly. All these attitudes are common to us, but Jesus never indulged himself under pressure or provocation. That is the way of love and it is the way for all followers of Jesus.

In the context of chapters 12–14, Paul is (at least indirectly) referring to jealousy, pride and selfishness in the church community at Corinth. Time and time again the same sins rear their heads: people resent others' success, blessings or gifts; dissatisfied with their own place and opportunities, they compete for more room, honour or recognition. Jesus, by contrast, quietly pursued the work to which he had been called; he rejoiced in the growth and success of others, encouraging them onward with sensitive wisdom, but never putting anyone down or ignoring anyone. He never needed to overplay his ministry or to blow his own trumpet. Exaggerated, let alone sensationalized, descriptions of the way God is using us betray a lack of confidence in our acceptance by God. Love does not boast. Indeed, Jesus never seemed at all interested in gaining recognition, let alone in demanding his rights. He left his reputation and his results completely in the hands of God. He was free not to insist on his

---

[10] E.g. Bittlenger, pp. 82ff.
[11] Cf. K. Barth, *Church Dogmatics* IV, 2, p. 825.

own way, entrusting himself to 'the one who judges justly' (cf. 1 Pet. 2:23), particularly when facing rejection and humiliation.

In a few deft strokes Paul paints a picture of the person who is moved and filled with the love of God. In so doing he also throws into relief the self-centredness of much Corinthian – and modern – church life. Only the love of God, keeping us in a deep experience of his complete acceptance of us as we are, can enable us to face up to our self-centredness, to renounce it and to look for light to shine in our inner darkness. In the love of God there is no place for asserting our rights, despising our gifts, envying our brothers and sisters, or treating them insensitively and boorishly. Such love, in any case, turns us outwards to look to the needs and the interests of others: when we notice that our behaviour or attitudes are damaging or offending another person, love propels us to deal with such inner darkness through the grace of the Lord. There is no local church anywhere which does not need more love for this very basic purpose.

b. Love and the darkness of others (13:5b–6)

Paul mentions three ways in which we can easily allow the weaknesses, sins and failures of others to force us into lovelessness. First, there are some people who simply provoke us, not perhaps deliberately or knowingly, but consistently and uncontrollably. It is tempting to blame such people for their impact upon us, instead of facing honestly the reality of our own touchiness. Jesus once more shows us the way by his patient forbearance towards those twelve disciples, whom he 'loved . . . to the end' (John 13:1). If we truly love people with the love of the Lord, we shall see their strengths and their potential rather than their quirks and their foibles. When they do or say something which angers us, we shall be able to treat that in the context of what they are in Christ, instead of magnifying what has happened so that it consumes our vision.

Second, Paul refers to actual 'evil' in others. Like ourselves, other Christians sin and transgress God's Word. We may well be among those who suffer as a result, either directly or indirectly. It is crucial to recognize the menace of holding on to any such behaviour, of gloating over the failures of another, and particularly of keeping a list of wrongs committed. The word in verse 5, *logizetai* (*resentful*), refers to keeping an account: love forgets as well as forgives and does not keep a record of things said or done against us.

Third, Paul focuses our attention on our attitude to sin and wickedness in general. There is a perverse streak in human nature, played on and pandered to by most communicators, which actually enjoys evil, particularly in others. We can fall into the trap of rejoicing, not in what is good and true, but in the murky and sordid. We find false solace in seeing others fail and fall, presumably because we imagine it gives us more leeway to trifle with sin ourselves. That is the reverse of love, which longs to see others stand and grow, which is saddened and hurt when another is defeated, which rejoices with those who rejoice and weeps with those who weep. A particular danger, selected on several occasions by Paul in the Pastoral Epistles for condemnation, is gossiping. Love does not gossip, particularly not under the cloak of sharing a need for prayer. Love 'covers a multitude of sins' (1 Pet. 4:8).

c. Love and apparent darkness in God (13:7)

The fourfold *all things* of this verse makes it plain that love is no human quality, but the gift of God himself. In the varied circumstances and relationships of our daily lives it is only his love in Jesus which can enable us to bear, to believe, to hope and to endure.

Frequently the Christian is asked by God to shoulder burdens (often the burdens of others and on every occasion burdens which God himself already bears) which wear us down and evoke the question: 'Why, Lord?' 'Love sacrifices the right to rebel against God',[12] however much we pour out our hearts before him. Especially when there is little to encourage faith, love strengthens us to trust in the dark, to penetrate through to the other side despite the mountains of doubt, knowing that our Father God is in control and will ultimately demonstrate his victory. More than that, love enables us to exercise a strong assurance that, however black it seems, God has not lost his way and has for us 'a future with hope' (Jer. 29:11).

Whatever happens, we hang on because it all has a purpose. God is chiselling out in us the image of his Son, Jesus. Oswald Chambers has written: 'God's batterings always come in commonplace ways and through commonplace people.'[13] Only love for God, released by his love for us, can keep such faith and hope alive and in control of our daily lives. When we

---

12 Bittlenger, p. 88.
13 Oswald Chambers, *My Utmost for His Highest* (Marshall, Morgan and Scott, 1963), p. 278.

realize afresh that Jesus loves us in this way – he bears everything we throw at him, he still believes in us and is quietly confident for us, he has endured even the cross for us – then we take heart again and know that only his love can sustain us and make us the people, the local churches, he wants us to become.

3. The endlessness of love (13:8–13)

If any vestige remains in our minds to suggest that such love can be reproduced by human beings on their own, the first words of verse 8 finally dispel it: *Love never ends*. The Greek word *piptei* literally means 'falls' or 'collapses'. This love never folds under pressure of the most intense and sustained kind. This love continues through death into eternity. This is the love of God. In order to underline the priority of love for all Christians in Corinth – and elsewhere – Paul then mentions the three gifts at the top of their list of priorities: tongues, prophecy and knowledge. Each of these will either become irrelevant or else be swallowed up in the perfection of eternity: for *when the complete comes, the partial will come to an end* (10).

Paul illustrates this general truth in two ways: first, he refers to growth from childhood into mature adulthood; second, he contrasts looking at someone reflected in a mirror with seeing the person face to face. The very best mirror, which in those days was made of metal and inevitably gave only a blurred and imperfect picture, is as nothing compared with this full encounter. We are told by John that, when we see Jesus face to face, 'we will be like him, for we will see him as he is' (cf. 1 John 3:1ff.). So full knowledge of ourselves will come only when we see Jesus and know him as fully and as perfectly as he now knows us (12).

So long as we have not seen Jesus as he is, we are still short of maturity, of adulthood as Christians. By his grace we have been given many gifts through which we may see more of his glory and will, even in the limitations of this mortal life. These gifts, all of them, are media of revelation into the nature and purposes of God. Every gift is valuable for our growth into maturity, but the heartbeat of our relationship with God now is that he knows us, not vice versa (12).[14] One day we shall also know him.

---

[14] See Paul's own self-adjustment in describing this truth in Gal. 4:9.

If the Corinthians majored on tongues, prophecy and knowledge, Paul focuses attention on faith, hope and love. These three qualities are the ones which *abide.*

1 Corinthians 14:1–40

14. Prophecy and tongues

1. What are they?

Having established the love of God as the unique priority in a local church, especially one so divided and immature as at Corinth, Paul returns to the question of spirituality, and specifically to two gifts: speaking in tongues and prophecy. He urges the Corinthian Christians to pursue love and, in that atmosphere, earnestly to desire 'spiritual gifts'. In 14:1, he actually uses a different phrase (the more general one used in 12:1, meaning 'spirituality') from the one used in 12:31, where he has described the Corinthians as competing for so-called 'greater gifts'. In their league table, speaking in tongues was way out on top. Paul encourages them all to 'prophesy' (1 and 5, 31 and 39).

At the outset we must stress that, as with the ministry of the first apostles, so with the prophets who with them became the foundation of the church, their authority is unique and unrepeatable. Whatever Paul means in encouraging the gift of prophecy, he does not suggest that any Christian can be on a par with those original prophets as organs of divine revelation. Any subsequent manifestation of this gift must be submitted to the authoritative teaching of the original apostles and prophets,[1] as contained in the canon of Scripture.

Is there, then, a subsidiary prophetic gift and ministry today? If so, what is it? It has often been equated with preaching, or with the kind of preaching which teaches biblical truth, notably expository preaching.

---

[1] Cf. Eph. 2:20; 3:5.

> The gift of prophesying . . . is basically the explanation of the present in the light of the revelation of God. The closest term we would call it by today is 'expository preaching', unfolding the mind of God and applying it to the daily struggles of life.[2]

As we shall see, expository preaching may well contain particular words of prophecy, but this equation cannot be sustained biblically. The New Testament draws clear distinctions between preaching, teaching and prophecy.

An important principle to follow is sketched by Paul himself, when he *both* stresses the special value of prophecy *and* wants every Christian at Corinth to use it. In other words, we must look for (and expect to find) an understanding of the New Testament gift of prophecy which is neither banal nor esoteric. It is presumably a gift which at the same time uniquely strengthens the church and is accessible to any member. We must not trivialize it in our attempts to understand it, nor must we make it so specialized that it lies beyond the reach of most Christians. To equate it with expository preaching is to fall into the latter danger. A church in which everybody is an expository preacher (or any kind of preacher, for that matter) would be a nightmare, and is manifestly not what Paul wants for the Corinthians. Equally, it is very easy to empty the gift of prophecy of its unique, immediate and distinctive content. It then becomes nothing more than sanctified common sense. The evidence of the Scriptures and of church history (early and current) makes such a conclusion invalid.

At this point it is, perhaps, helpful to take Michael Green's summary as a working definition of prophecy: 'a word from the Lord through a member of his body, inspired by his Spirit and given to build up the rest of the body'.[3] Such a ministry is available to every Christian, as the Holy Spirit 'allots to each one individually just as the Spirit chooses' (12:11). This gift is, therefore, for all Christians earnestly to desire, whether or not the Lord chooses to distribute it to all. If we take into account the rhetorical questions of the end of 1 Corinthians 12, we conclude that all Christians can be used in the gift of prophecy, but that only a few will be used with sufficient regularity for them to be recognized as gifts from God to the church as prophets; in other words, the gift of prophecy is to be

---

[2] R. Stedman.
[3] Michael Green, *To Corinth with Love* (Hodder, 1982), p. 74.

distinguished from the office and ministry of a prophet. Even then, such prophets are not on a par with the original prophets (either in the Old Testament or in the New Testament) and must come thoroughly under the authority of the Scriptures both in their conduct and in the content of their utterances.

There are, of course, many questions we might still ask in this matter. But it may prove more constructive to look at a passage from one of the mighty prophets of the Old Testament as a way in to the nature, content and impact of the gift of prophecy. In Isaiah 50:4–6 we read:

> The Lord GOD has given me
>> the tongue of a teacher,
> that I may know how to sustain
>> the weary with a word.
> Morning by morning he wakens –
>> wakens my ear
>> to listen as those who are taught.
> The Lord GOD has opened my ear,
>> and I was not rebellious,
>> I did not turn backwards.
> I gave my back to those who struck me,
>> and my cheeks to those who pulled out the beard;
> I did not hide my face
>> from insult and spitting.

Although it would be wrong to suggest that any Christian with a prophetic ministry today has the same authority as the man who spoke these words, this passage is important for several reasons. First, it clearly has a messianic thrust, and Jesus is seen throughout the New Testament revelation as the Prophet par excellence, fulfilling Moses' promise that such a person would arise (cf. Deut. 18:15). The Gospels see Jesus fulfilling this role.[4] Testimony to Jesus is 'the spirit of prophecy' (Rev. 19:10) – a testimony which is prospective in the Old Testament and retrospective in the New.

Second, the way of life through which God inspires a person with the gift of prophecy is clearly delineated in the passage from Isaiah. The daily discipline of spending time with God, in order to listen to him and to hear

---

[4] Cf. Matt. 16:14; Mark 6:4; Luke 7:16; 9:7–8; 13:33; 24:19; John 4:19.

his word, is fundamental to any authentic prophetic gift. Because every Christian is duty bound to discover and pursue that discipline which most effectively maintains personal contact with the Lord, therefore the fruits of such a devotional life (in terms of receiving a word from God for others) are available to every Christian.

Third, the emphasis in Isaiah 50 is on the strength and support which such a ministry will bring to 'the weary' – a perspective which Paul himself underlines in this chapter (14:3).

Fourth, the latter part of the passage stresses the need for both an open heart and a thick skin: open to God and impervious to opposition. It is clear from all sides that those who genuinely receive a prophetic gift need great courage and resilience in bringing it faithfully to the church. There may be hostility, even rejection.

This passage from Isaiah encourages us, therefore, to expect special insight to be given by God to any sensitive and obedient believer: insight into God's will for a specific situation, or into the application of God's Word to the times in which we live. Such prophetic insight does not have the inherent and permanent authority of those prophets who, with the apostles of Christ, provided the foundation of the church (cf. Eph. 2:20). But continuing prophetic ministry is essential today if the church is not going to settle down into a comfortable conformity to contemporary culture.

When the Spirit fell on the seventy elders outside the tent of meeting in the wilderness, Joshua was less than enthusiastic. But Moses replied with words fulfilled at the day of Pentecost: 'Would that all the LORD's people were prophets, and that the LORD would put his spirit on them!' (Num. 11:25–29).

Similarly, when Peter explained the Pentecostal phenomenon to the astonished crowds, he explained that the gift of the Spirit was in fulfilment of the prophet Joel's words:

> In the last days it will be, God declares,
>   that I will pour out my Spirit upon all flesh,
>   and your sons and your daughters shall prophesy . . .
> Even upon my slaves, both men and women,
>   in those days I will pour out my Spirit;
>   and they shall prophesy.[5]

---

[5] Acts 2:16–18; cf. Joel 2:28–29.

The second reference in Acts 2 to 'they shall prophesy' is not actually in the Joel passage, an addition which probably reflects the early Christian church's expectations for and emphasis on this manifestation of the Spirit.

It is important also to try to understand what Paul means by the gifts of speaking in tongues and interpretation of tongues. If we take the text of 1 Corinthians 14 at face value, speaking in tongues bypasses the mind (14), is addressed to God himself and not to other human beings (2), and is acknowledged to be for the individual's own edification (4), as well as being unintelligible because 'they are speaking mysteries in the Spirit' (2).

The Greek word *glōssa* (apart from referring to the tongue as the organ of speech) could be rendered either 'tongue' or 'language'. The New International Version uses the first translation in its text, and the second in the margin. This approach reflects two different understandings of the gift. The rendering 'language' is favoured by those who see Luke's description of the Pentecost event as determinative for 1 Corinthians 12 and 14, as well as for the other relevant passages in Acts (10:46 and 19:6) and in Mark (16:17).[6] Acts 2 is the only passage where the gift is explained, namely, as a miraculous power to speak intelligible, foreign languages. On that basis, it is argued, we must assume that Paul uses *glōssa* in the same way and is referring to the same phenomenon.

Those who think that the gift is the ability to speak a foreign language differ in their understanding of its nature: some think it is a miraculous power to speak in this way; others that it is nothing more unusual than being competent to speak in one or more languages other than that of one's birth or that of those listening.

As an exegetical principle, interpreting one scriptural passage by another is sound. There is, however, a problem in this case, because the context and the content of 1 Corinthians 14 are different from Acts 2.[7] Paul's situation at Corinth is the fellowship life of the local church at worship; the Pentecost experiences took place in the presence of large crowds of outsiders. All use of *glōssai* in the church at Corinth required interpretation; at Pentecost some hearers understood directly what was being said, because 'each one heard them speaking in the native language of each' (Acts 2:6). Paul himself thanks God (18) that he speaks in *glōssai*

---

[6] E.g. Hodge, pp. 248–250.
[7] Morris writes: 'Some commentators think that it is this gift of speaking in other languages which is meant here. This is an attractive solution, but nobody reading 1 Corinthians would think that this is what Paul had in mind' (p. 172).

more than all the Corinthians. It seems difficult to believe that he is here making what amounts to a 'quantity judgment' about his facility as a linguist over against every Corinthian Christian, whether through miraculous enabling or by his experience and education. The Greek of verse 18 actually precludes such an interpretation; if Paul had meant that he spoke in more languages than any Corinthian Christian, he would have used a comparative adjective (i.e. 'in more *glōssai*'). He actually uses an adverb, which stresses the phenomenon itself, not the number of languages.

It remains impossible to be certain whether the gift of *glōssai* at Pentecost and the gift described by Paul in 1 Corinthians are identical, similar but distinctive, or completely different. In 12:28 Paul refers to 'various kinds [Greek *genos*, from which we get 'generic'] of tongues'. This may leave room for many different forms and types. It is also unclear whether the content of such *glōssai* is *invariably* a distinguishable language. There have been several recorded instances of tongues being recognized in unusual circumstances as a specific language,[8] but Paul himself seems to allow the possibility of wide variation in his reference (13:1) to 'the *glōssai* of mortals and of angels', although in 14:10–11 he seems to assume that human languages can be involved. What is clear is that speaking in *glōssai* is a gift of God's Spirit, is therefore to be prized and used, and is valuable enough for Paul apparently to want all the Christians at Corinth to enjoy it for their own personal benefit.[9] When any individual Christian is built up, the whole fellowship is inevitably, if indirectly, strengthened.

Some commentators find the tone of Paul's remarks in this chapter to be rather sceptical towards any notion of *self*-edification. How, it is asked, can a spiritual gift (as Paul describes and applies them in chapters 12 and 14) be turned towards oneself? Paul does, however, say explicitly that 'Those who speak in a tongue build up themselves' (14:4): what he deprecates is any self-indulgent use of this gift in public worship, rather than a disciplined use in love, which (when accompanied by the gift of interpretation) serves to edify the church.

---

[8] E.g. John Sherrill, *They Speak with Other Tongues* (Hodder, 1967), especially pp. 108–111.

[9] The edifying benefits of such personal speaking in tongues include a particular sense of God's presence, relaxation from tension, strength to cope with pain, power in prayer to resist demonic onslaught, freedom in intercession when verbal prayer is inadequate or impossible, and freedom to worship God when 'lost in wonder, love, and praise'.

The relative unimportance of determining precisely the content of *glōssai* can be appreciated when we examine more thoroughly the gift of interpretation of *glōssai*. Invariably this is taken to mean 'translation'.

The Greek word rendered *'interpretation'* (*hermēneia*) does not necessarily or exclusively carry that meaning: for example, on the Emmaus road Jesus 'interpreted to them the things about himself in all the scriptures' (Luke 24:27). In classical Greek there were three nuances in the verb: to explain or interpret; to articulate or express clearly; and to translate. Colin Brown has written:

> It would seem that Paul is not thinking of interpretation in the sense of translating one language into another, which would presume that tongues had a coherent scheme of grammar, syntax and vocabulary. Rather, interpretation here seems to be more akin to discerning what the Spirit is saying through the one who is speaking in tongues.[10]

In addition to the linguistic perspective just given, the substance of most modern interpretations of a *glōssa* is a message *from* God *to* the people gathered, not vice versa. Now Paul is clear that speaking in *glōssai* is directed by the Spirit *from* the individual believer *to* the Lord (14:2). The interpretation is not, on this basis, a translation of that. Rather, it is the response of God the Father through the Spirit to the prayer (also through the Spirit) of his child.[11]

If this is correct, we are experiencing at such a time the Spirit's interpretation of the mind and heart of God back to his people in response to their turning to him. Individual members of the body are used as channels for this intimate communication between the Father and his children, one through the gift of speaking in tongues, another through the gift of interpretation. Apart from the pointlessness of public speaking in *glōssai* on its own because it is unintelligible, this perspective on the gift of interpretation adds further point to the edification factor so uppermost in Paul's thinking in this chapter. There is, prima facie, not as much edification in listening to a translation of another Christian's prayer in a *glōssa* as in

---

[10] In *Dictionary of New Testament Theology*, Vol. 3 (Zondervan, 1982), p. 1080. Cf. D. B. Burke in the *International Standard Bible Encyclopaedia*, Vol. 2 (Eerdmans, 1982): 'This sort of interpretation is clearly not to be understood in the sense of "translation" . . . The gift of interpretation is that of rendering intelligible the preconceptual spiritual ecstasy of the tongues-speaker.'

[11] This two-way relationship between the Father and his children in prayer through the inspiration of the Holy Spirit is described evocatively in Rom. 8:26–27.

receiving a direct communication in response from the heart and mind of God.

This perspective, incidentally, has two other merits. First, it explains why the interpretation of a *glōssa* invariably turns out to be much longer or shorter than the original spoken *glōssa*. If the interpretation is not a translation, this objection is removed – and it needs to be, because one often hears fairly sceptical and dismissive remarks about the whole phenomenon on such grounds. Second, we can see why Paul treats the gift of prophecy and the combined gift of speaking-plus-interpretation of *glōssai* as equivalent (14:5) – both are vehicles for God to communicate his mind to his people.

As with all spiritual phenomena in the Corinthian context, we must beware any gullible acceptance of any apparent speaking-in-tongues as God-given. Such a phenomenon was common in the Greek mystery-religions, is often found today in different cultures and cults of a pagan character, and must always be evaluated by the criteria which Paul has adduced in chapters 12–14. Some commentators go so far as to say that modern 'glossolalia' has nothing to do with what Paul is talking about in chapters 12 and 14, attributing current phenomena to purely psychological causes or even to satanic counterfeiting of the true biblical gift.

The rest of our exposition of this chapter is based on the understanding that this gift is available to us today and is being experienced constructively as such in many churches in different countries. For this reason the rendering of *glōssai* as 'tongues' will be followed. Hodge provides a thorough exposition of the chapter based on the rendering 'languages' on the analogy of the Acts 2 narrative.

The major concern on Paul's heart throughout this chapter is the 'edification' (or 'building up') of the church at Corinth: the word comes seven times (3, 4 [twice], 5, 12, 17, 26). Earlier, he has urged upon the Corinthians the use of the right materials in building properly on 'the church's one foundation . . . Jesus Christ her Lord' (cf. 3:10–16). He has also stressed the irreplaceable power of love as uniquely conducive to such edification, rather than the knowledge on which the Corinthians laid so much emphasis (8:1). Now he is determined that their corporate worship should strengthen, not split or shake, the building. The worship of a local church has an indispensable role in building up the faith and the discipleship of its members. When it is vital, participatory, expectant and attractive (the root meaning of the word translated 'decently' in verse 40), the whole congregation grows strong and steady in the Lord. As we look at some of Paul's teaching in this chapter, we will do well to ask ourselves whether the corporate worship of our own churches contains the ingredients Paul discusses here.

In verses 1–25, Paul compares and contrasts tongues and prophecy in terms of building up the church. In verses 26–36, he establishes a few guidelines for their proper use in the church. In verses 37–40, he concludes the matter with a few pithy instructions. At no stage does he decry, let alone dismiss, the gift of tongues. He is redressing an imbalance in Corinthian spirituality and correcting a confusion in Corinthian worship. He wants tongues to find their proper place in the life of the church – neither reckoned to be the most important gift of all, nor used in public worship without interpretation. He accepts readily the importance of tongues for the personal edification of believers; but he looks to the gifts of prophecy (5) and teaching (19) to build up the church as a whole, along with any other contribution brought by any member of the body 'when you come together' (26). It will be valuable to identify some of the principles which Paul elucidates as we go through the chapter.

2. The effect of prophecy (14:1–5)

Within the broad understanding of prophecy sketched earlier, we have here three helpful words (3) about the results which this gift will bring in the local church when it is properly used: *building up and encouragement and consolation*. Given Paul's concern for the church to be *built up* in the Lord, it is not surprising that he mentions this function first: any purported word of prophecy which undermines or shakes the faith of others is to be rejected. This is a major reason why prophecy must always be received in the fellowship of God's people, not in private conversation. There is a large amount of alleged prophecy which is nothing more than another, rather spiritualized way of one person manipulating or exercising influence over another. Such tendencies can be checked only as the gift of prophecy is encouraged in the gathered life of God's people. The gift is, in any case, intended for the edification of the whole church, not so much of an individual Christian. What is called by many today 'personal prophecy' is highly suspect on these – and other – grounds.

The second word is *encouragement* (*paraklēsis*), the same root as the word used in John (John 14:16 etc.) to describe the Holy Spirit as Paraclete,

Advocate, Counsellor. It literally means 'to be called in alongside' to assist and support. The ministry of prophecy has this function, as the Holy Spirit inspires a Christian to speak words which give strength to the life and witness of the local church, perhaps particularly to its witness, because the delight of the Spirit is to enable the church to bear consistent and convincing witness to Jesus as Lord.

Paul's third word to describe how a true word of prophecy will help the church is *consolation* (*paramythia*). This has the sense of whispering in the church's ear,[12] probably in the sense of allaying fear and enabling God's people to be calm under pressure.

> Consolation . . . calms the storms of fear, anxiety and despair. It helps us rest in the presence of Jesus . . . It leads us away from the hectic bustle of daily affairs, away from the restlessness of this life, into the great peace of God.[13]

The regular motif both of the Old Testament prophets and of Jesus, the great prophet, is 'do not fear'.

If this is something of the impact prophecy can have on the church, it is no wonder that Paul wants every Christian to desire such a gift.

3. The incompleteness of tongues (14:6–25)

Paul has indicated (5) that, within the sovereign economy of the Lord who distributes gifts as *he* chooses, he (Paul) would like every Christian at Corinth to speak in tongues (for personal edification) and to prophesy (for the edification of the church). At this stage, at any rate, he is far more concerned for the corporate than for the individual, and so he proceeds to underline the limitations of speaking in tongues as far as the building-up of the church is concerned. Paul spells out three major limitations in speaking in tongues: in intelligibility, personal wholeness and impact on outsiders.

a. Limitations in intelligibility (14:6–11, 16–17, 23)

Quite simply, anyone within earshot finds speaking in tongues to be gibberish. Indeed, there is no intelligible content to the speaker. In

---

[12] See Green, *To Corinth with Love*, p. 76.
[13] Bittlenger, *Gifts and Graces*, p. 106.

verse 11, Paul talks of the reaction of those present as being like the relationship between Greeks and barbarians (*foreigner*; 'barbarous'). Greeks were very proud of the beauty of their language and regarded every other language as boorish and grating. To them these languages sounded like a heavy 'bar-bar-bar' noise: hence the word 'barbarian'.

Speaking in tongues may often have a pleasant ring to it, although the phenomenon per se does not always sound attractive. Where the life of a local church is concerned, Paul's central criterion is: can it be understood by fellow believers, by 'fringe' people and by outsiders? If it is unintelligible, it should be restrained. The ministry of the Spirit brings harmony (7) and equips God's people for spiritual battle (8). Both matters cannot be 'fudged', and therefore it is crucial to channel enthusiasm for spiritual gifts in constructive directions: let the innate zeal of the Corinthian Christians be harnessed into *building up the church* (12).

The positive way forward for the person who speaks in tongues, and wants that gift to be used to build up the church, is to 'pray for the power to interpret' (13).[14] Paul seems to have no compunctions about the same person being gifted by the Spirit, first to speak in a tongue, and immediately to bring an interpretation of God's response. When it happens in a gathering of local Christians, we can instinctively feel uneasy, as if some hoodwinking or artificiality is being foisted upon us. Paul's position is a healthy corrective to such scepticism.

At the same time, Paul insists on the need to avoid the situation where anyone in range of the church at worship feels left out or lost. He seems to include both those uninitiated into the ins and outs of tongues (16) and those being instructed in or enquiring about Christian commitment (23). For this reason Paul has made it his firm resolve to expect the Spirit to use him in ministry to the church along lines which contain something more solid and easy to grasp, whether by *some revelation or knowledge or prophecy or teaching* (6). In one of these ways he will genuinely *benefit* the church, however much (i.e. in private prayers) he speaks in tongues (18).

b. Limitations in personal wholeness (14:13–17, 19–20)

Paul has stressed the personal benefits accruing to the Christian who speaks in tongues in his or her individual prayer life (4). It has been

---

[14] Morris makes the valuable point that verse 13 shows that 'there was nothing static about possession of the gifts. A man who had the gift of "tongues" need not take that as his end state. He might later receive other gifts . . . He should pray to this end' (p. 194).

suggested that these benefits have to do with 'the constructive building-up of the personality'.[15] Morton Kelsey, who, as a theologian and psychotherapist, has written extensively on the subject, says: 'There are people who without this experience would never have been able to come to psychological maturity. The experience of speaking in tongues opened them up to the unconscious and to a fuller, though more difficult, life.' Kelsey quotes a linguist with psychological training who writes: 'Speaking with tongues is one evidence of the Spirit of God working in the unconscious and bringing one to a new wholeness, a new integration of the total psyche, a process which the church has traditionally called sanctification.'[16]

In the distinctly emotional and enthusiastic atmosphere of the church at Corinth, with strong influences still hanging over from unregenerate experiences in the mystery-religions, the theme of wholeness needed to be tackled from a different angle. The Corinthian tendency was not to be over-cerebral, but to devalue the importance of the mind. Paul is concerned, therefore, to stress manifestations of the Spirit which do not bypass the mind. Speaking in tongues has real benefit for the individual, but his or her *mind is unproductive* (14). Paul wants the Christians at Corinth to be *adults* in their *thinking* (20): that requires exercising their minds through the Spirit to the full extent of their abilities. He mentions five areas of Christian living where this needs to be done: in prayer (15), in singing (15), in thanksgiving (16–17), in catechesis (or 'instruction', 19) and in thinking (20).

Christians who do not allow the Spirit to stretch and renew their minds in these five ways are resisting the work of God in sanctification, in wholeness. There were many believers at Corinth whose experience of the Spirit was confined to manifestations which bypassed the mind entirely. Paul expresses his own firm resolve to pray, sing and give thanks *with the spirit* and *with the mind also* (15).[17] He is so concerned to build up the church that he would far rather use a few intelligible, wise words to instruct Christians in the faith than *ten thousand words in a tongue* (19).

On the other hand, the imbalances of the Christians at Corinth led Paul to stress a proper balance between the rational and the non-rational, not

---

[15] Bittlenger, p. 99.

[16] Morton T. Kelsey, *Speaking with Tongues* (Hodder, 1965), p. 222.

[17] The use of the phrase 'my spirit' in verse 14 shows that Paul is not contrasting the use of his mind with the inspiration of the Holy Spirit in verses 14–16. The word 'spirit' should have a small 's' in each case.

to place one over against the other. The plea for maturity in verse 20 seems to hark back to the strong remarks about immaturity at Corinth made towards the beginning of the letter (cf. 3:1–4).

c. Limitations in impact on outsiders (14:16–17, 21–25)

Paul has one eye all the time on the way Christian worship affects *anyone in the position of an outsider* (16). He obviously expects, not merely that such people will normally be present on such an occasion, but that they will come under conviction by the Spirit's manifest presence in the midst. Both expectations constitute a challenge to our church life today. Are outsiders present? Do they meet the Lord?

The precise identity of these outsiders is difficult to discover. Two Greek words are used: *idiōtēs* and *apistos* (23). The first word (from which we get the word 'idiot') refers to someone who is not part of the group under consideration: for example, it is used of 'laymen over against priests, private citizens over against those in public life . . . "privates" over against officers'.[18] Some commentators believe that Paul is using the word to describe those not accustomed to the phenomenon of speaking in tongues, either in pagan cults or in the Christian church. The most likely explanation of *idiōtēs* is the one given by Morris. Paul uses a rather cumbersome phrase in verse 16, 'one who fills the place of the *idiōtēs*',

> which indicates that [these people] had their place in the Christian
> assembly. They would be 'inquirers', people who had not committed
> themselves to Christianity, but who were interested. They had ceased
> to be simply outsiders, but were not yet Christians.[19]

Any church with an evangelistic cutting-edge into the local community has people of this kind in its gatherings for worship. They are not yet believers; indeed, they are still 'unbelievers'. But they are on the verge of commitment. Nothing should be done, especially in a spirit of self-indulgence by a few enthusiastic Christians, to drive them back into an unbelief from which it will then be far more difficult to extricate them.

This sheds light on the apparent contradictions in verses 21–25, where Paul seems unable to decide whether speaking in tongues is intended for

---

[18] Morris, p. 195.
[19] Ibid., pp. 195f.

believers or unbelievers. Everything he has written so far has stressed that tongues are not simply for Christians, but for Christians in their private devotions – not to be used in public worship except with interpretation. In verse 22, he declares that *Tongues . . . are a sign, not for believers but for unbelievers.* The text (21) from Isaiah 28:11–12 (and even more the wider context in Isaiah 28 as a whole) indicates what kind of 'sign' Paul has in mind. Both there and in verse 23, he is showing that the impact on those without a living faith in God of speaking in unintelligible tongues is to confirm them in their unbelief. The very fact of unintelligibility feeds their unregenerate minds and stubborn wills; they conclude that Christians are *out of [their] mind* and have nothing new or true to offer.

The Greek words translated *you are out of your mind* (23) do not mean fit for the asylum, but under the influence of some spiritual force on a par with those active in the mystery-cults. In the Corinthian context, Paul means that the net result of believers all speaking in tongues in a time of worship is that the very people they are keen to win will become convinced that Christianity is like any other mystery-religion, into which they have to be properly initiated if they want to belong. They have not been initiated into the secret vocabulary and practices; therefore they leave. We find ourselves wondering how many modern inquirers find similar habits equally off-putting in our own churches.

This tragedy is all the more poignant when the positive alternative is studied. Paul describes what can and does happen when believers are sensitive to God's Spirit, to one another, to apostolic teaching, to interested observers and even to total unbelievers. The gift of prophecy, which is an unmistakable sign to all believers (22) of the Lord's personal commitment to his church, makes plain to everybody present that the Lord is in the midst of his people. The inevitable impact, on outsiders and unbelievers, of the reality of God's presence is that their consciences are stabbed awake (cf. John 16:7–11) and their true spiritual state is laid bare:

> the word of God is living and active, sharper than any two-edged sword, piercing until it divides soul from spirit, joints from marrow; it is able to judge the thoughts and intentions of the heart. And before him no creature is hidden, but all are naked and laid bare to the eyes of the one to whom we must render an account.
> (Heb. 4:12–13)

As God speaks with the immediacy of prophetic words, 'all are naked and laid bare' – believers, outsiders, unbelievers. That is why Paul looks to everyone to be used as a vehicle for God to speak in prophecy.

The quotation in verse 25 from Zechariah, 'Let us go with you, for we have heard that God is with you' (Zech. 8:23), emphasizes Paul's conviction that the gift of prophecy is one of the chief hallmarks of the new covenant, because the relevant passage in Zechariah looks forward to the time when 'ten men from nations of every language shall take hold of a Jew, grasping his garment and saying, "Let us go with you, for we have heard that God is with you."' In cosmopolitan Corinth, Jews and varied Gentiles had formed a new assembly of God's people, made possible by the death and resurrection of Jesus the Messiah. When the gift of prophecy was in full flow in such an assembly, the Zechariah vision became reality.

4. The need for congregational control (14:26–36)

Paul has just referred to occasions when 'the whole church comes together' (23). He now deals with what happens on such occasions – or what should happen, because at Corinth there was clearly a tendency towards disorder, if not chaos. Though different from the disorder he has had to rebuke in chapter 11, it is of a similar kind: individuals going ahead with their own personal preferences, instead of thinking of the needs and sensitivities of others.

When, incidentally, he writes of 'the whole church' (23) coming together, he is probably thinking of the different home churches at Corinth meeting together in the large house of one of the few wealthy Christians in the city. Such occasions, which would have been not nearly as frequent as the regular home-church gatherings, were the context in which Paul expected interested inquirers and other 'outsiders' to be present. In verse 26, on the other hand, he is probably thinking more of the regular gatherings of believers in different homes throughout the city – what elsewhere he calls 'the church in the house' of (for example) Aquila and Prisca (16:19). He envisages every member of the church bringing a distinctive contribution to its worshipping life: *a hymn, a lesson, a revelation, a tongue, or an interpretation* (26). The controlling factor is not personal enjoyment but general edification. Whether in the larger context of the city-wide church or in the microcosm of the home church, Paul sees the need for control.

a. Control of those with the gift of tongues (14:27–28)

Having made it clear that in the gathered church speaking in tongues must always be accompanied by interpretation, Paul now limits the number of such tongues-plus-interpretation in any one meeting: *let there be only two or at most three.* No doubt that would have sounded like heavy discipline for the Corinthian enthusiasts. Otherwise other important ministry will be squeezed out, and undue emphasis will once again fall on one particular gift – and inevitably on those who have it.

In addition, Paul limits the use of tongues by prohibiting any use of the gift if there is no interpretation forthcoming. In practice this means that, if the first tongue to be brought is not interpreted, others with the gift are to *be silent.* Silence means no noise, and distractingly speaking aloud in tongues to oneself is not obeying the apostolic injunctions in this chapter (cf. 37). Paul clearly knows (from his own experience?) that the one who speaks in tongues is well able to speak to him or herself and to God in silence, so as not to offend or divert the others. If there is no interpretation, we can safely assume that God intends to minister to the body in some other way.

A fundamental truth is implicit in Paul's teaching here. Speaking in tongues (and, indeed, prophecy – 30) is not an uncontrollable phenomenon. The person with the gift can choose either to use it or not to use it; can choose to use it in private or in public; can choose to keep it private and silent even in public. For this reason it is very misleading to use such language as 'ecstasy' (as in the NEB) to describe any of the Spirit's gifts, but particularly speaking in tongues. Such terminology reintroduces pagan concepts and experiences into the arena of God's operations. His Spirit does not override the wills and minds of human beings. On the contrary, in his love he wins our willing cooperation, and he never forces us to do anything. In all examination of spiritual gifts it is essential to assert this principle of personal self-control. Those presiding over the church's worship need to underline the principle consistently.

b. Control of those with the gift of prophecy (14:29–33a)

Paul lays down the same limitations for the use of prophecy in any one gathering of the church, presumably for much the same reasons. He reiterates that everyone should expect to be used in this ministry (31), which leads to the whole body being taught and encouraged. This principle hints at another perspective: any member of the body can be used at any meeting to bring any gift. We often allow ourselves to limit the Spirit by expecting certain gifts to come only through certain people, who have been used in that way before.

As far as any prophecy is concerned, it needs always to be weighed, tested, evaluated. When prophecy is rare, we tend to omit this control, and we often pay the penalty in lives being manipulated. In 1 Thessalonians 5:21 and 1 John 4:1ff. this weighing is seen to be the responsibility of the whole church. It is tempting to leave it to the leadership. It is also tempting for other prophets to assume the right to weigh such prophecies. Some of the criteria for such testing are: Does it glorify God? Is it in accord with Scripture? Does it build up the church? Is it spoken in love? Does the speaker submit to judgment by others? Is the speaker in control of him- or herself? Does the speaker go on too long? Is the speaker demonstrating the fruit of the Spirit in his or her life?[20]

Again Paul reinforces the fact of self-control (30, 32) in all genuine manifestations of the Spirit. 'A prophet cannot plead, as some in Corinth may have done, that he must continue speaking because the Spirit compels him to do so; if there is a reason for him to be silent, he can be silent.'[21] The apostle then roots this statement in the very character of God himself: *God is a God not of disorder but of peace* (33). When the Spirit is truly in control, he brings peace, not confusion. This is the strongest incentive for pressing on as a congregation to discover and use all the gifts of the Spirit.

c. Control of married women in the congregation (14:33b–36)

Whatever this section is teaching, it is not telling women to keep quiet in church. In 11:5, Paul has already referred to women praying and prophesying. The reference to *their husbands at home* (35) immediately indicates that the apostle is thinking about the behaviour of some married women at Corinth, behaviour which needed firm control of the kind which had clearly proved necessary *in all the churches of the saints* (33b). Although we cannot uncover the details of what was going on, we can discern some of the attitudes prevalent at Corinth. It seems that the principle of submissiveness was being ignored (they *should be subordinate*, 34), that a spirit of defiance was uppermost (*it is shameful* . . . , 35), and that an

---

[20] For an expansion of these criteria, see Green, *To Corinth with Love*, pp. 77–78.
[21] Barrett, p. 329.

isolationist tendency was turning these wives into arbitrators of their own church order and even doctrine (*did the word of God originate with you?*, 36). In other words, these married women were the source of some of the arrogance in the Corinthian church which Paul has already had cause to castigate.[22]

Some commentators think that Paul is checking these women's garrulousness in church gatherings. Something fascinating might have been taught or communicated, and they began to chatter about it as the worship continued. The Greek word translated *speak* (*lalein*) can carry the connotation of chattering, but Paul does not use it this way on other occasions. Barrett's comments are apt: 'it is not impossible that Paul should now use it in a new sense, but it is unlikely'.[23] Whatever the detailed explanation, this paragraph looks like a fairly localized example of what could well have been a general tendency among Christian wives in the early church. They had discovered a unique freedom in the life of the Christian community, and it is possible that this freedom had gone to their heads, or, more precisely, to their tongues. This lack of self-discipline was causing confusion and disorder in the worship of the church. Because Paul is so insistent on the priority of edification, he writes with some firmness – and not a little sarcasm – about the need for control.

5. Conclusion (14:37–40)

Paul ends the general discussion on spirituality (chapters 12–14) and the specific teaching on prophecy (chapter 14) with a strongly worded statement about his authority as an apostle: *what I am writing to you is a command of the Lord*. Obviously there were many Christians at Corinth laying claim to being really spiritual: Paul's response to such claims points out that true spirituality is not arrogant and self-assertive, but accepts the authority of those set over them in the Lord. To those Corinthians who prided themselves on being prophets – an attitude which often seems to characterize those used in the prophetic ministry – Paul also emphasizes the call to recognize the authority behind his remarks. Any tendency to think that we are right, while the rest of the church universal is wrong, is both arrogant and dangerous.

---

[22] 1 Cor. 4:7ff.; 5:2ff.; 6:1ff.; 8:1; 13:5.
[23] Barrett, p. 332.

Yet, whatever the dangers and the temptations facing those with the gift of prophecy, Paul concludes with another exhortation to the Corinthians to pursue it with eagerness. It seems that he may have been worried lest he had so played down speaking with tongues in public that the leadership would start to clamp down on it completely. So he urges them not to hamper, hinder, prevent or restrain speaking in tongues: any of these words is a more accurate translation of the Greek (*kōlyō*) than NRSV's *forbid* (39). This is another instruction, with the Lord's specific command behind it (37), which the church today needs to obey.

His final word on the matter is directly connected with the number one priority of edification: *all things should be done decently and in order* (40). The first word focuses on the way Christian worship appears to onlookers, the second on the ability of each individual Christian to function properly in his or her own place. As the latter is encouraged in an atmosphere of true love, so the net result will be a community life which attracts outsiders by its harmony and beauty.

6. Additional note on spiritual gifts

Some scholars and commentators believe that certain gifts of the Spirit are not generally available to the church in every generation. They rightly stress the uniqueness and unrepeatable authority of apostles and prophets in founding the church, and conclude that since those times there have been no apostles or prophets of comparable authority. Miracles and healings, it is further argued, tended to cluster round specific periods of divine revelation (e.g. the exodus, the giving of the law, the days of Elijah and Elisha, the ministry of Jesus and his apostles) and were intended to authenticate it. They should, therefore, not be expected today with the same frequency. Some writers also include speaking in tongues and interpretation of tongues as New Testament phenomena which are not in evidence today, and regard 'the utterance of wisdom' and 'the utterance of knowledge' as non-miraculous words of wisdom and knowledge.

Some writers go further still and categorically declare that no miracles of any kind have taken place since the apostolic age. In this case, the majority of the nine specific gifts in 12:8–10 are either consigned to the past history of the church or explained as 'sanctified common sense'. Classic Pentecostalism, either in reaction or in rediscovery, has stressed the supernatural nature of all these nine gifts, to the exclusion (generally speaking) of any ordinary manifestation of such gifts of God's grace in everyday Christian living.

This exposition of chapters 12 and 14 has sought to avoid both extremes. The basis of this approach is not a desire for compromise, so much as the essential conviction that God is both transcendent and immanent. Because he transcends this world, the church, our minds and our experience, we can expect him to manifest himself in ways consistent with his own revealed nature, however unpredictable in terms of our own finite limitations. Because he also holds the world and the church together and 'sustains all things by his powerful word' (Heb. 1:3), we shall find him constantly at work redeeming and renewing all the resources inherent in us because we have been created in his image.

We find it unhelpful, therefore, to introduce into this discussion of spiritual gifts any notions of 'natural' and 'supernatural', 'normal' and 'abnormal', 'usual' and 'unusual'. This terminology is not used by Paul or any biblical writer; it seems illegitimate therefore to import it into the text as an aid to exegesis, especially in any determinative fashion.

Because there is no *biblical* warrant for the total cessation of certain gifts (with the exception of the unique ministries exercised by the original apostles and prophets), we feel it right to focus our attention on the ascended Lord Jesus Christ, who remains the same today as ever, and who longs to see his church grow into maturity in both the fruit and the gifts of the Holy Spirit. Implicit in that focus is the expectation that there is always more to know and to share. In both tenor and thrust, the relevant biblical passages (including 1 Cor. 12 – 14) open up our horizons, increase our expectancy and broaden our vision of all that God by his Spirit wants to do in the body of Christ.

This uncertainty about what God might do with us as his church need not move us, in the face of spiritual phenomena of various kinds, either into childish gullibility or into sceptical rationalism. It does almighty God no service to be constantly spotlighting what some regard as exceptional and extraordinary. Nor is it honouring to him to preclude any manifestation of his power and glory which we find it hard to explain or control. The Corinthians wrongly concentrated on what they reckoned to be the more dramatic gifts – and Paul found them in disorder, heresy, immorality and division. Let us not, in reaction, adopt an understanding of spiritual gifts which effectively excludes a God who transcends our finite minds, and who in his love reveals himself unexpectedly in our mortal existence. We believe that a supreme miracle happens in conversion and regeneration: why not thereafter?

1 Corinthians 15:1–58

15. Resurrection – past, present and future

It is not until verse 12 that we discover the reasons which prompted Paul to write this remarkable chapter. There were Christians at Corinth who asserted that 'there is no resurrection of the dead'. For the apostle to the Gentiles who had proclaimed Jesus and the resurrection so fearlessly and pointedly that some of his hearers (at Athens) were convinced he was preaching about two separate gods (Jesus and Anastasis – the Greek word for resurrection – Acts 17:18), this uncertainty about the core of the gospel was appalling. He had, it is true, determined to preach nothing but 'Jesus and him crucified' at Corinth; but, however much he may have emphasized the meaning of the cross rather than the fact of the resurrection, the two events were inseparable both in his thinking and in his teaching. He preached Jesus, crucified and risen. How could any Christian, even at Corinth, dismiss the resurrection of the dead? What had given rise to such scepticism? What precisely did they believe anyway?

Several answers have been given. First, the common Greek belief (originally expressed with supreme brilliance by Plato nearly five hundred years earlier) was in the immortality of the soul. The body was seen as a prison, and death marked the release of the hitherto-captive soul to soar to the real world, of which everything on this earth is only a shadow. Greek Christians brought up with this philosophy found it difficult to discard. There were plenty of Gnostic trends in contemporary Christian circles capable of turning Christians away from apostolic truth into an over-spiritualized approach to life before and after death.

The second possibility assumes that Corinthians shared modern scepticism in the face of claims to Jesus' tomb being empty on the first Easter morning. 'Dead men don't rise' could have been the watchword of such an attitude. When making his defence before Agrippa at Caesarea, Paul threw out this challenge to all within earshot: 'Why is it thought incredible by any of you that God raises the dead?' (Acts 26:8). Likewise, both before the Sanhedrin and later in front of Felix, the Roman governor of Judaea, Paul stated his own position unequivocally when he declared: 'It is about the resurrection of the dead that I am on trial before you today.'[1] From the moment the news spread that the tomb of Jesus was empty, there were plenty of voices to be heard giving all kinds of explanations except resurrection, not least (we presume) those influenced by the Sadducees.[2]

Such voices will always be insistent, mainly because the resurrection of Jesus (if genuinely investigated) strips away the arguments and theories behind which people have always tried to hide from God. Paul's affirmation to the Athenians presents the implications of Jesus' resurrection with consummate precision:

> While God has overlooked the times of human ignorance, now he commands all people everywhere to repent, because he has fixed a day on which he will have the world judged in righteousness by a man whom he has appointed, and of this he has given assurance to all by raising him from the dead.
> (Acts 17:30–31)

The third way to understand Corinthian hesitations about the resurrection of the dead has the merit of being based in an attitude which Paul has already confronted earlier in this letter. In brief, this assumed that Christians enter into the fullness of their inheritance in Christ from the outset of their incorporation into Christ, spelt out in baptism. In 4:8, Paul has expostulated: 'Already you have all you want! Already you have become rich! Quite apart from us you have become kings! Indeed, I wish that you had become kings, so that we might be kings with you!' We have seen that this triumphalism failed to do justice to the paradox of 'already' and 'not yet' in biblical eschatology. The Corinthians wanted everything now, and saw constant victory over sin, sickness, suffering and Satan as the right-by-faith of every properly directed Christian. The logical

---

[1] Acts 23:26; 24:21.
[2] Cf. Acts 23:8; also Matt. 27:62–66.

conclusion of such an approach to Christian discipleship was to claim, with Hymenaeus and Philetus, that 'the resurrection has already taken place' (2 Tim. 2:18). Such a position does not necessarily deny the resurrection of Jesus, but does deny any future hope of resurrection for the Christian: all we can expect is what we have now. It is not surprising that Paul accuses Hymenaeus and Philetus of 'upsetting the faith of some' by such teaching.

Such triumphalist teaching has its modern counterpart in the 'prosperity churches' now burgeoning in many countries (i.e. 'trust God and you will be prosperous, healthy and successful'). In such circles there is no theology of suffering remotely linked to the New Testament. Their teaching appeals to those who want a comfortable life with a clear conscience; enslaves many who find the theory never fits the facts of their experience and are then made to feel guilty for not having 'enough faith'; and appals any whose circumstances make it virtually impossible for them to become in any sense prosperous and successful (into this group fall probably 75% of the world).

It is likely that the situation at Corinth did not fit neatly into any of these three categories. Nevertheless, Paul felt bound to return to absolute fundamentals, in order to deal properly with its inherent dangers. Throughout this chapter he expands the principle and the fact of resurrection as being the heart of the gospel. Christianity is concerned, not with mere immortality, nor with sheer survival, nor with the transmigration of the soul, nor with reincarnation, but with resurrection from the dead. For Paul, as for all the New Testament writers, this necessarily meant the raising of the whole person from the dead, not just the soul or the body or even the personality. Resurrection is consistently seen in the New Testament as a demonstration of God's power over death. Almost invariably it is God who raises Jesus from death; Jesus does not rise of his own accord (e.g. 15:16). If God raised Jesus from the dead, he will also raise all those in Jesus. The wider implications of this foundation truth Paul unfolds in this chapter.

1. The facts of the resurrection of Jesus (15:1–11)

In these verses Paul reiterates the basic content of the gospel which he had proclaimed to the Corinthians from the beginning. However much he unfolds further insights as he develops the theme of resurrection, it is important to note that here he is repeating the facts, not adding to them. When there is doubt in people's minds about certain theological issues, it is easy to conclude that these fundamental facts are either insufficient or untrustworthy. Paul entertains no such ideas: he reminds the Corinthians of the gospel which they heard him preach and which they *received* (1).

This word *received* (*paralambanō*) refers to an established tradition passed on personally, and almost certainly by word of mouth, from the original eyewitnesses of the facts involved in the death and resurrection of Jesus. Paul has used the same vocabulary in recording the institution of the Lord's Supper (11:23ff.). When we recollect that 1 Corinthians was written in the early fifties, we can see that these facts at the heart of the gospel message concerning the resurrection of Jesus go back to within twenty years of the actual events. We are, therefore, as close as we can possibly come to eyewitness accounts of what took place in Jerusalem in those days. Paul has no hesitation in answering Corinthian doubts about resurrection by means of such historical evidence. The gospel facts he proclaimed were those he himself received from eyewitnesses, probably when he visited Jerusalem to consult with Peter and James (cf. Gal. 1:18–19). His exposition of the *significance* of those facts he claimed to have received 'by revelation'.[3]

He affirms that such a gospel has brought them salvation (2, *through which also you are being saved*). His only reservation lies in the shakiness of their faith in Christ. 'If men's grip of the gospel is such that they are not really trusting Christ, their belief is groundless and empty. They have not saving faith.'[4] Paul understandably deprecates any attitude or ideas which undermine faith in such a way. We constantly need to reiterate the heart of the gospel, and that involves taking a firm grip on the historical facts (2, *hold firmly*).

What are these facts?

Christ died ... was buried ... was raised on the third day ... appeared to Cephas, then to the twelve. Then he appeared to more than five hundred brothers and sisters at one time ... Then he appeared to James, then to all the apostles.
(3–7)

---

[3] Cf. Gal. 1:11ff.; Eph. 3:1ff.
[4] Morris, p. 205.

Before we look at Paul's account of the resurrection appearances, it is worth noting his reference to the fact that *Christ . . . was buried* (4). 'Many scholars see here an oblique reference to the empty tomb',[5] and the phrase *he was buried* is probably included, not merely as a necessary and actual stage in the whole drama, but as confirming the reality both of death and of resurrection.

> If he was buried he must have been really dead; if he was buried, the resurrection must have been the reanimation of a corpse . . . If he was buried, and was subsequently seen alive outside his grave, the grave must have been empty, and may well have been seen to be empty.[6]

Paul includes in these gospel facts the statement that *Christ died for our sins* (3). There is no true proclamation of the gospel which does not explain, in New Testament terms, the link between human sin and the death of Christ. Indeed, there is no gospel at all unless the death of Christ can be seen to deal with sin once and for all. The fact of resurrection by itself says little about the heart of the gospel, unless it can be shown that 'The sting of death is sin' (15:56) and that the resurrection of Christ has therefore drawn that sting.[7]

The apostle's other factor at the heart of the gospel facts is that both the death and the resurrection of Christ were *in accordance with the scriptures* (3 and 4). We recall that Jesus, in the evening of Easter Day on the road to Emmaus with two disciples, 'interpreted to them the things about himself in all the scriptures' (Luke 24:26–27). As we also read the Old Testament Scriptures[8] in the light of the death and resurrection of Jesus, they will speak to us eloquently of him.

The Old Testament actually speaks in only very shadowy terms of anything remotely like resurrection. On the other hand, the hope of the psalmists that they will not be given up to Sheol (which basically denotes emptiness, if not oblivion) was based firmly on confidence in God's power over death.[9] This confidence contained the seeds of a sure hope in resurrection. Likewise, the salvation promised by God to the patriarchs and

---

[5] E.g. Bruce, p. 139.
[6] Barrett, pp. 339–340.
[7] E.g. Rom. 4:25; Gal. 1:1–4.
[8] Notably Isa. 52:13 – 53:12.
[9] E.g. Pss 16; 49; 73; 88.

their descendants implicitly contains the assurance of resurrection, particularly in view of the promise being rooted in an irreversible covenant. This, in fact, is at the heart of Jesus' own confrontation with the Sadducees (who denied any possibility of resurrection), where Jesus concludes: 'have you not read . . . how God said to [Moses], "I am the God of Abraham . . . Isaac, and . . . Jacob"? He is God not of the dead, but of the living; you are quite wrong' (Mark 12:18–27). In these two examples, from the psalmists and the patriarchs, Jesus himself pointed to the truth of Paul's statement that his death and resurrection were 'in accordance with the scriptures'.

The appearances of the resurrected Jesus recorded by Paul, passing on what has been handed on to him by the original eyewitnesses, differ in several ways from the narratives in the four Gospels. G. E. Ladd's examination of these differences is illuminating and constructive,[10] and we need not repeat his commentary. Paul's reference to a single appearance to over five hundred brothers and sisters all together is clearly a very strong lynchpin in his argument about the truth of Jesus' resurrection, particularly as most of them were still alive and could be consulted personally.

Perhaps the most significant phrase in this account of the gospel facts is in verse 8: *Last of all . . . he appeared also to me*. By this terminology Paul is saying at least two things: first, his own encounter with the risen Jesus (after the ascension) is of equal validity and identical in nature to the others he has just recorded;[11] second, once the risen Jesus had appeared to Paul, there were no further appearances of that nature (*Last of all*).

This is a necessary corrective to claims today to have had a vision of the ascended Jesus. Such an experience may well have taken place, but it is in no sense on a par with or of the same kind as Paul's experience on the Damascus road. The appearance to Paul was so unusual that the apostle calls himself *someone untimely born* (*ektrōma*). The word refers to a miscarriage or an abortion, and should probably not be taken too literally. Apparently the word was used as a term of abuse. 'Perhaps it had been hurled at Paul by his opponents. He was not a handsome man (2 Cor. 10:10), and they may have combined an insult to his personal appearance with a criticism of his doctrine of free grace.'[12]

[10] G. E. Ladd, *I Believe in the Resurrection of Jesus* (Hodder, 1975), pp. 105–106.
[11] Cf. 1 Cor. 9:1, 'Have I not seen Jesus our Lord?' NB To have been an eyewitness of the resurrection was a necessary qualification for being an apostle (cf. Acts 1:22).
[12] Morris, p. 207.

We can imagine such opponents declaring that, so far from being born again, Paul was an abortion. He was constantly overwhelmed by the sheer grace of God in forgiving, let alone calling as an apostle, one who had viciously persecuted the church (9–10). In that sense it was unnatural for him to encounter the risen Jesus in the same way as people like Peter and John. There is probably also a reference to the time factor: he came on the scene too late to qualify as one of the original apostles, but God overrode that handicap as well.

It is not surprising, in the light of Paul's background, that he regarded himself as *the least of the apostles, unfit to be called an apostle* (9). Only the grace of God could overcome such demerits: but because his grace *had* been lavished on such an unworthy person, Paul was not going to let anyone take either his position or his vocation away from him. To let that happen would be to treat God's grace flippantly. The only proper response to grace is total commitment with every fibre of our being (10). If God's grace does not produce such energetic single-mindedness, there is something seriously lacking in our faith.[13] In the last analysis, however, the identity of the preacher is irrelevant: faith is kindled by the preaching of this gospel. There is no other.

2. The centrality of the resurrection of Jesus (15:12–19)

If the gospel proclaimed to the Corinthians revolved around these crucial facts, culminating in the resurrection of Jesus, and if through this gospel their lives had been completely redirected and transformed, it was inconceivable that anyone should have asserted that *there is no resurrection of the dead* (12). If resurrection does not exist in any shape or form, then the consequences to Christian faith and discipleship are devastating. It is important, with Paul, to push people to see the logic of their beliefs, whether those beliefs are orthodox or heretical. Many Christians have never applied their faith either to their ordinary thinking or to their daily behaviour. Likewise, those who deviate from biblical truth must face up to the implications of what they assert and deny. This is what Paul does in verses 13–19. To deny resurrection is to strip the Christian message of seven essentials.

---

[13] Cf. Rom. 12:1ff.; Col. 1:27–29.

a. 'Christ has not been raised' (15:13, 16)

If there is no such thing as resurrection, then Jesus himself did not triumph over death. If dead people don't rise, then Jesus is still dead. Presumably, the Corinthian heretics never intended to suggest that Jesus was still dead; but Paul is pressing the logic of their position, in order to reveal its menace. 'The truth as it is in Jesus' is of a piece; it holds together with inner consistency; whatever the paradoxes inherent in the truth, it is not self-contradictory. To deny one lynchpin of this truth is to dislocate the whole structure. Of course, the truth itself is not imperilled, because it stands for ever into eternity, unshakeable and incontrovertible. But if people, like those at Corinth, decide to pick and choose which aspects of the truth they will accept, they will end up with no truth, that is, in falsehood. This is nowhere more obvious than in the case of resurrection. This attitude reveals, in general, the danger of coming to the person and work of Jesus with even one preconceived idea about what can and cannot be true, what can and cannot happen. This is frequently being done: 'dead people don't rise', 'miracles don't happen', 'there is no life after death', 'you can't change human nature'.

b. 'Our proclamation has been in vain' (15:14)

Paul regards himself supremely as a preacher of the gospel. He is, therefore, stating that his whole life has been a complete waste of time if there is no such thing as resurrection. All those persecutions, sufferings, tribulations, have been pointless.[14] The obvious implication is that not only has his life's ministry been founded on a fraud and a hoax, but so has every other apostle's – indeed every other believer's. The word translated *in vain* (*kenos*) literally means 'empty': in other words, take out the resurrection of Jesus, and there is nothing left to the Christian's proclamation. As Paul shows in the rest of the chapter, the whole sweep of salvation in time and eternity is based not merely on the resurrection principle, but on the fact of Jesus' resurrection.

c. 'Your faith has been in vain' (15:14)

Because their faith was based entirely on his preaching (15:1–2), the collapse of the ground of his preaching necessarily meant the collapse of their faith. Take out the resurrection of Jesus, and there is nothing left on

---

[14] Cf. 1 Cor. 4:11–13; 2 Cor. 6:4–10.

which to rest faith – only the decomposing corpse of an itinerant Jewish carpenter-turned-rabbi. Here, as everywhere, Paul underlines the truth that faith is produced by looking to Jesus Christ, crucified and risen. Faith is not created, sustained or increased by looking at ourselves or at others, but only by absorbing the reality and the implications of the resurrection of Jesus.

d. 'We are misrepresenting God' (15:15)

The very reputation, and even the character, of God is destroyed if there is no such thing as resurrection. Paul's vocation and ministry are consistently portrayed as given him by God, not assumed by himself. The gospel he proclaimed was not his own invention, but given him by God through revelation.[15] Specifically, Paul's claim (following the apostolic traditions handed on to him) was that *God ... raised Christ*: if he did nothing of the sort, if Jesus was another guru figure and in fact an impostor, it is nothing short of blasphemy to link the name of God almighty with such a person. The only convincing reason for linking God to the person and work of Jesus is the fact of his resurrection. Only God has power over death: if Jesus rose from the dead, God raised him.

e. 'You are still in your sins' (15:17)

In verse 14 Paul has referred to faith being empty, devoid of content. Here he writes of its being unable to secure any results, that is, being weak and ineffective. Of course, if it has no content, it will not achieve anything at all. But Paul's main thrust in this verse is that the sin-problem remains unsolved if Jesus did not rise from the dead. All talk of Christ dying for our sins in accordance with the Scriptures becomes meaningless if in fact he stayed dead. The unanimous testimony of the Scriptures is that 'the wages of sin is death' (Rom. 6:23): death marks the end result of that separation from God which sin inevitably produces. If Jesus stayed dead, there are only two possible conclusions: either he was not the sinless person everyone thought him to be and his death marked his final separation from God; or he might have been without personal sin, but his attempts to atone for the sin of the world by his death did not meet with divine approval. Either way, we are still in our sins, cut off from God and facing his judgment, like everyone else.

---

[15] Cf. Gal. 1:11–13; also Rom. 1:16–17; 1 Cor. 1:18; 2:1, 5; 4:1; 9:1–2.

f. 'Those also who have died in Christ have perished' (15:18)

Another awful consequence of there being no resurrection is that death remains, not just 'the last enemy' (26), but the one invincible terror. Death is not falling asleep in Christ and waking up to see his smile of welcome into the Father's house (cf. John 14:1ff.): it is hard confirmation of the lostness of all human beings, that we are all doomed to perish without hope and without God. It is no coincidence that Paul almost casually, if not unconsciously, introduces the pregnant phrase *in Christ* at this point. As we shall see, this is the core of his positive teaching about the implications of the resurrection of Jesus; but it becomes empty words if Christ turns out to be nothing more than a dead guru.

g. 'We are of all people most to be pitied' (15:19)

If Christ was not raised from the dead, any expectation of life beyond death with him evaporates. We are then left with a pseudo-gospel which purports at least to give some meaning to our life here on earth. This presumably takes the form of doing the best we can to follow the example of Jesus Christ, assuming that we select him as our mentor in preference to countless other teachers, wise men and women and leaders. Paul sees this attitude to Jesus as pitiable and pathetic: if there is no such thing as resurrection, much of Jesus' teaching falls to the ground and he is revealed to be a liar. Yet the Corinthian Christians had set their hope on Christ as Lord of life, death and eternity. If he was not raised from the dead, he is not Lord of anything. If life here on this earth is all there is, it makes no sense to base our hope on the groundless promises of one who made empty assertions about eternity. If the Christian faith is thus based on an empty gospel and a fraudulent saviour, 'anybody is better off than the Christian'.[16]

It is right at this stage to ask certain questions of those today who deny that there is such a thing as resurrection from the dead, and particularly dismiss the historical reality of Jesus' resurrection from the dead. With what premises do they come to the evidence? What is the actual content of their preaching? Does their teaching lead people to a saving faith? What kind of God are they presenting? Do they believe in the assurance of sins forgiven? Do they preach such assurance? Is there any firm expectation of life beyond death? Can they say, with Tertullian, 'Our people die well'?

---

[16] Morris, p. 212.

When an elderly churchgoer heard one such modern sceptic speaking on the radio, she concluded that everything she had hitherto believed by way of orthodox Christianity was unreliable, if not untrue – and committed suicide.

3. The consequences of the resurrection of Jesus (15:20–34)

a. Its consequences for the future (15:20–28)

We can almost hear the sigh of relief as well as the cry of confidence with which Paul declares: *But in fact Christ has been raised from the dead* (20). This *But* must rank with the great 'buts' of the Bible.[17] Here Paul is saying that a whole new age has dawned with the resurrection of Jesus Christ from the dead: he is the *first fruits* of an immense harvest, consisting of all those who are *in Christ* (22) and who *belong to Christ* (23). The word translated *first fruits* (*aparchē*) is echoed by the language of Colossians: 'he is the beginning [*archē*], the firstborn from the dead' (Col. 1:18). If Christ was raised from the dead, it is clear that all those who, through the grace of God, are now *in Christ* will also be raised from the dead.

Indeed, elsewhere Paul sees this union as so complete and real that, in spiritual terms, those in Christ have already been raised.[18] Yet this reality has still the limitations inherent in the mortality of our present physical bodies, which cannot anyway 'inherit the kingdom of God' (15:50). This is also the interim and balanced perspective of Romans.[19]

Paul is thus completely consistent in stressing *both* the union of believers with Christ in his death and resurrection, *and* the definite *order* (23; *tagma* is a military word) in which this will be consummated. He seems to be thinking of three groups: Christ, those who have *died in Christ* (18, 20), and those who are still alive *at his coming* (23, *parousia*). The latter two categories together form those who, being in Christ, belong to Christ and are therefore his care and responsibility. At this stage Paul is establishing that resurrection is a *future* event, but assured because it is continuous with the *past* event of Christ's own resurrection. This is the

---

[17] E.g. Rom. 3:21; 1 Cor. 6:11; Eph. 2:4.

[18] Cf. Eph. 2:4–7; Col. 2:12–13; 3:1–4.

[19] Rom. 6:3, 5, 11–13; 8:10–11.

thrust of verses 21–22, which stress the humanity of Jesus (as real as the humanity of Adam): in being born, living, dying and being resurrected as man, Jesus has opened up the way for humankind to be raised from the dead.

The emphasis on Jesus' humanity, with its necessary reference to Adam as the one whose sin marked the historic entry of death into the world, introduces the Pauline doctrine of the solidarity of the human race in sin (cf. Rom. 5:12–21). Adam's sin constituted the mass of humanity as sinners, because it introduced them into a society which is, as a whole, alienated from God. As members of the human race, which has departed from its original vocation in God's purposes, all men and women inherit death as their destiny. There are no exceptions to this pattern: all have sinned and *in Adam all die*.

Paul's language in verses 21–22 suggests, at first reading, that in the same way all men and women will be made alive with Christ and through Christ. But even in these few verses the 'all' at the end of verse 22 is qualified by the two phrases 'those also who have died in Christ' (18) and *those who belong to Christ* (23). So there are clearly exceptions to this second pattern, that is, those who do *not* belong to Christ and those who have died *without* being in Christ. Moreover, in several parts of 1 Corinthians Paul has referred to those who are 'perishing'.[20] We conclude, therefore, that the main point of Paul's parallelism between Adam and Christ (as in Romans 5) is that, like Adam, Christ is the progenitor of a race, of a new humanity. The resurrection marks the beginning of this new creation: Jesus is 'the firstborn among many brothers' (Rom. 8:29, margin): 'if anyone is in Christ, there is a new creation' (cf. 2 Cor. 5:17).

In verses 24–28 Paul picks up the suggestive thread of the parousia, that is, Christ's second coming, to show where history and time are heading. There will be a clearly demarcated *end* (24, *telos*). In verses 25–26 he talks of a time when Christ is reigning, but when he is gradually bringing more and more of his enemies under his control: this most naturally refers to the period between his first coming and his second coming. His second coming marks the final destruction of everything ranged against God, every rule, authority and power (24). Only then will death be finally robbed of its efficacy (26). If death is the *last enemy*, it is reasonable to assume that

---

[20] Cf. 1 Cor. 1:18; 3:17; 5:13; 6:9ff.; 9:27; 15:18.

the spiritual forces now ranged against Christ and his church still find scope for effective opposition in matters connected with death – through occult practices, in times of bereavement, by creating fear of death and dying, with teachings which question the fact and the implications of Christ's resurrection.

Once Christ has overcome every enemy of God and of humanity, he will voluntarily hand the sovereignty (24, *basileia* = 'kingship') to *God the Father*. As Barrett aptly comments, 'this does not necessarily imply difference of status, but it does imply difference of role and operation'.[21] The sense in which Christ thus submits to God is illustrated vividly in verses 27–28. Paul there quotes from Psalm 8, which describes the smallness and yet the greatness of men and women – finite and tiny by comparison with the cosmos, but mighty both in their capacity to subdue and control the cosmos and in being only 'a little lower than God' (Ps. 8:5). The Creator God has *put all things in subjection* under the feet of humanity, and Jesus has come as the second Adam (cf. 22, 45), the perfect man in human flesh, to bring everything back into submission to humanity and ultimately to God – *back*, because under the first Adam the world moved into rebellion against God, thus also prejudicing humanity's intended control. Once that has been finally achieved by Jesus, exercising by virtue of his resurrection his sovereign power over every enemy of God (including death), he will submit himself in his obedient manhood to God the Father. Thus God, in the eternal perfection of the Trinity, *may be all in all* (28).

This ultimate goal (of God being all in all, everything to everyone) will include the submission of every enemy of God to Jesus as Lord. To those who have steadily and deliberately rejected Jesus, God will then be revealed irrevocably as Judge. God will thus have the last word and in that sense *be all* to his enemies, that is, to those who have refused to accept Christ's ministry of reconciliation.

Before we move on from the consequences of the resurrection of Jesus for the future, we must pause to recollect how far Paul has come from reminding the Corinthians about the basic facts of the gospel. We can now see why he adjudged their shaky doctrine about the resurrection of the dead to be so perilous. To Paul's redeemed, renewed and uniquely inspired mind, there was an unbroken continuity between the empty tomb and the

---

[21] Barrett, p. 357.

perfection of heaven. Remove the fact of resurrection and you have excised the very life principle of the kingdom of God.

If the major consequences of Christ's resurrection bear on the future and on eternity, Paul was not so transported that he ignored the present. So he speaks of the present in the next six verses.

b. Its consequences for the present (15:29–34)

Three very different consequences crowded into Paul's thoughts: the first highly esoteric and almost unidentifiable; the second linked with the harsh realities of his own ministry; the third for the daily behaviour of the Christians at Corinth.

It seems that, on at least one occasion, the Corinthians had held a baptism service *on behalf of the dead* (29). Barrett describes this as 'a practice no doubt as familiar to them as puzzling to us'.[22] Morris assures us that 'between thirty and forty explanations have been suggested';[23] he believes that the most natural explanation is that some believers got themselves baptized on behalf of friends or relatives who had died unbaptized. In quoting the practice Paul was not expressing approval, but simply using their practice as an argument against their assertion that 'there is no resurrection of the dead'. If there is no such thing as resurrection, what is the point of the practice? Barrett suggests that there had perhaps been an epidemic or large-scale accident in Corinth, and many Christians had died unbaptized. Baptism was a powerful visual proclamation of death and resurrection: 'in this setting it is not impossible to conceive of such a rite, practised perhaps only once'.[24]

Of the many possible interpretations of this practice, G. W. Bromiley has suggested the following two as 'perhaps the most helpful': first, people were often baptized as a result of seeing Christians 'die well' or live consistently Christlike lives before their death. Second, baptism is *with a view to* the dead, that is, to their resurrection. In both cases it makes no sense if there is no resurrection.[25]

Far more apposite and intelligible is Paul's indignation about the value of his own sufferings. *I die every day!* (31) is his experience. Virtually every hour of the day he faced dangers of all kinds:

---

[22] Ibid., p. 362.
[23] Morris, p. 219.
[24] Barrett, p. 364.
[25] See *International Standard Bible Encyclopaedia*, Vol. 1 (Eerdmans, 1979), p. 426.

danger from rivers . . . bandits . . . my own people . . . Gentiles . . . in the
city . . . in the wilderness . . . at sea . . . from false brothers and sisters;
in toil and hardship, through many a sleepless night, hungry and thirsty,
often without food, cold and naked.
(2 Cor. 11:26–27)

He pressed on with such a dangerous life because he was convinced that
something infinitely better awaited him in the resurrection life of heaven.
He was prepared to persevere with such ministry because, in this carrying
about in his body the death of Jesus, life was released in the Corinthians (cf.
2 Cor. 4:8–12) – and that made him very proud of them (31). He had already
been sustained through the most daunting experiences by the resurrection
power of Jesus (cf. Phil. 3:10), even the ghastly horror of fighting *with wild
animals at Ephesus* (32).

Luke's description of Paul at Ephesus (Acts 19) makes it fairly plain that
the apostle is referring to direct encounter with occult forces and the
imminence of mob-lynching under the influence of frenzied devotion
to the local goddess, Artemis. The theatre at Ephesus is specifically
mentioned, the scene of literal battles-to-the-death with wild beasts:
Paul's memory of these events was probably jogged, as in Ephesus he
dictated this letter to his amanuensis. What is the point, asks the apostle,
of subjecting oneself to such a lifestyle if there is no resurrection? Only a
masochist would choose to live that way: *If the dead are not raised, 'Let us
eat and drink, for tomorrow we die'* (32). Thus Paul clinches the argument
by quoting an aphorism[26] which was in contemporary vogue in most
Greek society.

The final consequence of the resurrection mentioned by Paul is very
pragmatic: if the Corinthians surrendered faith in the resurrection, they
would open the door to lax moral behaviour. They would take on the
standards of those around them, because *Bad company ruins good morals*
(33) – a saying of the Greek poet Menander. In Paul's assertion that *some*
[of you] *have no knowledge of God* (34) we can detect another veiled attack
on the so-called knowledge of the Corinthians (cf. 8:1). Certain Christians,
who were claiming a special knowledge of God, were losing control of
themselves and sliding back into paganism. They needed Paul's blunt
command: 'Stop sinning!' Paul saw this sinfulness as the result of failing

---

26 Mentioned also in Isa. 22:13.

to think soberly (*Come to a sober and right mind, and sin no more*). Wrong thinking, about the resurrection or any other fundamental articles of faith, inevitably leads to wrong behaviour. Paul was not beyond shocking Christians into a sense of *shame* about the way they were behaving (34): they had allowed themselves to be led astray and to absorb error.

4. The nature of the resurrection body (15:35–50)

The glorious future to which Paul has been referring earlier in the chapter virtually beggars all human understanding, let alone description. Faced with such an immense hope, mortal men and women can resort only to very basic questions: *How are the dead raised? With what kind of body do they come?* (35). Paul answers this very understandable question in the ensuing verses: through them all runs one fundamental principle: *flesh and blood cannot inherit the kingdom of God* (50). These physical bodies of ours simply are incapable of coping with the glory of God. If we are going to be resurrected in Christ, we need also to be transformed into his likeness. Only Christlike people will be suitable for such a quality of life. Yet, however radical and total such a transformation must inevitably be due to the vulnerability of our present bodies, there is nevertheless a clear continuity between Christians now and Christians then: 'we shall be raised', not destroyed and reincarnated in a different existence altogether. This continuity guarantees the fulfilment of such natural desires as being able to recognize and enjoy those whom we have known here in this life, when we have come to share in the life of the world to come.

Paul illustrates from nature this continuity-cum-transformation (36–41). Jesus had himself used a similar picture to describe the absolute necessity of his own death if there was to be any such reality as resurrection: 'Very truly, I tell you, unless a grain of wheat falls into the earth and dies, it remains just a single grain; but if it dies, it bears much fruit' (John 12:24). Thus, the Creator has written into nature the principle of resurrection: without death and burial there is no new life. At present the whole creation is in bondage to the endless cycle of birth–life–age–death–birth, and so on (what Paul calls 'decay' – Rom. 8:21). The raising of Lazarus is an illustration of such life (John 11): he was raised from the dead, only to die again. Jesus, through his resurrection to an indestructible life (cf. Heb. 7:16), has broken out of this bondage to decay and has brought life and immortality to light through the gospel (2 Tim. 1:10). He died, was raised from the dead and will never die again. 'Much fruit' will result from his death and resurrection: he is the 'first fruits' of this bountiful harvest. So there has to be death before life, even in nature. What is sown in the ground will, however, reappear in a different form altogether. By taking examples from different aspects of the created order (39–41), Paul shows that the Creator God is accustomed to producing many varied kinds of *bodies*. He thus ensures that each is specially suited to its own particular environment: a star will not function in the water, nor will a whale cope with the sky. Each is perfectly suited to its own location. In the same way our physical bodies, ideal for this earthly existence in spite of their mortality, will be useless in the perfection of God's kingdom. They need, therefore, to be buried when their work is done, so that from such raw material God can produce *a spiritual body* (44), perfectly suited for inheriting the kingdom of God.

The contrast between the *physical body* and the *spiritual body* is underlined in verses 42–49, particularly in the succession of phrases in verses 42–43. The totality of that contrast is indicated by using opposite epithets. Paul does not mean that there is no honour or power in our physical bodies, but that the very greatest honour and power inherent in these bodies could not begin to cope with life in the kingdom of God in all its fullness. The fundamental reason for this is their bondage to decay (42).[27] There is no way in which this corruption can be halted; it can only be buried. Paul's choice of *glory* (*doxa*) and *power* (*dynamis*) in verse 43 to describe life in the kingdom of God evokes the ascription at the end of the Lord's Prayer: 'Yours is the kingdom, the power and the glory, for ever and ever.' These two words summarize Paul's consistent vision of the consummation of God's kingdom.[28]

Paul then returns to the contrast between Jesus and Adam (45–49). Again, the perspective is of two humanities, each under its federal head. All human beings share in the characteristics of Adam. 'the Lord God formed man from the dust of the ground, and breathed into his nostrils the breath of life; and the man became a living being' (Gen. 2:7). Adam – and every human being – *was from the earth, a man of dust* (47). We have all *borne the image of the man of dust* (49). It is important to recognize that this was all by the fiat and express purpose of God, as the Genesis account

---

[27] The phrase translated *perishable* echoes Paul's language in Rom. 8:21 and is literally 'in decay'.

[28] Cf. 2 Cor. 3:18 – 4:18; Phil. 3:20–21.

makes plain. *The last Adam*, Jesus, himself partook of flesh and blood, eventually being put to death and buried.

Everything that happened from that point onwards revealed the resurrection. From that point of no return he *became a life-giving spirit* (45); raised from the dead, he revealed his true origin as *the . . . man . . . from heaven* (47) – truly and fully man, not condemned to lie in the dust, but destined to resume his place at the right hand of God the Father. All those who belong to him will bear his image (49), both in the sense of being made like him and in the sense of sharing his resurrection body. Indeed, it is probable that Paul's description of Jesus in these verses provides us with the only intelligible category for appreciating the nature of his resurrection appearances prior to his ascension. He was recognizable as the crucified One – there was continuity with his past existence; but he was released into a quality of life unshackled by mortality and the finiteness of time and space – there was discontinuity. So the resurrected Jesus, indwelt by the Spirit of God, was able to give life in a new dimension to all who trusted him. What happened to Jesus after his death and resurrection will happen also to all those in Jesus when they are all together raised on the last day (cf. 51–53).

In the whole of this section, we are particularly hamstrung both by the limitations of English in rendering key Greek words, and by popular views of humanity which divide our nature into different parts (e.g. body, mind and spirit). The Greek word *psychē*, often translated 'soul', is used by Paul to describe our natural physical existence as human beings.[29] Paul here is contrasting the body which expresses this natural human life (44, *sōma psychikon*) with the body which will eventually express the supernatural life of God's Spirit in the fullness of his kingdom (*sōma pneumatikon*). Even now God's Spirit dwells in our mortal bodies (cf. 6:19): but the more the Spirit makes us like Jesus, the more these mortal bodies groan under the strain of anticipating their own demise and the freedom of totally new bodies designed for glory and power. Therefore the English words used in this section can bring more confusion than clarity. Perhaps the most helpful single clue is to note Paul's contrast between the bodies we have now for our natural human existence and the bodies we will be given when we enter into our full inheritance in heaven. The first body

---

[29] Cf. 1 Cor. 2:14, where the *psychikos* is contrasted with the *pneumatikos*, i.e. the person who has the Spirit of God, who is born again by the Spirit.

has all the limitations of our earthiness; the second body has all the capacity of God's Spirit. From this perspective it is obvious that the first body (*flesh and blood*) cannot inherit the kingdom of God, because decay and corruption cannot be part of what is eternally incorruptible (50).

In summary, we must acknowledge that in this whole discussion Paul is struggling to describe the indescribable. As Ladd says,

> Who can imagine a body without weakness? or infection? or tiredness? or sickness? or death? This is a body utterly unknown to earthly, historical experience . . . it is an order of existence in which the 'laws of nature' . . . no longer obtain. In fact, when one puts his mind to it, it is quite unimaginable.[30]

5. The moment of the resurrection of the body (15:51–57)

At this stage Paul explains that he is revealing *a mystery* (51). Previously[31] he has used this word to describe the open secret of the gospel, revealed by the Spirit to the apostles and prophets. Here he suggests strongly that what he is saying has been unveiled to him by special revelation. Is the content part of what he obliquely refers to in 2 Corinthians 12:1–4? However sealed his lips have been about the full content of such revelations, he now feels constrained to divulge something of what will take place at the last day.[32]

He again uses the picture of sleep to describe the condition of those who die as Christians (51, NRSV margin). The word 'sleep' seems most naturally to describe a state of unconsciousness: in other words, at death Christians fall asleep in Christ and their next conscious experience is being woken to see Jesus at 'the general resurrection on the last day'. The moment of death marks a person's transition from time into eternity. 'The last day' marks both the final consummation of 'things temporal' and the full unveiling of 'things eternal'. Paul thus envisages those who have died before the parousia being woken by *the last trumpet*, being united with Christians still alive at that point, and then the whole church together

---

[30] Ladd, *I Believe in the Resurrection of Jesus*, pp. 115, 117.

[31] 1 Cor. 4:1; cf. Col. 1:26–27.

[32] What Paul describes in this passage needs to be read alongside 1 Thess. 4:13ff., where a similar panorama is spread out.

being transformed *in a moment, in the twinkling of an eye* (52) as each Christian is given his or her imperishable, immortal resurrection body (53). It is a completely open question, on the evidence of this passage, whether Paul anticipated being alive at the return of Christ. Whether dead or alive at the coming of Christ, *we will all be changed* (51–52).

The three vivid phrases in verse 52 used to describe this climax to history each have a particular nuance: *in a moment* signifies the smallest possible amount of time (Greek *atomos*, from which we get 'atom'); *in the twinkling of an eye* refers to the length of time it takes to blink; *at the last trumpet* draws attention to the occasions in the Old Testament, in the teaching of Jesus and in contemporary Judaism when the sound of the trumpet signals celebration and triumph. It is this full and final victory over death, that 'last enemy', which will then be consummated. Then, and only then, will the prophecies of Isaiah and Hosea be truly fulfilled: 'he will swallow up death for ever. Then the Lord GOD will wipe away the tears from all faces' (Isa. 25:8); 'O Death, where are your plagues? O Sheol, where is your destruction?' (Hos. 13:14).

Despite Paul's confident expectation about Christ's ultimate vindication and victory, there is no superficial triumphalism in his attitude to death. Not only does he refuse to regard its enmity as truly overcome until the return of Christ, but he acknowledges the bitterness of its *sting:* 'the word refers primarily to the sting of bees, serpents, and the like'.[33] Death is not just a natural and unpleasant phenomenon, but a punishment from God. Death is, therefore, an evil which exists only because of humanity's rebellion against God. In that sense it is completely alien, and we can appreciate the crucial importance of rooting the meaning of Christ's death in the need for sin to be properly dealt with (cf. 15:3).

Paul adds the further statement, *the power of sin is the law* (56). The best commentary on this phrase is Paul's own exegesis of the law in Romans 7, where he explains that, however 'holy and just and good' it might be, the law condemns all people by its strict requirements. It even throws the reality and seriousness of sin into sharp relief through its precise definition of sin as transgression of God's commandments. Indeed, our inner propensity to rebel and disobey actually makes us want to do the opposite of what God's law requires: we see the sign 'No Trespassing' and its very presence makes us want to trespass. In these ways sin exerts

---

[33] Morris, p. 234.

its inexorable grip over us, and the law serves only to spell out the seriousness and the strength of that grip.

Death . . . sin . . . the law – all have been broken wide open in the death and resurrection of Jesus. Even now we can experience victory over this trio, but the full fruits of the victory of God through our Lord Jesus Christ are only for the last day. As with all that God has done for us in Christ, this victory is a gift of his grace: *thanks be to God, who gives us the victory*, now and then.

6. Conclusion (15:58)

Because this is the glorious hope in front of the Christian, Paul urges the Corinthians (with a particularly warm form of address, *my beloved*) to be steady and unshakeable in pressing on with the Lord. There can be little doubt that 'the hope of glory' (cf. Col. 1:27) is the strongest incentive for *excelling in the work of the Lord*, especially when the going is tough or simply unexciting. One of the inevitable and common results of a false triumphalism – as distinct from authentic victory in Christ in all circumstances – is later disillusionment, and even disappearance from Christian fellowship.

In the instant mood of modern society there are many switched-off Christians who, having been led to believe that complete victory in Christ was to be expected now rather than later, have an inbuilt cynicism towards any authentic experience of the risen Christ. We need a sober realism (as Jesus himself provides in the parable of the sower – Mark 4:13ff.), imbued with a fervent hope in resurrection. Such a combination will tackle the Lord's work with unswerving dedication, recognizing that it involves real *labour*, or toil (*kopos*): the word talks of 'the fatigue involved in hard work'.[34] Modern Christians need that kind of 'stickability' and Paul states the incentive with typical understatement: *in the Lord your labour is not in vain*.

This final clause is, in fact, a summary of the whole chapter and contains two specific phrases which recall key arguments concerning resurrection: *in vain* and *in the Lord*. If resurrection is ruled out of court altogether, Christian preaching and even faith in Christ are *in vain*, that is, empty (15:14). But if resurrection is real and certain, the whole of a

---

[34] Ibid., p. 236.

Christian's life and work is full of purpose and hope. The other phrase, *in the Lord*, recapitulates the major theme of this chapter: those who are in Christ will be resurrected in the same way and with the same body as Christ himself was raised from the dead. Indeed, the Greek text ends with the phrase *in the Lord*, thus adding even further emphasis to the significance of being in Christ.

1 Corinthians 16:1–24

16. An international church

After the grandeur of chapter 15, anything is bound to be something of an anticlimax. The contents of this chapter are essentially practical and therefore prosaic. A closer look will yield fascinating insights into the life of the New Testament church. These insights can best be summarized, not so much by consecutive exposition of the text, as by a more panoramic overview of the chapter as a whole. We thus discover:

1. A church which is international but also interdependent

Although Paul has mostly personal comments to make, the context is markedly international. At least five Roman provinces are mentioned: Galatia (1), Judaea (3), Macedonia (5), Achaia (15) and Asia (19). These areas of the Roman Empire reflect very different cultures and conditions: European and Eastern, Jew and Arab, Greek and Roman, urban and rural. We see a church which has penetrated into all these situations, such is the power of the Christian gospel. It is fascinating to note how mobile this international church proved to be in the Mediterranean world of the first century. This mobility was immeasurably improved by the efficiency of the Roman Empire. Roman roads radiated throughout the provinces. Roman legions ensured that travel was reasonably safe: indeed, Pax Romana (the peace of Rome) became a byword. The Romans also had a very effective postal system, and various hostelries dotted the main roads. Throughout the whole region the Greek language was the lingua franca.

The vision and dedication of men and women, married couples, business-men and missionaries produced an international church which took full advantage of the situation.

The interdependence of this far-flung church was expressed in several ways. In this chapter we see a generous sharing of both money and ministry. The chapter begins with Paul's heartfelt concern for the church in Jerusalem (1–4). He was burdened with the needs of the mother church, which had been facing very straitened circumstances for a long time as a result of a severe famine (this had been foretold by Agabus in a word of prophecy – Acts 11:27–30), a natural disaster that would have hit Judaea particularly hard because it was not a very wealthy area, especially around Jerusalem. In every church for which he was responsible Paul stressed the opportunity, privilege and responsibility of thus meeting the needs of *the saints* (1) in Jerusalem.[1] There was no better or more tangible way of cementing relationships between Jewish Christians and Gentile Christians.

In order to regularize and organize this *collection* (1), Paul urged on the Corinthians the habit of setting aside a regular amount each week. The reference to *the first day of every week* (2) shows that he saw such disciplined giving as part of the regular worshipping life of the church at Corinth. The amount should be determined by what each Christian experiences at God's hands by way of prosperity. But the fact that Paul instructed *each of you* to take part indicates that relative poverty should not prevent such planned, systematic giving. In fact, Paul seems to see such giving as combining the systematic with the spontaneous: the spon-taneity controlling the amount given, the system ensuring regularity. Paul made it plain (3–4) that everything thus collected would be scrupulously handled – a model which needs to be constantly emulated.

Sharing our material prosperity is only one way of demonstrating our interdependence in the body of Christ. This chapter also reveals the generous way in which the early church shared its resources in personnel. Paul's own travelling ministry is obvious (5–7), but we read of an imminent visit from Ephesus to Corinth by *Timothy* (10–11). That would not have been without considerable cost for Timothy: he was a sensitive, nervous and hesitant minister, who constantly needed a boost to his morale. Clearly, Paul believed that Timothy had an important ministry to bring to

---

[1] Cf. Acts 24:17; Rom. 15:26; 2 Cor. 8 – 9.

the church at Corinth. He encourages them to put him at his ease and, his work done, to send him on his way rejoicing.

Paul refers also to *Apollos* (12), who had already brought great strength to the fledgling church at Corinth (cf. Acts 18:24ff.). He is more than ready to make another visit to Corinth, *with the other brothers* if necessary (the same travelling companions are referred to in connection with Timothy's visit: cf. verse 11). Although Apollos was not ready to go to Corinth at that particular moment, *He will come when he has the opportunity.*

The traffic was not all one way: Paul has been greatly *refreshed* by the visit from Corinth to Ephesus of *Stephanas, Fortunatus* and *Achaicus* (17–18), even if other news from Corinth has caused him much heartache. One further reference underlines the importance of this interdependence in the churches of the Mediterranean: *Aquila and Prisca* (19). This couple had been of immense importance in nurturing the church in at least three key centres: Rome, Ephesus and Corinth. The New Testament evidence indicates that they were involved in a family business (tentmaking – Acts 18:3) which entailed a lot of travelling. Wherever they settled, they became the focus for *the church in their house.*

Such giving and receiving of ministry between churches in completely different cultures is equally constructive today. In particular, the church in the West, which has for nearly two centuries been exclusively on the sending side of shared ministry, stands in urgent need of learning to receive ministry from churches in the Global South. There can still be a patronizing attitude among many Western Christians towards fellow Christians from Africa, Asia and Latin America. Until this is repented of and renounced, the spiritual riches in these continents will remain distant.

2. A church which faces opportunities but also opposition

A wide door for effective work has opened . . . and there are many adversaries (9). Paul is describing the situation during his two and a half years at Ephesus, recounted in Acts 19. He spent longer there than anywhere else. One of the main reasons for his long stay was the number of openings for the gospel he discovered. He 'dialogued' daily in a public lecture room, the Hall of Tyrannus, which he used during the midday siesta period (11 am to 4 pm). As a result of this public teaching, the whole of the province of

Asia 'heard the word of the Lord' (Acts 19:10) – a wide-open door indeed. It seems likely that Epaphras, a resident of Colossae in the Asian hinterland, was converted to Christ during his lunchbreaks from his business in the city. He then returned home and founded churches, not just in his home town, but in the neighbouring towns of Laodicea and Hierapolis.

Not surprisingly, Luke tells us that 'the word of the Lord grew mightily and prevailed' in Ephesus (Acts 19:20). Paul talked eloquently of the thorough, sacrificial and costly ministry which he pursued in Ephesus: the account is in his farewell speech to the elders of the Ephesian church at Miletus (Acts 20:17ff.).

If Paul faced great opportunities in Ephesus, he also met bitter and concerted opposition. To this he also bears testimony in his farewell speech:

> You yourselves know how I lived among you the entire time from the first day that I set foot in Asia, serving the Lord with all humility and with tears, enduring the trials that came to me through the plots of the Jews. (Acts 20:18–19)

Luke's account in Acts 19 tallies with Paul's own reference to fighting with wild beasts at Ephesus (1 Cor. 15:32). This vicious opposition was focused in three particular experiences. First, Paul's confrontation of evil powers in many Ephesians led to some very dramatic experiences, culminating in a public bonfire when the books of magic arts so rife in Ephesus were consigned to the flames. All those who have found themselves face to face with occult forces in Christian ministry will testify to the immense cost involved: opportunities, indeed, but also immense opposition.

The second focus for opposition to Paul and to the gospel was the guild of silversmiths, led by Demetrius. The preaching of the gospel was so powerfully successful that their lucrative trade of making silver statues for the worship of Artemis was dramatically diminished. Quite simply, Ephesians in large numbers were turning from idolatry to serve the living God, and no longer wanted to have silver statues of the local goddess around the home. Demetrius and his colleagues were understandably furious with Paul, raised a public outcry against the evangelists, and dragged Paul and his companions into the local amphitheatre, where they were all but lynched. Wherever the gospel is faithfully preached, it always challenges economic vested interests and will make many wealthy and influential people very nervous. The true church has always been opposed, not by the poor, but by the wealthy (cf. Jas 2:6–7).

The third source of opposition in Ephesus was the Jewish hierarchy, representing the religious establishment of the day. The history of the church from the outset has shown clearly that all times of strategic opportunity for the gospel have been accompanied (and sometimes actually caused) by opposition from official leadership in religious matters.

There is one simple lesson, above all others, to be learnt from Paul's experience: the presence of opposition does not mean that we have moved out of the will of God. There were many in Corinth then, as indeed there are many today, who at least intimated that everything goes smoothly when we are properly in touch with the Lord. The New Testament teaches differently.

3. A church which has resources but also responsibilities

We have already seen Paul's insistence on the Corinthians' responsibility to share their financial resources. We have also noted the way Aquila and Prisca made their home available to the fellowship of believers. The most penetrating comment on such responsible sharing of resources comes with Paul's description of *the household of Stephanas* (15–16): *they have devoted themselves to the service of the saints; I urge you to put yourselves at the service of such people, and of everyone who works and toils with them.*

Barrett sees these apparently innocuous phrases as the beginning of what we now know as the Christian ministry.[2] Stephanas's extended family (the contemporary meaning of the word *household*, that is, relatives and retainers included) had seen the priority in the Christian community of simply being available, with the gift of hospitality, to wait on the needs of *the saints*. So they *devoted themselves* (the word speaks of a dedicated and disciplined lifestyle) to serving others. As these folk began to meet the needs of their fellow Christians, people began to recognize in them the marks of true Christian leadership. Paul felt able to urge the Corinthians *to put [themselves] at the service of such people* – in other words, to respect their leadership gifts.

---

[2] Barrett, p. 394.

This insight challenges our notions, but particularly our practice, of leadership. We tend to give leadership to those who have received one particular kind of education, who have a measure of articulacy and general ability to think and speak on their feet, who measure up to worldly criteria of leadership. Do we ever take with proper seriousness the perspective Paul provides on leadership as service? Jesus taught the same truth: 'whoever wishes to be great among you must be your servant' (Matt. 20:26). This indicates that the authentic, solid leadership of a local church will come from people who give themselves to serving the saints. Such leadership does not depend on education, qualifications, degrees or natural charisma. It comes from the grace of God equipping his people with gifts which enable them to be servants of others in the fellowship of believers (cf. 1 Cor. 12:5). The whole household of Stephanas lived like that: as a family they served others – adults, teenagers and children; master of the house and domestic servants; the elderly and the very young. Indeed, Barrett's conclusion that 'since the household of Stephanas have taken upon themselves the service of the saints, they must be adults'[3] must be rejected. Children are very good at serving others; they often relish the opportunity and seize it without being solicited. One of the most effective testimonies to the reality of the risen Christ is the servant lifestyle of a Christian family.

Such resources for Christian ministry are present in every local church. Every home, every person, is a resource and therefore constitutes a responsibility for those resources to be used for the glory of God. This chapter speaks of the body's responsibility to minister to its ministers, as well as the ministers' responsibility to the body. Both are vital, if the church of God is to grow up to maturity.

Such growth is always close to Paul's heart, and his instructions to the Corinthians in verses 13–14 summarize the responsibility incumbent upon every Christian: *Keep alert, stand firm in your faith, be courageous, be strong. Let all that you do be done in love.* In the course of this letter he has pinpointed many areas of discipleship where they have either fallen asleep, or started to totter, or lost their nerve. He has challenged them to take firm action to put right what has gone wrong. Above all, he has stressed the absolute priority of love for everything they do as a church. These words stand, therefore, as the nub of Paul's instructions to a lively,

---

3 Ibid.

divided, exuberant and precarious church. They articulate accurately what lay close to Paul's heart.

4. Epilogue (16:21–24)

Paul now takes the pen from his amanuensis and records his personal farewell *with my own hand*. His parting shot must be aimed at certain troublemakers in Corinth: *Let anyone be accursed* [*anathema*] *who has no love for the Lord* (22). Paul clearly does not mean unbelievers, but those within the church at Corinth who have been causing such chaos to believers and such heartache to the apostle. 'If a man's heart is not aflame with love for the Lord, the root of the matter is not in him.'[4] The use of the word *anathema*, recalling the strange reference in 12:3 to someone as if under the inspiration of the Spirit saying that Jesus is *anathema*, might indicate that Paul knew who at Corinth had made that outrageous claim about Jesus, and that he is referring obliquely to the same person in these closing, personally written, remarks.

The words *Our Lord, come!* translate an Aramaic phrase, *Maranatha*, which must go back to the early days of the church in Palestine.[5] It expresses very concisely one of the deepest convictions of the primitive church from its very youngest days. It takes on even more profound meaning in the wake of Paul's magnificent tour de force in chapter 15. 'It expresses the eager longing felt by the Church in those early days for the speedy return of the Lord.'[6] Is our expectation and eager longing as fervent as this?

So Paul concludes with a message of grace and love. God's grace is coveted for *all* the Corinthians, even or especially those who have caused him the greatest problems and put up the fiercest opposition. Above all else, nothing can quench Paul's love for them all – *in Christ Jesus* (24). The best manuscripts omit the final 'Amen'. This would mean that Paul's last word to the Corinthians was a reaffirmation of his central conviction: 'in Christ'. That has been the hub of his message throughout the letter, and with that truth he is content to leave the matters brought to his notice by the church at Corinth, 'those sanctified in Christ Jesus' (1:2).

---

4 Morris, p. 247.
5 Ibid.
6 Ibid., p. 248.

Study guide

The aim of this study guide is to help you get to the heart of what the author has written and to challenge you to apply what you learn to your own life. The questions have been designed for use by individuals or by small groups of Christians meeting, perhaps for an hour or two each week, to study, discuss and pray together.

The guide provides material for each of the sections in the book. When it is used by a group with limited time, the leader should decide beforehand which questions are the most appropriate for the group to discuss during the meeting and which should perhaps be left for group members to work through by themselves or in smaller groups during the week.

In order to be able to contribute fully and to learn from the group meetings, each member of the group needs to read through the section or sections under discussion, together with the passages in 1 Corinthians to which they refer.

It is important not to let these studies become merely academic exercises. Guard against this by making time to think through and discuss how what you discover works out in practice for you. Make sure you begin and end each study by focusing on God in praise and prayer. Ask the Holy Spirit to speak to you through your discussion together.

Introduction (pp. 1–8)

1 What do we know about first-century Corinth (pp. 1ff.)? In what ways is where you live like Corinth?

1. Paul at Corinth

2 Why does Paul describe himself as arriving in Corinth in 'fear and in much trembling' (pp. 3ff.)?

3 What encouragements does he find there (pp. 5ff.)?

4 What is 'the secret of all Christian ministry' (p. 7)? How have you found this to be the case?

2. The Corinthian correspondence

5 Can you trace the sequence of letters and events into which 1 and 2 Corinthians fit (pp. 7f.)?

(Q) 1 Corinthians 1:1–9
1. The perfect church (pp. 9–16)

1. Paul's greeting to the church at Corinth (1:1–3)

1 What is 'uppermost in Paul's mind as he ponders the relationship between the Corinthian church and himself' (pp. 10f.)?

2 'We often speak too loosely of "my church" or "our church"' (pp. 10f.). In your experience, what problems has this led to?

3 To what has God called you (p. 11)? How do you know?

2. Paul's confidence in the church at Corinth (1:4–9)

....

'The church is a fellowship of sinners before it is a fellowship of saints.' (p. 12)

....

4 Which 'primary truth' (p. 13) do we need to register before looking at anything else that is true of the church? Why?

5 Why do we need one another in the church (pp. 13f.)?

6 What does Paul hint at about the role of 'special gurus' (p. 14)? How does this apply to your church?

7 'Bare preaching is not adequate' (p. 15). Why not? What more is needed?

8 What does it mean to be called into the fellowship of God's Son (pp. 16f.)?

9 Are you 'unreservedly committed to the church of God where he has placed' you (pp. 16f.)? What factors encourage or inhibit you?

(Q) 1 Corinthians 1:10–17
2. Cliques at Corinth (pp. 17–27)

1 What lay behind the divisions in the church at Corinth (pp. 17f.)? Can you identify similar factors in your own church?

2 At what point does a justifiable 'selectivity' become 'heresy' (p. 18)? What particular emphases do you hold? How do you treat those who take a different point of view?

1. The four groups

3 Paul mentions four particular cliques which had developed. Can you identify them (pp. 19ff.)? What particular emphases are thought to have characterized each of them?

4 With which of these four parties do you have most in common?

5 Summarize Paul's 'three powerful arguments against disunity' (pp. 24ff.).

2. Focus on Jesus Christ

'There is no single truth more eloquent or productive of true unity between Christians than the cross of Christ.' (p. 26)

6 How does David Prior's discussion of Holy Communion and baptism fit into what he has to say about unity (pp. 26f.)?

Q 1 Corinthians 1:18 – 2:16
3. Wisdom – true and false (pp. 28–42)

1 In what four senses does Paul use the word 'wisdom' (p. 28)?

2 How does the 'unbelieving world' attempt to construct its own way to God (pp. 28ff.)? In what ways might your views have become contaminated by such thinking?

3 In what ways is worldly wisdom a 'serious threat to the gospel and to the church' (p. 30)?

'Jesus himself warned plainly about a religion which is expressed in orthodox language but does not result in a changed lifestyle.' (p. 31)

1. The word of the cross (1:18–25)

4 In the light of what Paul says about wisdom, is preaching a waste of time (p. 32)?

5 What exactly do you think it means to preach 'the message about the cross' (p. 32)?

6 How has God destroyed 'the wisdom of the wise' (p. 34)?

2. *The ways of God (1:26–31)*

7 How do you judge someone's importance? How does God? Can you explain any difference there might be (p. 35)?

8 What 'false standards' does God overthrow and what methods does he use (pp. 35f.)?

....

'God is constantly and deliberately bringing proud people to their knees, so that they can enter his presence in repentance and faith.' (p. 36)

....

3. *The ministry of the Spirit (2:1–16)*

9 Why is there such a 'close relationship between the cross and the Spirit' (p. 37)?

10 In what ways does this section provide 'the perfect touchstone for all preaching' (p. 38)? If you are a preacher, how do you match up?

11 Paul writes about 'the rulers of this age' in verses 6 and 8. What does he mean (pp. 39f.)?

12 'We never, therefore, move on from the cross of Christ' (p. 40). Why not? In what ways do you try to do this?

13 What is Christian maturity (pp. 40f.)? What does Paul tell us here about how it comes about?

14 'Paul must have felt so frustrated by . . .' what (p. 42)? Would he feel the same way about you? What can you do about it?

15 'To have the mind of Christ is essentially a corporate experience' (p. 42). What implications of this statement can you think of?

(Q) 1 Corinthians 3:1 – 4:21
4. Fools for Christ's sake (pp. 43–56)

1. *Babies and adults (3:1–4)*

1 What marks of immaturity does Paul identify here (pp. 43f.)? To what extent are these things true of you and the fellowship to which you belong?

....

'Mere lapse of time does not bring Christian maturity.' (C. K. Barrett, quoted on p. 44)

....

2. Planting and watering (3:5–8)

2 What is so wrong with personality cults in the church (pp. 44f.)? How much do you think this is a problem in modern Christianity? What can be done about it?

3 Where does 'truly Christian authority' come from (pp. 45f.)? Why?

4 How would you answer someone who suggested that perhaps we should try to do without leaders altogether (pp. 45f.)? What reasons would you give?

3. Foundations and buildings (3:9–17)

....

'Pastors and preachers move on and die: only a church built on Jesus Christ survives.' (p. 46)

....

5 What sort of activities do you think Paul has in mind when he writes about building the church (p. 46)?

6 What are the implications of the fact that the quality of our work will not be known until the Day of the Lord (p. 47)?

7 What determines whether our work will survive or be burned up (pp. 47f.)? What determines whether we ourselves will survive or be burned up?

4. Worldly wisdom (3:18–23)

8 Why is it 'totally out of place to boast about people' (p. 48)?

5. Servants and stewards (4:1–7)

9 Do you tend to follow 'big names' (p. 49)? Which ones? Why? What is wrong with this?

....

'All true ministry in the church, whoever brings it and of whatever kind it is, is provided by God: it is ridiculous to "be puffed up in favour of one against another".' (p. 51)

....

10 What is significant about Paul's reference to himself and other Christian leaders as 'stewards' (p. 49)? How does this apply to you?

11 Why is verse 4 'of special interest' (p. 50)?

6. Kings and paupers (4:8–13)

12 What lay at 'the heart of the boasting at Corinth' (p. 52)? Could a similar criticism be levelled at you?

. . . .

'For people who . . . are concerned for their own status, reputation and popularity, authentic Christian ministry is immensely difficult to accept, let alone to embrace.' (p. 53)

. . . .

13 What 'three principles for Christian ministry need to be stressed from this metaphor of kings and paupers' (pp. 53f.)? How do these apply to you?

7. Fathers and children (4:14–21)

14 What does Paul mean by referring to himself as a 'father' to the Christians at Corinth (pp. 54f.)? Do you think of anyone as 'father' in this sense? Why or why not?

(Q) 1 Corinthians 5:1–13; 6:9–20
5. Flee fornication (pp. 57–91)

1. The problem stated (5:1–2a)

1 What does Paul mean by 'immorality' (pp. 57f.)? What is it that so concerns him about the Corinthians' attitude to it?

. . . .

'The history of the church shows that strong temptation in sexual matters is one of Satan's most frequent tactics in attempting to quench spiritual vitality.' (p. 58)

. . . .

2. The need for discipline (5:2b–13)

. . . .

'If, in the eyes of God, it is right and good for a particular person to suffer in this life in order that he or she might ultimately be saved, then let it be so.' (p. 59)

. . . .

2 How can Paul pronounce sentence with such 'finality and . . . absolute authority' (p. 59)? Can we do the same today?

3 From what does 'the failure in today's church to exercise proper church discipline' often stem (pp. 60f.)? Why is this so?

4 In what ways are the implications of this passage 'very encouraging as well as admonitory' (pp. 61f.)?

5 What parallel does Paul draw between the life of the Christian community and the Jewish celebration of Passover (pp. 63f.)?

6 What does David Prior identify as 'the kernel of Paul's theology and the essence of his incentive for holy living' (p. 65)?

7 'Celebration is a distinctive mark of the Christian community' (p. 65). Why? Is it a mark of yours?

....

'For the true Christian it is always Easter, always Pentecost, always Christmas.'
(Chrysostom, quoted on p. 65)

....

8 How had the Corinthians misinterpreted Paul's previous warning against mixing with immoral people (p. 66)? Do you tend to do the same?

9 What do you think is 'the most common and destructive sin in the Western church' (p. 67)? How does David Prior suggest a Christian from the Global South would reply?

10 Which idols enslave the members of your community (p. 68)? Where does freedom come from?

11 Paul mentions three other areas which call for discipline to be exercised by the church (pp. 68f.). What are they? Why is such discipline necessary?

12 What does David Prior identify as 'the tragedy of so much modern Christianity' (p. 69)? What can you do to contribute towards the answer rather than being part of the problem?

13 In what way do purity in the church and penetration of the world 'interact creatively' (p. 71)?

14 When is it right to 'judge' someone else (pp. 71f.)? Why?

3. *The need for clear convictions (6:9–11)*

15 'The unrighteous cannot inherit the kingdom of God' (p. 76). Why not? What implications does this have for the life of the church?

16 In his list of those excluded from the kingdom of God, why does Paul mention homosexuals (p. 77)?

17 Why is 'And this is what some of you used to be' such an 'exciting and energizing' statement (p. 78)?

'Every Corinthian Christian was living evidence that God's answer to sophisticated Greek wisdom was not clever arguments but changed lives.' (p. 79)

4. The need for purity (6:12–20)

'Walking in the Spirit is always a matter of steering the middle and narrow course between too much licence and too many rules and regulations.' (p. 81)

18 David Prior suggests that Paul's slogan 'All things are lawful for me' could be taken as 'Do what you feel like doing, and if you don't feel like doing it, don't do it' (p. 82). But what three 'crucial qualifications' must we add (pp. 82ff.)? Why?

19 Can you summarize the five truths Paul sets out about the body (pp. 86ff.)? How do these contradict 'the mood of his contemporaries' (p. 86)?

20 What does it mean to 'glorify God in your body' (p. 90)?

(Q) 1 Corinthians 6:1–8
6. Settled out of court (pp. 92–101)

1 What 'important thread' might explain the switch in what Paul writes from sexual morality to litigation between Christians (pp. 92f.)?

2 Under what circumstances would Paul go to court (p. 94)? Why? Have you ever been in a similar position?

1. You are flaunting your failures (6:1)

3 Is it ever appropriate to confess sin publicly (pp. 94f.)? When?

2. You are forgetting your destiny (6:2–4)

4 According to Paul, what does the future hold for Christians (pp. 95ff.)? How does this affect the issue he is tackling?

5 'One of the most insidious and pervasive attitudes among evangelical Christians is the importance attached to "top people"' (p. 98). Is this true of you? What does it lead to?

3. You are bypassing your resources (6:5–6)

6 How should disagreements between Christians be sorted out (p. 99)?

....

'Paul believed that in every church resided everything needed to express the love of Christ.' (p. 99)

....

4. You are betraying your calling (6:7–8)

7 Rather than going to court, what is the 'much better way' for Christians to deal with situations where they are wronged by others (pp. 100f.)? How do you react to this?

1 Corinthians 7:1–40
7. Marriage and singleness – two gifts from God (pp. 102–126)

1. Married couples (7:2–5)

1 How would you answer someone who claimed that Paul was a misogynist (p. 102f.)?

2 What is 'God's purpose for marriage' (p. 103)? Why?

3 Why does Paul insist on 'husband and wife giving each other their due' (pp. 103f.)? What does this tell us about (a) equality within marriage and (b) the purpose of sexual intercourse?

4 How does Paul qualify his one exception to the instruction given in verse 3 (pp. 105f.)?

5 How would you answer someone who claimed that sexual activity is 'morally neutral' (p. 107)?

6 How do you react to David Prior's observation that 'couples often find praying together the most difficult part of their whole relationship' (p. 107)?

2. Paul's personal remarks (7:6–9)

7 How does Paul rehabilitate 'both celibacy and marriage as manifestations of the grace of God' (pp. 108f.)?

8   Do you see your own singleness or marriage as a 'gift' (p. 108)?
    What difference does this make?

3. Marriage and divorce (7:10–16)

9   What issues are raised by Paul's phrase 'not I but the Lord' in verse 10
    (pp. 109f.)?
10 What would you say to a Christian who feels that his or her marriage
    is a mistake (pp. 109ff.)?
11 What does Paul say about the situation where a newly converted
    Christian is married to an unbeliever (pp. 112ff.)? How does he
    back this up?
12 What does it mean for an unbelieving partner to be 'made holy'
    through his or her Christian spouse (p. 113)?
13 How does the principle that 'It is to peace that God has called
    you' apply here? Do you think that what Paul says about not
    being 'bound' would allow divorce and possible remarriage
    (pp. 116f.)?

4. Christian vocation (7:17–24)

14 What are the 'three basic priorities in the apostle's mind' (p. 117)?
    How do you measure up?
15 What modern equivalents can you think of to the difficulties caused
    by the issues of circumcision and slavery (pp. 117f.)?

....

*'What matters is obedience to the Lord's commandments, and that has nothing
to do with ritual religious acts.' (p. 119)*

....

16 What is 'the key to making their present situation count' (p. 118)?
    How does this apply to you?

5. Virgins (7:25–35)

17 'One factor stands out in Paul's mind' (p. 120). What is it? Does it stand
    out in yours?
18 *X* says that it's better to be single than to be married. *Y* disagrees
    and maintains that marriage is better than singleness. Who is right
    (pp. 123ff.)? Why?

6. Engaged couples (7:36–38)

19　What is the 'primary point' (p. 125) that Paul is making here?
How does it apply to you?

7. Widows (7:39–40)

20　On what does Paul base his advice to widows (pp. 125f.)?

Ⓠ **1 Corinthians 8:1–13**
8.　Freedom and sensitivity to others (pp. 127–136)

1　What are the 'two sides' to the question of food offered to idols
(pp. 128f.)? What is the basic 'battle on two fronts' which Paul needs
to address? Can you think of similar issues which face us today?

1.　The overriding principle: love builds up (8:1–3)

....

*'Any true knowledge does not lead to pride in what we know, but to humility
about what we do not know.' (p. 130)*

....

2　Why is it so important that knowledge should be controlled by love
(pp. 130f.)?
3　How does the principle of love apply to the 'particular question of food
offered to idols' (pp. 130f.)?

2.　The fundamental truth: there is one God (8:4–6)

4　How would you answer someone who said that it doesn't matter what
or whom we worship because we are 'worshipping the same God, but
by different names and in different ways' (p. 131)?
5　Is it enough simply to say that idols have no reality and leave it at that?
What lies behind idol worship (pp. 132f.)? Why is this so important for
us today?

3.　The supreme consideration: the fellow Christian for whom Christ died (8:7–13)

6　What arguments does Paul use to persuade the 'strong' person to
restrict his or her freedom voluntarily (pp. 134f.)?
7　What does it take to be a 'strong' person (p. 136)? How strong are you?

1 Corinthians 9:1–27
   9. Freedom to restrict our freedom (pp. 137–151)

1. *Paul's freedom in Christ (9:1–6)*

   1 What marks of an apostle does Paul set out here (pp. 137ff.)? What sort
      of 'rights' do you have? When might it be appropriate for you to refuse
      to claim them?

2. *Forgoing his rights (9:7–18)*

   2 List the five reasons Paul sets out for having rights (pp. 140ff.).
      How does he then go on to argue the case for giving them up?

....

*'A man who is ready to endure anything for the gospel is not interested in his
rights.' (p. 144)*

....

   3 What does the author suggest would have been Paul's 'ultimate
      catastrophe' (p. 144)? How do you react to his perspective here?

3. *Choosing slavery to all (9:19–23)*

   4 Would the writer of your obituary be able to say that 'the gospel
      dominated [your] whole life' (p. 146)? What does this mean in
      practice?
   5 What was Paul's 'fundamental philosophy' in the way he went about
      evangelism (pp. 146f.)? How does this apply to you?
   6 'There were dangers in Paul's own methods of evangelism' (p. 148).
      What were these? How can they be avoided?

....

*'The task of identification with and incarnation into our contemporary
paganism, of all kinds, is one of the biggest tasks confronting the church.'
(p. 149)*

....

4. *Running to win (9:24–27)*

   7 What does Paul mean by the possibility that he might be 'disqualified'
      (pp. 150f.)?
   8 In what ways do you need to exercise 'self-control' and 'pummel' and
      'subdue' your body (pp. 149ff.)?

ⓠ 1 Corinthians 10:1 – 11:1
10. Freedom and its dangers (pp. 152–163)

1. The danger of presumptuousness (10:1–13)

1 On what 'two particular facets' of the experiences in the life of God's people during Moses' time does Paul concentrate (pp. 153f.)? Why?

....

'To receive blessing is by no means the same as to enter into the privilege and responsibilities of blessing.' (p. 154)

....

2 Can you think of any examples where you allow yourself 'the indulgence of thinking that sin does not matter' (p. 155)? How did the Corinthians get into this 'perilous position'?

3 How should the exodus be 'accurately expounded and properly applied' (p. 157)?

4 In this area, how have you experienced the truth that 'God is faithful' (pp. 158.)?

2. The danger of compromise (10:14–22)

5 On what does Paul base his argument that idolatry must be rejected (pp. 159ff.)? What modern equivalents of idols can you identify?

3. The danger of legalism (10:23–30)

6 In this summary paragraph, how does Paul draw together 'the threads of the last three chapters' (p. 162)?

4. Conclusion (10:31 – 11:1)

7 What are 'Paul's five ground rules for life together in Christ' (p. 163)? How can you put them into practice?

ⓠ 1 Corinthians 11:2–34
11. The Christian community at worship (pp. 164–176)

1. Introduction (11:2)

1 What does Paul mean by 'the traditions' (pp. 164f.)?

2. *The behaviour of the women (11:3–16)*

2 What lies behind Paul's instructions about women wearing veils (pp. 165ff.)?

3 What is the significance of the fact that Paul 'starts from the doctrine of creation, not from the doctrine of redemption' in this paragraph (pp. 166.)?

4 What is 'the pattern of relationships which God has written into the Christian community' (p. 166)? What are the implications of this for public worship? How does the Christian community to which you belong match up to what Paul says?

5 'If we are as concerned as Paul for the glory of God to dominate our worship as his people, we shall not go far wrong' (p. 169). What does this mean in practice for you?

6 'Christian worship is expressed best when . . .' what (p. 170)? If you are married, how does this perspective affect you?

7 'As Creator . . . God intends that men and women should have different, but complementary, functions' (p. 170). Why? What differences does Paul have in mind? How does this work out for you?

3. *Attitudes to the Lord's Supper (11:17–34)*

8 What are the dangers in 'theological "soundness"' (p. 172)? How may they be guarded against?

9 'When you come together, it is not really to eat the Lord's supper' (verse 20). Why not? What is needed for such a meeting to qualify as 'the Lord's Supper' (pp. 172ff.)?

10 How should we approach the Lord's Supper (pp. 174ff.)? Why is this so important?

11 How do you respond to David Prior's question on p. 175: 'How much weakness and illness is, in fact, part of the wise, loving, painful but productive, discipline of a perfect Father?'

ⓠ 1 Corinthians 12:1–31
12. **Concerning spiritual gifts (pp. 177–208)**

1. *Proclaiming Jesus as Lord (12:1–3)*

1 How do you experience spiritual reality (pp. 178f.)? Are you ever misled in the same way as the Corinthians?

2 What is Paul's 'overall criterion of genuineness in this matter of spirituality' (p. 179)? How does the church fit into this? Is this how you see it?

3 What is the 'particular uniqueness' of the phrase 'Jesus is Lord' (pp. 179f.)?

'To be truly "spiritual" drives a person . . . into the life of the local church as an expression of his or her personal commitment to Jesus as Lord and to his body here on earth.' (p. 180)

2. For the common good (12:4–7)

4 What main purpose of the church does Paul focus on here (pp. 180f.)? How does it fulfil this function? To what extent does your church do this?

5 What different sorts of variety are there in God's gifts to his church (pp. 181f.)?

6 Where does 'the church's lack of credibility as the community of the Holy Spirit' lie (p. 182)? Does this need to be put right in your situation? How?

3. God's grace in action (12:8–11)

7 What distinctions are there between natural and supernatural gifts (pp. 183f.)? Why are they important?

8 Paul goes on to list six particular supernatural gifts. What are they (pp. 184ff.)? What is distinctive about them? What experience do you have of them?

9 What misunderstandings and pitfalls in this area does Paul answer in these verses (pp. 185ff.)?

10 Why is it so important that these gifts are 'exercised within the worshipping life of the body of Christ' (p. 194)?

11 'The three verbs in verse 11 are all crucial for a proper approach to these gifts' (p. 195). Which verbs? Why are they so important?

4. Unity in diversity (12:12–13)

12 What different interpretations are there of verse 13 (pp. 195f.)? Which is right? Why?

13 'We must not allow fear of wrong or superficial experiences to keep us from the birthright of the church from Pentecost onwards' (p. 197). Is such fear a problem for you? How may it be overcome?

'The more we today draw on the richness of the worldwide community of believers, the more pungent and attractive will be our testimony.' (p. 198)

5. We are Christ's and each other's (12:14–27)

14 Why do we need one another in the body of Christ (pp. 198f.)? How is this need expressed in practice?

15 Why does diversity in the body tend to be stifled (pp. 199f.)? How can we guard against this?

16 How should Christians care for one another (pp. 200f.)? What is your experience of receiving and giving such ministry?

'The way the Christian community faces and uses suffering is crucial to the integrity of its testimony.' (p. 200)

17 What is the difference between 'individuality' and 'individualism' (p. 201)? Why is this distinction so important?

6. God has appointed . . . (12:28–30)

18 Are there 'apostles' in the church today (pp. 202ff.)? If so, how do they differ from those in the early church?

19 What is distinctive about 'teachers', 'forms of assistance' and 'forms of leadership' (pp. 204ff.)? What happens where each of these ministries is undervalued?

7. The more excellent way (12:31)

20 Are Paul's words '[you] strive for the greater gifts' a statement or a command (p. 208)? What difference does this make?

21 How would you respond to someone who suggests that the 'way of love' is set out as an alternative to spiritual gifts (pp. 208f.)?

ⓠ 1 Corinthians 13:1–13
13. If I do not have love . . . (pp. 209–218)

1 Why is it so important that this chapter be 'studied in the context of the rest of Paul's letter to the church of Corinth' (pp. 210f.)?

1. The absence of love (13:1–3)

2 What 'three strong statements' does Paul make about the Christian who is without love (pp. 211ff.)? Do these apply to you? How?

....

'God cannot use loveless Christians for his glory.' (p. 212)

....

2. The nature of love (13:4–7)

3 Why is it 'important that Paul uses *verbs* in describing such love' (pp. 213f.)?

4 'There is no local church anywhere which does not need more love' (p. 215). Why? Where does love like this come from?

5 How does love cope with the 'weaknesses, sins and failures of others' (pp. 215f.)? Can you think of specific examples?

3. The endlessness of love (13:8–13)

6 How does Paul dispel the illusion that 'such love can be reproduced by human beings on their own' (p. 217)? Where does it come from, then?

ⓠ 1 Corinthians 14:1–40
14. Prophecy and tongues (pp. 219–239)

1. What are they?

1 What does David Prior stress 'at the outset' (p. 219)? Why is this so important?

2 How would you respond to someone who equated prophecy with expository preaching (pp. 219f.)?

3 How do you react to Paul's desire that 'I would like all of you . . . to prophesy' (verse 5)?

4 What lessons does David Prior draw from Isaiah 50 (pp. 221f.)?

'Continuing prophetic ministry is essential today if the church is not going to settle down into a comfortable conformity to contemporary culture.' (p. 222)

5 What does Paul tell us here about the gifts of speaking in tongues and interpretation of tongues (pp. 223f.)?
6 Why is there a problem in interpreting this chapter in the light of Acts 2 (pp. 223f.)? What conclusion do you come to about the nature of this particular gift? Why?
7 Does 'interpretation of tongues' mean 'translation' (pp. 225f.)? Why is this an important question?
8 What, according to Paul, are these gifts basically for (pp. 226f.)? Have they done this in your experience? How?

2. The effect of prophecy (14:1–5)
9 What are 'the results which this gift will bring in the local church when it is properly used' (pp. 227f.)? Does your church need more of these things?

3. The incompleteness of tongues (14:6–25)
10 What are the 'three major limitations in speaking in tongues' which Paul sets out here (pp. 228ff.)?
11 What are the 'apparent contradictions' in verses 21–25 (pp. 231f.)? How can they be resolved?

4. The need for congregational control (14:26–36)
12 What controls does Paul prescribe (pp. 233ff.)? Why?
13 'Whatever this section is teaching, it is not telling women to keep quiet in church' (pp. 235f.). How do we know? What *is* it saying, then?

5. Conclusion (14:37–40)

'Any tendency to think that we are right, while the rest of the church universal is wrong, is both arrogant and dangerous.' (p. 236)

14 Does your church tend to ignore verse 39 or verse 40 (p. 237)? Why are both important?

6. *Additional note on spiritual gifts*

15 Do you agree or disagree that 'certain gifts of the Spirit are not generally available to the church in every generation' (p. 237)? How do you arrive at your conclusion?

ⓠ 1 Corinthians 15:1–58
15. Resurrection – past, present and future (pp. 240–261)

1 Why might some of the Christians at Corinth have been asserting that 'there is no resurrection of the dead' (pp. 240ff.)? What modern equivalents are there to these views?

1. *The facts of the resurrection of Jesus (15:1–11)*

2 What is the significance of the fact that Paul had 'received' the gospel message he preached (pp. 243f.)?

3 List the facts that Paul mentions (pp. 243ff.). What is significant about each of them?

4 How would you answer someone who claimed that Jesus appeared to him or her in the same way that he appeared to Paul (pp. 245f.)?

2. *The centrality of the resurrection of Jesus (15:12–19)*

5 What 'seven essentials' are lost if we deny the truth of the resurrection (pp. 246ff.)?

....

'When an elderly churchgoer heard one such modern sceptic speaking on the radio, she concluded that everything she had hitherto believed by way of orthodox Christianity was unreliable, if not untrue – and committed suicide.' (pp. 250f.)

....

3. *The consequences of the resurrection of Jesus (15:20–34)*

6 What consequences for the future does Paul infer from Christ's resurrection (pp. 250ff.)? How does this perspective help us now?

7 Why might the Corinthians have been baptized 'on behalf of the dead' (pp. 253.)? Which suggestion do you find most persuasive?

8 How does the resurrection help us face (a) suffering and (b) temptation (pp. 253ff.)?

4. *The nature of the resurrection body (15:35–50)*

9 What 'fundamental principle' runs through Paul's thought on this issue (pp. 255f.)?

10 How are we to understand the continuity between our lives now and our lives after death (pp. 255ff.)?

5. *The moment of the resurrection of the body (15:51–57)*

11 How does the analogy of sleep help us to understand death and resurrection (pp. 258f.)?

12 Why does Paul refer to the 'sting' of death (p. 259)? Why is it important to acknowledge this?

13 What does Paul mean by 'the power of sin is the law' (p. 259)?

6. *Conclusion (15:58)*

14 How does what Paul has said provide the incentive we need for 'excelling in the work of the Lord' (p. 260)? What work of the Lord are you excelling in?

(Q) 1 Corinthians 16:1–24
16. An international church (pp. 262–268)

1. *A church which is international but also interdependent*

1 How was the interdependence of the church expressed then (pp. 263f.)? How is it expressed now?

2. *A church which faces opportunities but also opposition*

2 What is the 'one simple lesson, above all others, to be learnt from Paul's experience' (p. 266)? How is this relevant for you?

3. *A church which has resources but also responsibilities*

3 Which particular 'insight challenges our notions, but particularly our practice, of leadership' (p. 267)? How does it affect your view of leadership?

....

'One of the most effective testimonies to the reality of the risen Christ is the servant lifestyle of a Christian family.' (p. 267)

....

4. *Epilogue (16:21–24)*

4 How do you react to what Paul says in verse 22 (pp. 268f.)? Do you feel
strongly enough about the church to be able to say the same?

5 What has been 'the hub of his message throughout the letter' (p. 268)?
To what extent is it your central conviction too?

Listen to God's Word
speaking to the world today

The complete NIV text, with over 2,300 notes from the Bible Speaks Today series, in beautiful fine leather- and clothbound editions. Ideal for devotional reading, studying and teaching the Bible.

Leatherbound edition with slipcase
£50.00 • 978 1 78974 139 1

Clothbound edition
£34.99 • 978 1 78359 613 3

The Bible Speaks Today: Old Testament series

The Message of Genesis 1 – 11
The dawn of creation
David Atkinson

The Message of Genesis 12 – 50
From Abraham to Joseph
Joyce G. Baldwin

The Message of Exodus
The days of our pilgrimage
Alec Motyer

The Message of Leviticus
Free to be holy
Derek Tidball

The Message of Numbers
Journey to the promised land
Raymond Brown

The Message of Deuteronomy
Not by bread alone
Raymond Brown

The Message of Joshua
Promise and people
David G. Firth

The Message of Judges
Grace abounding
Michael Wilcock

The Message of Ruth
The wings of refuge
David Atkinson

The Message of Samuel
Personalities, potential, politics and power
Mary J. Evans

The Message of Kings
God is present
John W. Olley

The Message of Chronicles
One church, one faith, one Lord
Michael Wilcock

The Message of Ezra and Haggai
Building for God
Robert Fyall

The Message of Nehemiah
God's servant in a time of change
Raymond Brown

The Message of Esther
God present but unseen
David G. Firth

The Message of Job
Suffering and grace
David Atkinson

The Bible Speaks Today:
New Testament series

The Message of 1 Timothy and Titus

The life of the local church

John Stott

The Message of 2 Timothy

Guard the gospel

John Stott

The Message of Hebrews

Christ above all

Raymond Brown

The Message of James

The tests of faith

Alec Motyer

The Message of 1 Peter

The way of the cross

Edmund Clowney

The Message of 2 Peter and Jude

The promise of his coming

Dick Lucas and Christopher Green

The Message of John's Letters

Living in the love of God

David Jackman

The Message of Revelation

I saw heaven opened

Michael Wilcock

The Bible Speaks Today: Bible Themes series

The Message of the Living God
His glory, his people, his world
Peter Lewis

The Message of the Resurrection
Christ is risen!
Paul Beasley-Murray

The Message of the Cross
Wisdom unsearchable, love indestructible
Derek Tidball

The Message of Salvation
By God's grace, for God's glory
Philip Graham Ryken

The Message of Creation
Encountering the Lord of the universe
David Wilkinson

The Message of Heaven and Hell
Grace and destiny
Bruce Milne

The Message of Mission
The glory of Christ in all time and space
Howard Peskett and Vinoth Ramachandra

The Message of Prayer
Approaching the throne of grace
Tim Chester

The Message of the Trinity
Life in God
Brian Edgar

The Message of Evil and Suffering
Light into darkness
Peter Hicks

The Message of the Holy Spirit
The Spirit of encounter
Keith Warrington

The Message of Holiness
Restoring God's masterpiece
Derek Tidball

The Message of Sonship
At home in God's household
Trevor Burke

The Message of the Word of God
The glory of God made known
Tim Meadowcroft